THE STONE AND THE GLORY

LESSONS ON THE TEMPLE PRESENCE AND THE GLORY OF GOD

GREG HARRIS

Published by:

P.O. Box 132228
The Woodlands, TX 77393
www.kressbiblical.com

Unless otherwise indicated, Scripture taken from the *NEW AMERICAN STANDARD BIBLE*®, © Copyright 1960, 1962, 1963, 1968, 1971, 1972, 1973, 1975, 1977, 1995 by The Lockman Foundation. Used by permission.
www.Lockman.org

ISBN 978-1-934952-07-8
Cover Design: Mario Kushner
Text Design: Valerie Moreno

To Drs. Jim Rosscup and Robert Thomas,

men of God and scholars of the Word,

whose godly teaching ministry has eternally affected the lives of thousands,

mine deeply among those

Jesus said to them, "Did you never read in the Scriptures,

'The Stone which the builders rejected, this became the chief cornerstone; this came about from the Lord, and it is marvelous in our eyes?'"

— Matthew 21:42

CONTENTS

days to come" or literally "the end of the days" (Gen. 49:1). Throughout the remainder of the Bible every "stone prophecy"—and there are dozens of them—reveal intricate details about the life and work of the Messiah, including His initial rejection by His own people before the Jewish nations receives Him as King.

The New Testament picks up on these Messianic promises, showing their fulfillment in Jesus Christ. One Person alone *must* fulfill every one of these prophecies, down to the smallest detail. As you will see as you read this book, each stone prophecy bears witness that Jesus alone is the promised Messiah; each stone prophecy reveals some specific attribute of deity in the Messiah; and each stone prophecy ultimately and intimately links Jesus with God's Temple in Jerusalem, in both His first *and* second advents, even to the point where His feet will stand on the Mount of Olives (Zech. 14:1-4). Satan knew this—and knows this—and fears this, even employing a stone prophecy in one of his encounters with Jesus. Satan by no means wants people to be aware of the stone prophecies of the Messiah because they ultimately reveal aspects of his own demise and eternal judgment.

In *The Stone and the Glory*, Greg Harris takes his readers on a profound journey through the Scriptures as they explore these glorious realities. The journey begins in Genesis with the Patriarchs; it continues with the Israelites wandering toward the Promised Land and ultimately to the house where God Himself has promised, "I will put My name there forever, and My eyes and heart will be there perpetually" (1 Kings 9:3); it summons the nation to observe Messiah's final Passover that He observed with them before His cross—but not the last Passover He will ever celebrate (Luke 22:14-18)—as God the Father bore repeated witness to His Son in His Holy Word; it continues with the stone prophecies in the book of Acts, and it culminates with Messiah's return in glory. Along the way, readers will joyfully find themselves identifying with the biblical characters, pondering how they would have responded if they themselves were living in Bible times. Like a skilled tour guide, Dr. Harris brings the Scripture to life in a way that insightfully weds biblical exegesis, Christ-centered theology, and practical application.

This is a book about the magnanimous covenant promises of God, given to His people throughout the ages. For those interested in Jewish evangelism or apologetics, I highly recommend this Bible-rich study. These promises are exact and meant to be understood as they unfold in the text of Scripture. *The Stone and the Glory* traces these promises to their inevitable conclusion, that Jesus Christ is the Son of God and the

FOREWORD

Perhaps more than any other substance in nature, bedrock is solid, immovable, impenetrable, and fixed. So it's no wonder that the Bible repeatedly uses the imagery of a stone or rock to refer to God, especially to depict the certainty of His salvation and deliverance.

Before entering the Promised Land, Moses recalled the greatness of Israel's God with these words: "The Rock! His work is perfect, for all His ways are just; a God of faithfulness and without injustice, righteous and upright is He" (Deut. 32:4; cf. vv. 15, 18, 30–31). The metaphor of a rock reminded the Israelites of a miracle they had experienced earlier in their wilderness wanderings, when water gushed from solid stone to create a stream in the desert (Exod. 17:6; cf. Num. 20:10–11). What a sight that would have been! But there was more happening than just literal water flowing from physical stone. As the Apostle Paul explained: "All [of the Israelites] drank the same spiritual drink, for they were drinking from a spiritual rock which followed them; and the rock was Christ" (1 Cor. 10:4).

Other Old Testament writers drew on this same imagery to describe God's saving character. To the rhetorical question, "Who is a rock, except our God?" (Ps. 18:32), the answer is abundantly clear: "There is no rock like our God" (1 Sam. 2:2); for "The Lord is my rock and my fortress and my deliverer, my God, my rock, in whom I take refuge" (Ps. 18:2; cf. 31:3; 71:3). Believers of any age can exult in the truth of these words: "The Lord lives, and blessed be my rock; and exalted be the God of my salvation" (Ps. 18:46).

The Messianic hope of the Old Testament is similarly grounded in the symbolism of stone beginning in Genesis 49:24, "from there is the Shepherd, the Stone of Israel" with even the context of this prophecy specifically stated as "what will befall you [the Jewish nation] in the

Savior of the world, who will one day return to claim what is rightfully His and gather His own to Himself. May your heart be greatly encouraged as your eyes are drawn to Christ, the author and perfecter of faith, in the pages that follow.

John MacArthur

1

THE STONE

S tones, stones, stones, stones — stones! The one thing the Middle East does not lack is stones. They are everywhere. Even in the most fertile places in the Holy Land, stones lie readily visible, often marking land or crop boundaries with fences composed of carefully and strategically placed stones. In some places, including the wilderness where Satan tempted Jesus, virtually no vegetation exists; all that can be seen are stones.

What makes a stone a stone? Is there any difference between a stone and a rock, or are they synonymous? For instance, David used five smooth stones when going into battle against Goliath. Do these stones differ in any way from rocks? In some way they may. Webster's dictionary defines stone as "the hard, solid non-metallic mineral matter of rock." So can a stone exist within a rock?

This is something worth pondering because the Bible contains many references to both God the Rock and God the Stone. David writes in Psalm 18:1-2, "I love You, O LORD, my strength. The LORD is my rock and my fortress and my deliverer, my God, my rock, in whom I take refuge." In presenting Himself as the God who declares and controls all world events past, present, and future, God attests to Himself, asking, "Is there any God besides Me, or is there any other Rock? I know of none" (Isa. 44:8).

An interesting pronouncement occurs in Genesis when the elder Jacob/Israel blessed his children, declaring, "The archers bitterly attacked him, and shot at him and harassed him; but his bow remained firm, and his arms were agile, from the hands of the Mighty One of Jacob (from there is the Shepherd, *the Stone of Israel*)" (Gen. 49:23-24). Jacob actually indicated two separate designations of the One who would come from the Mighty One of Jacob — namely, the Shepherd and the Stone of Israel.

Jacob knew the requirements and qualities of shepherds because he had been one most of his life (Gen. 30:25-43). So it would be fitting for the elder Jacob to testify as he blessed Joseph, "The God before whom my fathers Abraham and Isaac walked, the God who has been my shepherd all my life to this day" (Gen. 48:15). Among other things, shepherds look after, lead, and defend their sheep. Jacob acknowledged this shepherding aspect of God's care long before David would pen the twenty-third psalm almost a thousand years later:

> The LORD is my shepherd, I shall not want. He makes me lie down in green pastures; He leads me beside quiet waters. He restores my soul; He guides me in the paths of righteousness for His name's sake. Even though I walk through the valley of the shadow of death, I fear no evil, for You are with me; Your rod and Your staff, they comfort me.
> You prepare a table before me in the presence of my enemies; You have anointed my head with oil; my cup overflows.
> Surely goodness and lovingkindness will follow me all the days of my life, and I will dwell in the house of the LORD forever.

Each element fits with God's care of Jacob—and likewise with God's care of His own who walk with Him. Even a casual reading of the New Testament shows how Jesus fulfills the role of the Shepherd. He discloses in John 10:14 that He is "the Good Shepherd." Peter refers to Jesus as "the Chief Shepherd" (1 Pet. 5:4). The author of Hebrews presents Him as "the great Shepherd of the sheep" (Heb. 13:20). Many additional references appear throughout the Bible.

God the Shepherd or Jesus the Good Shepherd we readily acknowledge, but a stone as a descriptive name for God, we generally do not. Yet, that is how Genesis 49:24 depicts him: "the Shepherd, the Stone of Israel." As we will see, the Genesis 49 Stone reference is merely the first of many contained within Scripture. We will do well to take notice of this often overlooked aspect of God's revelation to us. The Trinity must have specific aspects or qualities that They desire for the beloved to know—and the truths these verses reveal are astounding.

When Jacob made his Stone attestation in Genesis 49, he was an old man. Decades earlier, God had changed him into the new creature whom He named Israel, who became the father of the twelve tribes of the nation that shared his new name. But before God changed him, Israel was Jacob, in fact, Jacob to the core: deceiver, supplanter, heel-grabber. Jacob had much to learn—and much to become—from the Shepherd, the Stone of Israel. We have as well.

Genesis 25:19-26 gives the account of the birth of twins, Esau and Jacob. Years earlier, God kept His promise by giving Abraham and Sarah their promised child, Isaac. After Isaac married Rebekah, they were childless for years, which caused them as much consternation as being childless for so long had cause Isaac's parents. "Isaac prayed to the LORD on behalf of his wife because she was barren; and the LORD answered him, and Rebekah his wife conceived" (Gen. 25:21). In one way God granted the prayer with Rebekah's pregnancy. Yet, the pre-natal wrestling match inside the womb raised additional concerns. Rebekah inquired of God why this blessing He gave was so difficult. The Lord revealed the reason for the intense struggle within her: "Two nations are in your womb; and two peoples will be separated from your body; and one people shall be stronger than the other; and the older shall serve the younger" (Gen 25:23).

God gave fiat pronouncement that the older shall serve the younger. Although God declared it, this did not necessarily mean that everyone would accept it. Nonetheless, events would transpire precisely as God had said, in spite of any human efforts or hindrances, and in spite of the brotherly feud that began even in the womb. Esau was born first, but came into this world with his little brother already gripping him by his heel—which is the basis of the name Jacob (Gen. 25:26). The birth only openly initiated the ongoing struggle between the older brother and his little brother—the grabber—that would last for almost all of their lives.

The Genesis account also describes the growth and development of the brothers. When the boys grew up, Esau became a skillful hunter, a man of the field, but Jacob was a peaceful man living in tents. The friction between the two boys also became a wedge between Isaac and Rebekah, for the unwise parental favor of one child over the other became a way of life. "Now Isaac loved Esau, because he had a taste for game, but Rebekah loved Jacob" (Gen. 25:28)

One monumental development occurred when Esau sold his birthright in Genesis 25:29-34:

When Jacob had cooked stew, Esau came in from the field and he was famished; and Esau said to Jacob, "Please let me have a swallow of that red stuff there, for I am famished." Therefore his name was called Edom.
But Jacob said, "First sell me your birthright."

> Esau said, "Behold, I am about to die; so of what use then is the birthright to me?"
> And Jacob said, "First swear to me"; so he swore to him, and sold his birthright to Jacob.
> Then Jacob gave Esau bread and lentil stew; and he ate and drank, and rose and went on his way. Thus Esau despised his birthright.

The admirable aspect of this narrative is that Jacob wanted the birthright blessing due the older much more than Esau wanted it. Although not specifically mentioned in the text, Rebekah probably had informed her beloved son Jacob of God's pronouncement before the birth of her twins. Far less admirable were the means that Jacob employed to procure this blessing. God had previously divinely decreed; Jacob chose, instead, to grab and supplant, seizing as he had at birth when he latched onto Esau's heel. At this point in his life, Jacob was neither believing nor trusting God to bring His promise to fulfillment. However, from Jacob's viewpoint, an unwitnessed transaction between brothers in the field is hardly binding. Because he did not trust Esau, Jacob next began procuring the blessing by means of deceit (Gen.27). This hurriedly arranged deception came as Isaac intended to bless Esau. Perhaps Isaac did not believe Rebekah's account of God's answer about the older child serving the younger; after all, Scripture gives no indication that God had told him this. Nevertheless, God had stated it, and it would come about exactly as He had said. The Holy One used even human folly to accomplish His will. Disguising himself as Esau, the supplanter Jacob cautiously approached his vision-failing father to receive the blessing that once given was binding. When Isaac was convinced that his son was Esau, he pronounced this bonded declaration on Jacob: "Now may God give you of the dew of heaven, and of the fatness of the earth, and an abundance of grain and new wine; may peoples serve you, and nations bow down to you; be master of your brothers, and may your mother's sons bow down to you. Cursed be those who curse you, and blessed be those who bless you" (Gen. 27:28-29).

Immediately after Isaac's pronouncement, Esau returned to receive his expected birthright. Notice that he made no mention of having previously forfeited his inherited blessing to Jacob; his actions strongly indicate that he had no intention of keeping his sworn word. Both Isaac and Esau soon realized that Jacob had deceived them and had received the binding consequences of Isaac's pronouncement:

> And he [Isaac] said, "Your brother came deceitfully and has taken away your blessing."

Then he [Esau] said, "Is he not rightly named Jacob, for he has sup-
planted me these two times? He took away my birthright, and behold,
now he has taken away my blessing." And he said, "Have you not
reserved a blessing for me?"
But Isaac replied to Esau, "Behold, I have made him your master, and
all his relatives I have given to him as servants; and with grain and
new wine I have sustained him. Now as for you then, what can I do,
my son?" (Gen. 27:35-37)

Fearing Esau's violent retaliation, Rebekah hastily arranged for Jacob
to depart and live with her relatives in her old homeland. So the spiritually young deceiver left his home, his parents, his friends, his way of
life, and he would not return for over twenty years (Gen. 31:38, 41).
Jacob got what he wanted—and more—because God was about to
intervene and to begin changing and training him with lessons that
would break and renew him in the process. God had much to root out
of the supplanter, but the Master Teacher knew exactly how to transform a deceiver into a prince, beginning with a most unexpected
encounter with the God whom Jacob did not know very well.

Many young children learn the story of Jacob's ladder in Sunday
school or in Children's Church because this is one of the all-time great
flannel board lessons in Scripture. The problem is that most people
who know the account do not realize its significance. For instance, they
assume the story depicts God *rewarding* Jacob by giving him a revelatory dream. However, from before his birth up through Genesis 28,
nothing that Jacob has done is good, pure, or admirable. What God performs in this chapter is sheer grace upon grace—matching such grace
that He demonstrates in our own lives.

Exceedingly beyond this divine display of grace, God was also
keeping His Word. God had made and ratified a binding covenant
decades before with Jacob's grandfather Abraham involving the land,
a promised seed (lineage), and a blessing that ultimately would be to
all the nations (Gen. 12:1-3). In God's design, all would eventually culminate in the life and ministry of the Messiah. In the fulness of time
God would eventually send forth His Son to be born into Abraham's
very family lineage (Matt. 1:1-17; Luke 3:23, 34). From the time of
Genesis 12 onward, God had to maintain the seed lineage in order to
fulfill both His Word and His will. By God's divine selection, Jacob—
not Esau—had been designated as the progenitor seed lineage, which

had been determined before the twins were ever born, as Romans 9:10-13 demonstrate:

> And not only this, but there was Rebekah also, when she had conceived twins by one man, our father Isaac; for though the twins were not yet born, and had not done anything good or bad, so that God's purpose according to His choice would stand, not because of works but because of Him who calls, it was said to her, "The older will serve the younger."
> Just as it is written, "Jacob I loved, but Esau I hated."

So one of the most vital aspects of what God was about to do involved His truthfulness *and* His capacity to fulfill the covenant He had sworn by Himself to fulfill. Simply put, this story is not about Jacob—this account is about God.

Genesis 28:12-15 describes Jacob's most memorable night, as God reaffirmed with Jacob the land, seed, and blessing promises He had previously made with Abraham:

> He [Jacob] had a dream, and behold, a ladder was set on the earth with its top reaching to heaven; and behold, the angels of God were ascending and descending on it. And behold, the LORD stood above it and said, "I am the LORD, the God of your father Abraham and the God of Isaac; the land on which you lie, I will give it to you and to your descendants. Your descendants will also be like the dust of the earth, and you will spread out to the west and to the east and to the north and to the south; and in you and in your descendants shall all the families of the earth be blessed. Behold, I am with you and will keep you wherever you go, and will bring you back to this land; for I will not leave you until I have done what I have promised you."

Two other verses reveal Jacob's thoughts after his encounter with God: "Then Jacob awoke from his sleep and said, 'Surely the LORD is in this place, and I did not know it.' He was afraid and said, 'How awesome is this place! This is none other than the house of God, and this is the gate of heaven'" (Gen. 28:16-17). What Jacob stated is a childlike theology or understanding of God. Note how he repeatedly focused on "place" (twice), "house" and "gate"—all are inanimate objects. From Jacob's standpoint—who lived his life attempting to determine who owned what—he had not only stumbled onto God, but he also had unknowingly entered into God's territorial abode: the very place, house, and gate of God.

The revelatory dream that God gave Jacob greatly affected the habitual deceiver. Jacob responded as best he knew how at this very early part of his spiritual pilgrimage:

> So Jacob rose early in the morning, and took the stone that he had put under his head and set it up as a pillar and poured oil on its top. He called the name of that place Bethel; however, previously the name of the city had been Luz. Then Jacob made a vow, saying, "If God will be with me and will keep me on this journey that I take, and will give me food to eat and garments to wear, and I return to my father's house in safety, then the LORD will be my God.
> "And this stone, which I have set up as a pillar, will be God's house, and of all that You give me I will surely give a tenth to You" (Gen. 28:18-22).

An aspect of this last statement by Jacob is intriguing: "This stone, which I have set up as a pillar, will be God's house" (Gen. 28:22). This was Jacob's first association with God and a stone, in this case an anointed stone, a pillar for God's house. Again, this is relatively early in God's progressive revelation of Himself and His redemptive plan. When Solomon dedicated the Temple in Jerusalem over a thousand years later, the young king confessed how ridiculous the thought was that any structure — let alone one simple stone — could possibly contain God's presence. In 2 Chronicles 6:18, David's son declared in amazement, "But will God indeed dwell with mankind on the earth? Behold, heaven and the highest heaven cannot contain You; how much less this house which I have built." That was in reference to the beautifully constructed temple and in accordance with God's design. Jacob's design was much simpler: "And this stone, which I set up as a pillar, will be God's house" (Gen 28:22).

God neither confirmed nor rebuked Jacob for his statement, but ultimately God rejected Jacob's offer. In the eternal agreement of the Godhead before creation, They had already decided what would be – and even more — Who would be.

No, God Himself, not Jacob, would select the Stone. God would also anoint His Stone. He, too, would set His Stone in His own designated house — in the future, in the fullness of time — in the divinely ordained life and ministry of Jesus. And wonders of wonders — God Himself would actually indwell His own Stone.

We must skip over much of Jacob's life and leave many details for additional studies. Suffice it to say for the present that Jacob eventually returned to the Promised Land (Gen. 32). For over twenty years, he had not seen his brother whom he had deceived. The last time Jacob had seen Esau, Jacob had known that his brother intended to kill him at the first available opportunity. As far as Jacob knew, nothing had changed. After an absence of so many years, Jacob prepared to meet Esau and was most fearful (Gen. 32:3-8). Jacob was becoming a changed man. Instead of using his previous means of deception, Jacob voiced his concern directly to God. Notice how the content of his prayer dramatically changed over the years:

> Jacob said, "O God of my father Abraham and God of my father Isaac, O LORD, who said to me, 'Return to your country and to your relatives, and I will prosper you,' I am unworthy of all the lovingkindness and of all the faithfulness which You have shown to Your servant; for with my staff only I crossed this Jordan, and now I have become two companies. Deliver me, I pray, from the hand of my brother, from the hand of Esau; for I fear him, that he will come and attack me and the mothers with the children. For You said, 'I will surely prosper you and make your descendants as the sand of the sea, which is too great to be numbered'" (Gen. 32:9-12).

Note also the shepherding aspects that Jacob acknowledged or asked of God: "lovingkindness," "faithfulness," "deliver me," "You said, 'I will prosper you.'" This differs significantly from Jacob's previous grabbings. His prayer is also much more mature than the childishly foolish *"If* you bless me, *then* you will be my God" prayer of Genesis 28:20-21.

Jacob prepared to meet Esau, but, instead, once more unexpectedly encountered God (Gen. 32:24-32). In this extremely rich section of Scripture—we must not linger around this gold mine at the present time—God changed Jacob's name to Israel. Israel still grabbed, but this time he grabbed God, telling Him: "I will not let you go unless you bless me." God extended grace and blessed Israel much in the way that God had already promised back in Genesis 28.

After having striven with God, Jacob's meeting his brother Esau must have been anticlimactic for the newly named Israel (Gen. 33). Once the reunion occurred in proper fashion, the two brothers parted in peace. Israel had returned to the Promised Land as God had disclosed to him years earlier.

What takes place next is an eternally momentous occurrence, although we usually casually read many such sections. Genesis 33:18-20 states:

Now Jacob came safely to the city of Shechem, which is in the land of Canaan, when he came from Paddan-aram, and camped before the city. He bought the piece of land where he had pitched his tent from the hand of the sons of Hamor, Shechem's father, for one hundred pieces of money. Then he erected there an altar and called it El-Elohe-Israel.

In keeping with what Jacob (now Israel) declared in Genesis 28:20-21, in his "If you will bless me, then you will be my God" prayer, Israel fulfilled his word. He built an altar and named it in our translation, "God, the God of Israel." Here was his personal testimony of the faithful God Who had been exceedingly faithful to him.

There is something else vital that we must note. Years later when the aged Israel knew he would soon die, he summoned his faithful son Joseph in order to bless him and his children (Gen. 48). It is in this same context that Israel said, "The God who has been my shepherd all my life" (48:15). Because of Joseph's great qualities and kindness, Israel blessed him above his brothers, stating, "I give you one portion more than your brothers, which I took from the hand of the Amorite with my sword and my bow" (Gen. 48:22). Joseph was to receive one extra portion — and what a portion that turned out to be. Lost in our English reading is exactly what Israel passed on to Joseph. The Hebrew word for portion is *shechem*, meaning shoulder or ridge. It would eventually take on the proper name Shechem, a town that played vital roles in the nation's history. Centuries later, Shechem would be the place where the elder Joshua gathered Israel for the final time (Josh. 24:1), where he demanded that the people, "choose for yourselves today whom you will serve . . . as for me and my house, we will serve the LORD" (Josh. 24:15). Furthermore, Shechem would be the place where a temple would be erected centuries later to compete with the legitimate one that Solomon had previously constructed in Jerusalem.

But beyond this, Shechem would also be the place where, almost two thousand years later, the Shepherd — the Stone of Israel — would purposely seek and redeem a lost lamb.

He comes there alone. Having left Judea, Jesus journeyed north toward Galilee and through the region of Samaria. If you had asked the opinion of many of the day, they would have readily told you that Jesus had unwisely traversed through enemy territory. Samaritans: half-breed bastards who had mingled their sacred Jewish blood with that of their Assyrian conquerors over seven centuries earlier. Later in

His ministry, when accosted by His opponents, Jesus received one of the harshest accusations ever made against Him in John 8:48: "Do we not say rightly that you are a Samaritan and have a demon?" So great was this Jewish disdain that they attempted to make little distinction between Samaritans and demoniacs. Common custom and Jewish good sense mandated that one must circumvent Samaria when traveling from Judea into Galilee. Although avoiding Samaria made the trip much longer, it was better to have a lengthier walk than to have the accompanying contamination one bore by mere association with the Samaritans. Nonetheless, Jesus entered the region unashamedly. He feared neither public perception nor personal defilement. Although He, too, was weary from His journey, He comes there under divine mandate—both to receive and to give water.

The account of John 4 indicates that Jesus was sitting alone by the well (John 4:6)—but this was not just any well in the region. Jesus sat at *the* well. John revealed vital details for understanding much of the conversation that would follow: "So He came to a city of Samaria called Sychar, near the parcel of ground that Jacob gave to his son Joseph; and Jacob's well was there. So Jesus, being wearied from His journey, was sitting thus by the well. It was about the sixth hour" (John 4:5-6). This is the same well that Jacob had given to Joseph back in Genesis 48:22, and this is the context from which Jacob attested to "the God who has been my shepherd all my life" (Gen. 48:15). The well was functional because it supplied water, but beyond that, this was a well of Samaritan history and pride. Although the Jews disdained the Samaritans (and the Samaritans the Jews), the Samaritans were quite proud of their ancestral lineage. This well was their Plymouth Rock; Jacob's well was their heritage.

Here the Shepherd stations Himself. Jesus sits alone by Jacob's well of stone, not many yards away from where Jacob had made an altar to Him, naming it "God, the God of Israel." Here Jesus waits for the lamb who will unexpectedly encounter Him, much in the same way her ancestor Jacob unexpectedly experienced his life-changing encounter with God almost nineteen hundred years earlier.

She comes to the well alone. She is an outcast among a people of outcasts—a Samaritan among Samaritans. Sychar was a very small village about one-half mile north of Jacob's well. A dirt path worn from centuries of wear led to the well. This woman had walked this path so many times before, almost every time — if not all times — by herself. As she performed her arduous labor, she had no companions with whom to engage in friendly conversations; no discourse with mothers about family affairs or household solutions to everyday matters; no trusted friend to confide deep-heart secrets and hopes.

John noted, "it was about the sixth hour" (John 4:6). If he employed Roman time, the hour was 6:00 P.M. If he used Jewish time, which seems more likely, it was about 12:00 noon. Women usually drew water earlier in the morning or at the end of the day and usually in groups; however, she does not draw water then. She comes during the heat of the day — alone.

She is a whore. A married whore, or at least she had been, but why bother now. Later when Jesus asked her to go get her husband, she replied, "I have no husband." In the penetrating revelation of the eyes of God, Jesus said to her, "You have correctly said, 'I have no husband'; for you have had five husbands, and the one whom you now have is not your husband; this you have said truly" (John 4:17-18).

Two scenarios are possible. Perhaps each of her five husbands had died. Years later during Passion Week, in tempting Jesus, the Sadducees described a woman who was married seven times, each time the previous husband had died (Matt. 22:25-27). Had the Sadducees heard of this account that would later be recorded in John 4 and purposely used it as the basis for their attempt to prod Jesus? If so, they knew that Jesus could not deny this possibility because He had previously encountered such a woman years before. If this was their thinking, the Sadducees concluded that they would force Jesus to respond. He could neither claim ignorance nor deny the plausibility of such a story.

The second possibility is much more likely: the Samaritan woman had been passed from husband to husband. Under the Law of Moses, and according to the Matthew 22 account, such a widow was to marry the brother of her husband. The Samaritans held to the Pentateuch, which contains this teaching concerning widows (Deut. 25:1-10). But John did not state that she married brothers. If she had been widowed, she could have revealed this detail to Jesus. If she had been widowed, the women probably would have treated her with a degree of respect and sympathy, as Ruth's mother-in-law Naomi was treated in the Book of Ruth, unless they placed some superstition over one associated with so many deaths. Who were these men who had married her? Did some die? Did some abandon her? Did all? Who in this small village would marry a woman who had been married five times already? The types of men she bound herself to were most likely of the basest nature.

We know nothing of her early background. She may have entered into the first marriage at a very young age, perhaps arranged by others for myriad reasons, all usually funneling down to money. This woman may have loved none of her husbands nor they her. Whether the first one died, divorced, or abandoned her, we do not know. What we do know is that four more husbands followed, each sharing one common characteristic: either by choice or by death, they all left her. Receiving kindness, let alone love, was an alien concept to her. With her sixth partner, why marry? What did it mean, anyway, other than a temporary abode before being turned out and picked up by the next "husband" who had no intention whatsoever of a "til death do we part" relationship. Even in the biblical account, unlike so many other characters throughout the Bible, her name is never given. She is simply "a woman of Samaria" or "the woman." After all, with whose name would she associate herself?

So she comes to the well alone. If she passed other women on the path, they likely would divert their eyes and perhaps especially cover the eyes of their children, choosing to stray off the path so as not to become defiled in her presence. Men of low morals, however, would pay her much more attention, hoping to gain sexual favors from one who had the reputation of so freely giving them. Sychar was a village, not a town. In village life, not many secrets stay hidden long. Her situation, plus whatever else the gossip rounds added in elaborate detail, made her the subject of many conversations that she was not present to hear. Just as well; she would be spoken of either in contempt or in laughing mockery, which, after all, inflicts a far deeper sting of contempt.

And then in the midst of her drudgery she unexpectedly encounters Jesus. She was not looking for Him—not even aware that He existed—yet He purposely sought her. The account in John 4 is so vivid it speaks for itself:

> There came a woman of Samaria to draw water. Jesus said to her, "Give Me a drink." For His disciples had gone away into the city to buy food.
> Therefore the Samaritan woman said to Him, "How is it that You, being a Jew, ask me for a drink since I am a Samaritan woman?" (For Jews have no dealings with Samaritans.)
> Jesus answered and said to her, "If you knew the gift of God, and who it is who says to you, 'Give Me a drink,' you would have asked Him,

and He would have given you living water."

She said to Him, "Sir, You have nothing to draw with and the well is deep; where then do You get that living water? You are not greater than our father Jacob, are You, who gave us the well, and drank of it himself and his sons and his cattle?"

Jesus answered and said to her, "Everyone who drinks of this water will thirst again; but whoever drinks of the water that I will give him shall never thirst; but the water that I will give him will become in him a well of water springing up to eternal life."

The woman said to Him, "Sir, give me this water, so I will not be thirsty nor come all the way here to draw" (John 4:7-15).

Obviously, two levels of conversation took place: namely, those regarding physical and spiritual water. Each was necessary to life, both physical and spiritual; however, the woman knew only the physical. Note in John 4:12 how the woman referred to her ancestor Jacob and to the well. Jesus understood this and lovingly nudged her to spiritual truths. When the woman asked, "You are not greater than our father Jacob, are You?" The way she asked, as recorded in the Greek text, indicates that she obviously expected the obvious answer, "No, I am not." Jesus answered in such a way as to lead her to another conclusion (John 4:16-19):

He said to her, "Go, call your husband and come here."

The woman answered and said, "I have no husband." Jesus said to her, "You have correctly said, 'I have no husband'; for you have had five husbands, and the one whom you now have is not your husband; this you have said truly."

The woman said to Him, "Sir, I perceive that You are a prophet."

Most people who read the Bible would not consider Jacob to have been a prophet, yet he did prophesy in Genesis 49, speaking to the twelve tribes, "what shall befall you in the future" [or literally in the Hebrew, "the last days" or "end of the days"] (49:1). The woman reached a conclusion after asking, "You are not greater than our father Jacob, are You?" — "Obviously you must be, at least to a degree, because I have never met you, and yet you tell things about me that no one told you." Having recognized and designated Jesus as a prophet, the woman turned toward spiritual matters that had long puzzled her. Few would have considered this type of woman as having any interest whatsoever in the things of God. Jesus knew better, which was one reason that He was there. With the woman's background, she probably would have had no one else to ask. What an Audience God granted her to ask about spiritual matters! This woman had been born into a feudal conflict that had lasted for almost eight hundred years. She wanted to know who was right—Jew or Samaritan:

> "Sir I perceive that You are a prophet. Our fathers worshiped in this mountain, and you people say that in Jerusalem is the place where men ought to worship."
> Jesus said to her, "Woman, believe Me, an hour is coming when neither in this mountain nor in Jerusalem will you worship the Father. You worship what you do not know; we worship what we know, for salvation is from the Jews. But an hour is coming, and now is, when the true worshipers will worship the Father in spirit and truth; for such people the Father seeks to be His worshipers. God is spirit, and those who worship Him must worship in spirit and truth" (4:19-24).

Jesus disclosed to the woman His teaching that would so infuriate the Jewish officials not long thereafter. Note that the woman directed her questions about *where* to worship God. The Jews and the Samaritans worshiped the same God of the Old Testament. Her question was not Who, but where, on this *mountain*, or is Jerusalem *the place* where people ought to worship? All throughout His ministry, whenever Jesus encountered hearts earnestly seeking the Truth, He kept revealing God's Word to them—whether to this woman or to Nicodemus in the previous chapter of John 3. Although not denying God's divine choice of Jerusalem and its irreplaceable importance even in the future return of Messiah, Jesus took the question away from the place and redirected it to the spiritual status of the individual: "But an hour is coming, and now is, when the true worshipers will worship the Father in spirit and truth" (John 4:23). She asked about the past; Jesus responded about the present and the future. Although divinely important in God's plan, the place of worship is not the ultimate issue. The essential spiritual qualities and requirements of the true worshiper receive emphasis: spirit (Spirit?) and truth.

Many of Jesus' adversaries would later respond along the lines of, "I don't believe you! You are mad! This is *our* mountain, and I won't leave it for anyone" If the woman had responded using similar or other reasons that people give for not receiving God's truth, the story would have ended there. Instead, this little lamb goes deeper with her questions, as she nuzzled closer to the Shepherd without any fear. Twice Jesus had corrected the Samaritan woman on what she did not know. Once He said, "if you knew" (4:10), and then a more generalized, "You [plural—Samaritans] do not know" (4:22). Perhaps to indicate that she did, in fact, know something that is true, the woman said, in effect, "I do know this: Messiah is coming (He who is called Christ); when that One comes, He will declare all things to us" (John 4:25).

John 4:26 records that Jesus said to her, "I who speak to you am He."

Actually, in the culture and the setting, Jesus said much more. Literally in the Greek, John 4:26 reads, "I AM (*ego eimi* — God's name), the One who is speaking to you." Later in John 8 the Jews asked the same question that the Samaritan woman asked, but they took it even further: "Surely You are not greater than our father Abraham?" (John 8:53). The Greek wording made the expected answer obvious: "Of course not." Instead, Jesus answered with the same base component that He had used months earlier with the Samaritan woman, "Truly, truly I say to you, before Abraham was born, I AM (*ego eimi*)" (8:58). The Jews fully understood His statement and considered it brazenly sacrilegious, and they immediately took up stones to stone this blasphemer. But Jesus hid Himself. He had revealed divine Truth; they had rejected it. At this point there was no reason to offer any more. But for the one in John 4 who sought the truth, heard it, and received it unto herself, He offered more — He offered Himself — and she readily received Him. True worshipers — even the spiritual newborns — always worship in spirit and truth.

When we get to heaven we will see the biblical accounts complete with the facial expressions of those present. It would be understandable if Jesus had replied with the radiant smile of the Shepherd who had found the lost sheep, literally in the Greek, "I AM," — employing His own name of God, — "the One who is speaking to you." God is speaking to you, right now, just as He did then — even beyond what He had spoken with your father Jacob. In the presence of the one whom He had sought, who became a worshiper of the Father in spirit and truth, Jesus revealed God to the woman — and she would never be the same again throughout eternity.

One more quick aspect to note: John added that the woman left her water pot and went into the city and said to the men (as she possibly had no women to go to), "Come, see a man who told me all the things that I have done; this is not the Christ, is it?" (John 4:28-29). In John 1:45 Philip found Nathanael and declared to him, "We have found Him of whom Moses in the Law and also the Prophets wrote — Jesus of Nazareth, the son of Joseph." Nathanael hardly believed this report from his friend, asking with noted sarcasm, "Can any good thing come out of Nazareth?" Yet, pagan Samaritans, with only one sentence by an outcast woman, caused men to go immediately and to investigate. Why?

Part of the reason may be that Sychar was such a small village. The sins associated with this woman were never performed alone. Her statement "come see a man who told me all the things I have done" may not have been welcomed news to the assembled men. *All* the things? "Yes, *all* the things." In a village this small, "all the things" may have involved some of the very ones with whom she spoke. Better go and investigate this before the women do. The next line in John reads, "They went out of the city, and were coming to Him" (John 4:30). We will find out in heaven whether in their haste they turned over tables and chairs on the way out to discover exactly how much this One did know.

Jesus had originally asked the woman to, "Give me a drink," but He never got one. The woman left her water pot as she raced back to the village. Still, Jesus was more than content with the outcome. He actually had given water—and life eternal—to one who needed it much more than He needed physical refreshment.

She would never be an outcast again; she would never be alone. Even in the future as she walked the path to the well, each trip would vividly remind her of the Shepherd she had so unexpectedly encountered there. Her water vessel even looked different, and she could never consider it totally empty again, for it would become a constant reminder of the day that she received the Water of Life. Since John recorded that many of the Samaritans first believed because of her word (4:39), and then later because of the words of Jesus, many more believed (4:41), she also picked up a new family of faith who likewise drank from the Savior's spring. The Good Shepherd likely would have divinely nudged other newborn sheep to walk alongside this first Samaritan lamb in rejuvenating sisterhood.

She came to the well that day an outcast among outcasts. She ran back to her village a princess.

Jesus and the woman are the main characters of this biblical account, but one other is mentioned whom we generally overlook. John 4 actually presents three vital participants in this salvation drama. The three share a common characteristic: they each seek. Three different seekers—three different scenarios. The Shepherd seeks a lost lamb. The woman seeks something that she does not really know—"Lord, give me this living water." She eventually seeks the Someone who had first sought her. As the Shepherd seeks, so does the Father. In John 4:23 Jesus reveals, "But an hour is coming, and now is, when the true worshipers will worship the Father in spirit and truth; for such people the

Father *seeks* to be His worshipers." God the Father seeks: present tense, continuous on-going activity. This is not limited to the Savior seeking lost sheep. The day of salvation begins the process of knowing God, but it does not end there. God not only wants people saved, but God the Father also actively seeks for true worshipers to worship in spirit (or Spirit?) and truth. Scripture gives no indication that the seeking by God has ceased or declined in any way whatsoever.

We are on our way to Mount Zion, the city of the Great King. As with physical travelers over the centuries who would journey three times yearly to the great national feasts of Israel, we, too, have begun our own journey. But before we see the vistas of Jerusalem that God so delights in showing His children, we, too, have some land to traverse, but instead of walking miles to Jerusalem, our pilgrimage is through the pages of Scripture—often through some dark passages and often through obscure books for most readers of the Bible. But as with the earthly pilgrims, our journey promises to be more than worth any effort we exert.

How arduous it must have been during biblical times for mothers with small children or infants to travel up to one hundred miles or more on donkey or on foot. As the Jewish mothers no doubt used to encourage their weary and impatient children on their pilgrimage to Jerusalem, "Hush, child! We are not there yet. We have a ways to go. Settle down. Be patient. It will be worth it when we arrive. We are going to the Holy City of God"—the same holds true for us. But we have work to do. We must drop down into the Word "to see with their eyes and hear with their ears" the events and truths that God reveals. As always, God's Word contains marvelous mysteries and markers that God Himself has set before us. But we must be good Bible detectives. Expressed in another way, we are mining for gold from God's gold mine—not only with Divine permission, but also with Divine delight. Mining for riches, however, takes careful consideration and sifting. In order for us to worship God in spirit and truth, we need to know—and sift through—some biblical history and chronology, and recognize a gold nugget when we see one.

Behold! The life-giving Shepherd is at the well—and He still speaks to us today.

Behold! If we knew the gift of God and Who is speaking, we, too, would run to the well, and then away from it to tell others.

Behold! God has set forth His Stone all throughout Scripture for us to see.

After all, the Father still seeks—presently seeks—worshipers to worship Him in spirit and truth. And He passionately desires for us to know, love, and worship the Shepherd, the Stone of Israel—Whom God Himself selected.

2

THE PLACE

The Samaritan woman of John 4 questioned Jesus about which place of worship was legitimate. In John 4:20 she stated, "Our fathers worshiped in this mountain [referring to the mountain that God had given Jacob in Genesis 33:18-20], and you people say that Jerusalem is the place where men ought to worship." Although Jesus would expand the concepts of true worship to her, actually the place designated by God is of utmost importance. After all, it is His choice. That the woman asked no frivolous question is seen in Jesus' response: "You worship what you do not know; we worship what we know, for salvation is from the Jews" (John 4:22). In a rebuttal that at first may seem strong, Jesus spoke the truth: you Samaritans have the wrong place. Second Chronicles 7:15-16 is one of many Old Testament passages where God Himself made promises regarding His Temple in Jerusalem: "Now My eyes shall be open and My ears attentive to the prayer offered in this place. For now I have chosen and consecrated this house that My name may be there forever, and My eyes and My heart will be there perpetually."

The woman traced her people's rights to the mountain back to Jacob in Genesis 33. This was the best she and the Samaritans could do. Yet, Jacob was third, not first, in line: Abraham, Isaac, and then Jacob. By the time Jacob was born, God had already revealed and accomplished much. To begin the Samaritan's history with Jacob would be like beginning the history of the United States with the Civil War.

One item that the woman had not mentioned, which Jesus could have, was that Shechem was the first capital of the divided kingdom after Solomon. Just a few decades earlier, God had ratified the Davidic Covenant that granted forever the right to kingship to David's lineage. The covenant made by God was eternal and everlasting. God had chosen

Jerusalem for His abode and had allowed His Temple to be built. Then He had filled it with His own glory, much in the same way that the Book of Exodus ends with God's glory filling the tabernacle (Exod. 40:34-38). Eventually, because of Solomon's blatant disobedience, God divided the kingdom into two separate parts. The ten northern tribes kept the name Israel, and the two southern tribes of Judah and Benjamin took the name Judah.

The first king of the new Northern Kingdom was Jeroboam. First Kings 12:25 indicates that "Jeroboam built Shechem in the hill country of Ephraim," but that was hardly his last act. Fearful that his kingdom would fall, Jeroboam concocted his own strategy for self-preservation, as 1 Kings 12:25-32 reveals:

> Then Jeroboam built Shechem in the hill country of Ephraim, and lived there. And he went out from there and built Penuel.
> Jeroboam said in his heart, "Now the kingdom will return to the house of David. If this people go up to offer sacrifices in the house of the LORD at Jerusalem, then the heart of this people will return to their LORD, even to Rehoboam king of Judah; and they will kill me and return to Rehoboam king of Judah."
> So the king consulted, and made two golden calves, and he said to them, "It is too much for you to go up to Jerusalem; behold your gods, O Israel, that brought you up from the land of Egypt." He set one in Bethel, and the other he put in Dan. Now this thing became a sin, for the people went to worship before the one as far as Dan. And he made houses on high places, and made priests from among all the people who were not of the sons of Levi.
> Jeroboam instituted a feast in the eighth month on the fifteenth day of the month, like the feast that is in Judah, and he went up to the altar; thus he did in Bethel, sacrificing to the calves which he had made. And he stationed in Bethel the priests of the high places which he had made.

Everything about Jeroboam's actions was sinful. God reacted in holy wrath because of one golden calf in Exodus 32; two golden calves erected in blatant covenant disobedience would hardly go unnoticed. God had mandated that the tribe of Levi through Aaron's sons would be His designated priesthood; northern Israel now had a different priesthood comprised of people from all the tribes. Jeroboam instituted another feast in the eighth month, possibly rivaling the Feast of Tabernacles that God instituted in the seventh month. First Kings 12:33 gives the best summary phrase of Jeroboam's action. Although referring specifically to the feast he invented ("even in the month which he had devised in his own heart") the term "devised in his own heart" fits every other component as well. Every aspect of Jeroboam's religion was a willful rejection of God's revelation, replaced, instead, with a man-devised substitute. At Shechem—the very place where Joshua had demanded in Joshua 24:15, "Choose you this day whom you will serve"—Jeroboam and the northern tribes had already decided whom they would serve. If you had asked the participants at the time who was their God, they would have replied, "The God of Israel." If you could have asked God, He would have answered differently.

With this initial fracturing of the spiritual foundation, it is not surprising that the ten northern tribes fell to Gentiles. What is surprising is that God actually permitted the nation to exist for almost two hundred years. The Assyrians, the dominant world power at the time, eventually overthrew Israel and deported most of its inhabitants, although some of the godly remnant of the ten northern tribes migrated to the south before the exile, resulting in the fact that the tribes did not become extinct (2 Chron. 11:17-18; 15:8-12). If God had not miraculously intervened during Hezekiah's reign, the southern kingdom of Judah also would have fallen immediately afterward (2 Chron. 32).

Once Assyria defeated a nation, it not only deported a majority of the population, it usually repopulated the land with people of its own choosing. Thus began the lineage of what came to be known as the hated Samaritans of the New Testament. They had rejected God and the Davidic Covenant. They eventually constructed their own temple in an attempt to rival the true one in Jerusalem. In His own predetermined time, God severely punished His rebellious nation as He had repeatedly warned in His Word that He would do (Lev. 26; Deut. 28). However, to the Jews of Jesus' day, the most horrendous feature was that the Samaritans had permanently defiled their Jewish heritage by intermarrying with Gentiles.

Thus here was the background that formed the basis of the Samaritan woman's question: "Our fathers worshiped in this mountain, and you people say that in Jerusalem is the place where men ought to worship" (John 4:20). The division between Samaritan and Jew was a deep one. Jesus responded to her, "You worship what you do not know; we worship what we know, for salvation is from the Jews" (4:22). Everything about worship with the Samaritans was wrong: "you (plural) do not know." How could they know, at least know in truth? Jeroboam had concocted most of the religious practices of the nation, and he did so purposely to keep his people from worshiping in Jerusalem. As to the mountain on which the Samaritans worshiped, it was true that Jacob had previously worshiped at that place and had given the well to Joseph's children. But there would have been no Jacob without Abraham or Isaac—or even more to the point— without God. To trace one's heritage only as far as Jacob is to omit much of God's previous revelation. Jacob was part of the seed lineage, not the originator. God Himself had already ratified the eternally important Abrahamic covenant back in Genesis 15. Among other things, God had granted specific land promises. Abraham's grandson, Jacob, was in line as part of the promised seed blessing; however, he was in the line of succession—not its head.

Once more Jesus enlarged the Samaritan woman's understanding by broadening her biblical basis. Jesus spoke with certainty of the Holy Mountain in Jerusalem.

He should know: He Himself created it.

He should know: God Himself had designated the place.

He should know: He, too, is God.

He should know: before Abraham was, I AM.

He should know, because He was present for it all.

He should know, because ultimately the Stone aspect of His Person and work would manifest itself there, as the Godhead had so determined long before the foundation of the world.

Abraham had previously completed some long journeys with God, both physically and spiritually. Yet, in so many ways this was the longest. The God he had trusted—the God with whom he had walked for years; the God Who had blessed beyond logic—now called him to walk by faith and obedience, which earthly reasoning and natural instincts continually resist by their very nature.

In Genesis 22:1 God said, "Abraham!" Abraham responded by saying, "Here I am." An excited anticipation likely accompanied Abraham's answer. Each time God had called him or had appeared to him before, some new blessing or divine promise followed. Abraham was currently walking in obedience with God. He had no reason to expect anything different. Instead came the chilling but clear command: "Take now your son, your only son, whom you love, Isaac, and go to the land of Moriah, and offer him there as a burnt offering on one of the mountains of which I will tell you" (Gen. 22:2).

Although many who read the Bible know this story, we usually miss spiritual nuggets within this account. For instance, God does not merely tell Abraham what to do (that is, offer Isaac as a burnt offering); God tells him *where* to do it: "on *one* of the mountains which I will tell you." Not in any direction you wish. Not on one of several mountains within your sight. Not on one hill within the general vicinity. One mountain: one that the Creator God formed for His own choosing (Ps. 95:4-5). If this were simply the act of sacrificing his son, anywhere — including somewhere back of his current dwelling or inside his own tent — would suffice. Yet, God wanted this performed precisely where He had designated. Genesis 22:3 notes, "So Abraham rose early in the morning and saddled his donkey, and took two of his young men with him and Isaac his son; and he split wood for the burnt offering, and arose and went to *the place* of which God had told him." Again, "On the third day Abraham raised his eyes and saw *the place* from a distance" (Gen. 22:4) — a mountain in the land of Moriah (Gen. 22:2).

God had chosen Moriah for this divinely mandated sacrifice. The name Moriah is appropriate for the place where God sent Abraham. Lost in translation are sublime biblical nuances, almost puns of the original language. Moriah is a combination of three Hebrew words meaning, "the place," plus the verb "to see," and finally the "Yah" of Yahweh. *Moriah: the place to see God.* Yet, even beyond this, the word can be translated (with a few subtle changes to the root words) with either an active voice or a passive voice, with different results for each translation. The active voice makes the word mean, "The place where God provides or furnishes." The passive voice renders it, "The place where God appears." Both are correct grammatically; both are correct biblically; both factor in with the conversation between Abraham and Isaac.

Notice how the verb form in "Moriah" adds detail in Genesis 22:7-8:

> Isaac spoke to Abraham his father and said, "My father!" And he said, "Here I am, my son." And he said, "Behold, the fire and the wood, but where is the lamb for the burnt offering?"
> Abraham said, "God will *provide* [Literally, from the verb "to see" — God will see] for Himself the lamb for the burnt offering, my son." So the two of them walked on together.

Abraham's statement when paraphrased could be, "God will provide on Moriah, the place where God provides." And provide God did:

> Then they came to the place of which God had told him; and Abraham built the altar there and arranged the wood, and bound his son Isaac and laid him on the altar, on top of the wood. Abraham

stretched out his hand and took the knife to slay his son.
But the angel of the LORD called to him from heaven and said, "Abraham, Abraham!" And he said, "Here I am."
He said, "Do not stretch out your hand against the lad, and do nothing to him; for now I know that you fear God, since you have not withheld your son, your only son, from Me."
Then Abraham raised his eyes and looked, and behold, behind him a ram caught in the thicket by his horns; and Abraham went and took the ram and offered him up for a burnt offering in the place of his son (Gen. 22:9-13).

In a preliminary way, God had indeed "seen" for Himself a sacrifice. Note the connection Abraham made with what God accomplished. Genesis 22:14 states, "Abraham called the name of that place, 'The LORD Will Provide,' as it is said to this day, 'In the mount of the LORD it will be provided.'" This place became both a name and a proverb—and a promise—of God. Moriah: "the place where God appears." Moriah: "the place where God provides." Each translation is accurate, both grammatically and theologically.

Interestingly, the Samaritans (including the woman at the well in John 4) based their belief on the Samaritan Pentateuch, a re-translation of the first five books of the Old Testament. This work identified the mount where Abraham had attempted to sacrifice Isaac at Mount Gerizim, just outside of Shechem—not Mount Moriah. The Samaritans did not accept the rest of the Old Testament account as truthful.

But as picturesque and significant as the Hebrew word plays are, surprisingly, the word "Moriah" occurs in only one other place in the entire Bible. This reference is just as or even more important than the first account. Moriah was the same place as before, but with a different provision of God—and ultimately the residence for the Stone of Israel.

Everything about Second Samuel 24 and its parallel chapter First Chronicles 21 is perplexing at face value. In this account King David ordered his general Joab to conduct a census, an act that had been done at various times before in the history of Israel. In fact, much of the Book of Numbers is basically a census of the Exodus generation. Yet, when David took his census, everything was different. First Chronicles 21:7 states, "God was displeased with this thing, so He struck Israel." Why would God be displeased? Also, how could David's military commander Joab sense God's displeasure beforehand by warning David,

"Why does my Lord seek this thing? Why should he be a cause of guilt to Israel?" (1 Chron. 21:3). Nonetheless, David prevailed. The census was taken, followed by God's punishment of the king and his nation.

Actually, God responded in total harmony with His revealed Word. Earlier in His divinely decreed law, God had given the procedure whenever a census would be taken:

> The LORD also spoke to Moses, saying, "When you take a census of the sons of Israel to number them, then each one of them shall give a ransom for himself to the LORD, when you number them, so that there will be no plague among them when you number them.
>
> "This is what everyone who is numbered shall give: half a shekel according to the shekel of the sanctuary (the shekel is twenty gerahs), half a shekel as a contribution to the LORD. Everyone who is numbered, from twenty years old and over, shall give the contribution to the LORD. The rich shall not pay more and the poor shall not pay less than the half shekel, when you give the contribution to the LORD to make atonement for yourselves.
>
> "You shall take the atonement money from the sons of Israel and shall give it for the service of the tent of meeting, that it may be a memorial for the sons of Israel before the LORD, to make atonement for yourselves" (Exod. 30:11-16).

The sin was not that David took the census. The sin was that he disregarded God's Word about the ransom offerings, much in the same way that David had failed to follow God's instructions years before when transporting the Ark in a manner that God had not commanded (cf. 2 Sam. 6). Through pride or laziness or human rationalization, David purposely chose not to obey God's Word—and he immediately confessed his sin when later confronted with it.

However, there is more to this than merely David's sinful act. Beyond the physical events, the Bible also reveals behind-the-scenes activities in the spiritual realm. Both biblical texts begin with the spiritual realm—not the physical. Yet, even in this they differ, which only adds to the perplexing nature of these accounts. Second Samuel 24:1 states, "Now again the anger of the LORD burned against Israel, and it incited David against them to say, 'Go, number Israel and Judah.'" The parallel account in First Chronicles 21:1 raises even more questions, in this case by revealing additional information: "Then Satan stood up against Israel and moved David to number Israel." This is intriguing, but it raises questions. Why would Satan move David to number Israel? What did he intend to accomplish by his temptation—

or did he even know how God would respond?

So one account begins with God's activities; the other begins with Satan's. We would be totally unaware of either unless God in His sovereignty revealed it in His Word. Yet, since God did disclose these truths, they must be important. Still, knowing that something took place is not the same as understanding its significance. At the very least, however, something important must have occurred—and obviously something vastly beyond the mere human realm.

Satan appears in only the one verse, but God appears throughout the entire account. It reasons that we should follow God's leading in where He takes us. We need to see how the Lord responded, and if possible, why. God never does anything capriciously. If He chose to reveal these two glimpses into the spiritual world behind world affairs, we would do well to mark them.

Once David completed his census, God struck Israel. David confessed to God, "I have sinned greatly, in that I have done this thing. But now, please take away the iniquity of Your servant, for I have done very foolishly" (1 Chron. 21:8). The Lord then commanded His prophet to proclaim God's Word to David:

> The LORD spoke to Gad, David's seer, saying, "Go and speak to David, saying, Thus says the LORD, 'I offer you three things; choose for yourself one of them, which I will do to you.'"
> So Gad came to David and said to him, "Thus says the LORD, 'Take for yourself either three years of famine, or three months to be swept away before your foes, while the sword of your enemies overtakes you, or else three days of the sword of the LORD, even pestilence in the land, and the angel of the LORD destroying throughout all the territory of Israel.' Now, therefore, consider what answer I shall return to Him who sent me."
> David said to Gad, "I am in great distress; please let me fall into the hand of the LORD, for His mercies are very great. But do not let me fall into the hand of man" (1 Chron. 21:9-13).

The account reveals that 70,000 men of Israel died from the pestilence that God had sent (1 Chron. 21:14). Beyond this, "God sent an angel to Jerusalem to destroy it; but as he was about to destroy it, the LORD saw and was sorry over the calamity, and said to the destroying angel, 'It is enough; now relax your hand.' And the angel of the LORD was standing by the threshing floor of Ornan the Jebusite" (21:15). Jebus was the ancient name for Jerusalem; thus the inhabitants were called Jebusites.

The utter seriousness of the situation became evident when "David lifted up his eyes and saw the angel of the LORD standing between earth and heaven with his drawn sword in his hand stretched out over Jerusalem. Then David and the elders, covered with sackcloth, fell on their faces" (1 Chron. 21:16). David then said to God, "Is it not I who commanded to count the people? Indeed, I am the one who has sinned and done very wickedly, but these sheep, what have they done? O LORD my God, please let Your hand be against me and my father's household, but not against Your people that they should be plagued" (21:17). The angel of the LORD then commanded Gad to tell David that he "should go up and build an altar to the LORD on the threshing floor of Ornan the Jebusite" (21:18). Even in the midst of divine chastisement, God sovereignly directed the events so that David went back to the exact designated place that God had chosen.

The account continues in First Chronicles 21:19-25:

> So David went up at the word of Gad, which he spoke in the name of the LORD.
> Now Ornan turned back and saw the angel, and his four sons who were with him hid themselves. And Ornan was threshing wheat. As David came to Ornan, Ornan looked and saw David, and went out from the threshing floor and prostrated himself before David with his face to the ground.
> Then David said to Ornan, "Give me the site of this threshing floor, that I may build on it an altar to the LORD; for the full price you shall give it to me, that the plague may be restrained from the people."
> Ornan said to David, "Take it for yourself; and let my Lord the king do what is good in his sight. See, I will give the oxen for burnt offerings and the threshing sledges for wood and the wheat for the grain offering; I will give it all."
> But King David said to Ornan, "No, but I will surely buy it for the full price; for I will not take what is yours for the LORD, or offer a burnt offering which costs me nothing."
> So David gave Ornan 600 shekels of gold by weight for the site.

First Chronicles 21:26 notes, "Then David built an altar to the LORD there and offered burnt offerings and peace offerings. And he called to the LORD and He answered him with fire from heaven on the altar of burnt offering."

Usually, when we read lengthy Old Testament accounts, we generally know what took place, but rarely do we make the connections that God reveals in Scripture. For David and the nation Israel, this event became an act of judgment tendered with divine mercy. Interestingly, David responded somewhat like Jacob had centuries earlier in Genesis, saying, "This is the house of the LORD God, and this is the altar of burnt offering for Israel" (1 Chron. 22:1). Even more importantly, it is from this account that the Temple preparations began:

> So David gave orders to gather the foreigners who were in the land of Israel, and he set stonecutters to hew out stones to build the house of God. David prepared large quantities of iron to make the nails for the doors of the gates and for the clamps, and more bronze than could be weighed; and timbers of cedar logs beyond number, for the Sidonians and Tyrians brought large quantities of cedar timber to David.
> David said, "My son Solomon is young and inexperienced, and the house that is to be built for the LORD shall be exceedingly magnificent, famous and glorious throughout all lands. Therefore now I will make preparation for it." So David made ample preparations before his death (1 Chron. 22:2-5).

Yet, tucked away, almost without notice, is a one-sentence revelatory nugget that draws the entire account together. Nothing about this episode with David and the census and God's response merely happened haphazardly. God *led* David to the place, leading for three days as God had previously led Abraham for three days. Strategically, God led David to the exact place where He had led Abraham centuries before. Second Chronicles 3:1 uncovers a three-word goldmine: "Then Solomon began to build the house of the LORD in Jerusalem *on Mount Moriah,* where the LORD had appeared to his father David, at the place that David had prepared on the threshing floor of Ornan the Jebusite."

Moriah—the place where God appears. Note this same significance in 2 Chronicles 3:1: "Mount Moriah, where the LORD *appeared* to his father David"—again with a play on words from the verb part of the word Moriah.

The Samaritans, of which the woman of John 4 was representative, were wrong. God had selected Mount Moriah in Jerusalem—not Shechem in Samaria. Only twice does Moriah appear in the entire Bible: each instance depicts God's specific leading; each time requires God's specified sacrifice at His designated place. Both references look beyond the immediate participants to the greater work of God.

On Moriah: God will prepare (literally, "see") for Himself a lamb (Gen. 22:8).

Abraham named the place "The LORD will provide."

As it is said to this day, both proverbially and prophetically: "On the mountain of the LORD it will be provided" (Gen. 22:14).

Moriah: the place where God will provide for Himself a Lamb.

Moriah: the place where God will provide for us.

Moriah: the place where the Lord appeared to David (2 Chron. 3:1), becomes the Temple mount God chose to inhabit—*and* to place His name there forever (2 Chron. 7:16).

Moriah: the place to see God becomes the promised place where the LORD will appear. As His Holy Word would later reveal, "'And the LORD, whom you seek, will suddenly come to His Temple, and the messenger of the covenant, in whom you delight, behold, He is coming,' says the LORD of hosts" (Mal. 3:1).

Each element is true historically.

Each element is true for the future—especially in view of the Stone of Israel, whose dwelling it actually is.

3

THE DWELLING

fter God redeemed the people of Israel out of Egypt, He entered
into an additional covenant relationship with them. Over 430
years before the giving of the Law (Gal. 4:30), God had ratified the
Abrahamic Covenant that began what would eventually become the
nation of Israel (Gen. 15). In this covenant God promised a specific
land, a seed lineage, and that "in you all the families of the earth will
be blessed" (Gen. 12:1-3). Scripture repeatedly presents the Abrahamic
Covenant as an eternal one; it is just as valid today as it was on the day
it was ratified. For instance, regarding the title deed to the land, God
promised Abraham, "for all the land which you see, I will give it to you
and to your descendants *forever*" (Gen. 13:15). Later in Genesis 17, God
again emphasized the eternal nature of the Covenant that He had
entered into with Abraham, declaring, "And I will establish My
covenant between Me and you and your descendants [literally, "seed"]
after you throughout their generations for *an everlasting covenant*, to be
God to you and to your descendants after you" (Gen. 17:7). Not only
had the people entered into an everlasting covenant, but once more the
significance of the land comes into view. In the next verse, Genesis
17:8, God reiterated, "And I will give to you and to your descendants
after you, the land of your sojournings, all the land of Canaan, for *an
everlasting possession*; and I will be their God." Dozens of more verses
throughout Scripture bear holy witness to this.

The covenant that God made after the Exodus differed considerably
from the Abrahamic Covenant. The Mosaic Covenant, frequently referred
to generically as "the Law," was a conditional covenant of the way the
newly redeemed people were to live before their God and with each
other. The Abrahamic Covenant ratified by God alone was a covenant of
promised blessing. The Mosaic Covenant, however, contained promises

of either blessings or curses, which depended directly on the obedience (or lack thereof) of the nation of Israel. If the people obediently walked with Him, then God would bless them beyond measure. However, if the nation abandoned the true God for idols—which happened regularly throughout the rest of the Old Testament—God would severely punish them. Deuteronomy 28 reveals fifty-four verses of curses that God promised would come on the rebellious nation, including being exiled to the farthest ends of the earth (Deut. 28:64; cf. also 30:1). Although the Mosaic Covenant was a gracious outworking of God's salvation program, it, nonetheless, demonstrated the on-going biblical mandate, "to whom much is given, much is required" (Luke 12:48). Still, no matter the degree of sinfulness of any particular Jewish generation, the Abrahamic Covenant biblically requires that the Jewish people exist—as long as there is an earth, sun, and stars (Jer. 31:35-37).

The Bible clearly shows when the Mosaic Covenant came into existence. Just as had been the case with the Abrahamic Covenant, God ratified the Mosaic Covenant in blood:

> Moses wrote down all the words of the LORD. Then he arose early in the morning, and built an altar at the foot of the mountain with twelve pillars for the twelve tribes of Israel. He sent young men of the sons of Israel, and they offered burnt offerings and sacrificed young bulls as peace offerings to the LORD.
> Moses took half of the blood and put it in basins, and the other half of the blood he sprinkled on the altar. Then he took the book of the covenant and read it in the hearing of the people; and they said, "All that the LORD has spoken we will do, and we will be obedient!"
> So Moses took the blood and sprinkled it on the people, and said, "Behold the blood of the covenant, which the LORD has made with you in accordance with all these words" (Exod. 24:4-8).

However, the giving of the Law was not merely a divine listing of "do's and don'ts." A major purpose of the Mosaic Covenant was to protect the Jewish people from intermingling with various pagan tribes that surrounded them. Israel depended on the One true God; all of the surrounding nations served idols. If the Hebrew people obeyed the Mosaic Covenant (which both the Bible and history shows was rare and always short-lived), they would be protected from the harmful influences of the pagan false gods. As the Old Testament unfolded, the Hebrew people frequently and rebelliously pursued idolatry, and they committed other sins that God had warned against. God responded by sending His promised judgment. Even more to the point, a foundational component of the Mosaic Covenant was that God Himself would dwell among His very own redeemed people.

Notice how the aspect of God dwelling in the midst of His people is just as much a part of the Law as the giving of the Ten Commandments. With the covenant officially ratified, Moses returned to God for further instruction. Exodus 24:15-18 indicates that during this time God manifested a degree of His glory to Israel: "Then Moses went up to the mountain, and the cloud covered the mountain. The glory of the LORD rested on Mount Sinai, and the cloud covered it for six days; and on the seventh day He called to Moses from the midst of the cloud. And to the eyes of the sons of Israel the appearance of the glory of the LORD was like a consuming fire on the mountaintop. Moses entered the midst of the cloud as he went up to the mountain; and Moses was on the mountain forty days and forty nights."

God then gave directions concerning something that had never been done before in the history of His creation:

> "Let them construct a sanctuary for Me, that I may dwell among them. According to all that I am going to show you, as the pattern of the tabernacle and the pattern of all its furniture, just so you shall construct it" (Exod. 25:8-9).

For the first time since the expulsion of Adam and Eve from His presence in Genesis 3, God Himself would dwell in the very midst of His creation. This was totally God's idea — and highly unexpected.

Once the people had arrived at Mount Sinai and God's glory descended on it, the young nation responded in abject fear, terror, and dread to this small display of God's power (Deut. 5:22-27; Heb. 12:18-21). Yet, to dwell in the very midst of the people He had redeemed was God's desire and His intent. However, certain essential elements had to be addressed. For instance, God is holy — mankind is not. How can a holy God dwell in the midst of a sinful people? How can a holy God be approached in holiness if there are no holy humans on earth? God realized this; consequently, the heart of His earthly abode was to be the means for the atonement of sin. He gave specific instructions regarding this in Exodus 25:17-21:

> "You shall make a mercy seat of pure gold, two and a half cubits long and one and a half cubits wide. You shall make two cherubim of gold, make them of hammered work at the two ends of the mercy seat. Make one cherub at one end and one cherub at the other end; you shall make the cherubim of one piece with the mercy seat at its two

ends. The cherubim shall have their wings spread upward, covering the mercy seat with their wings and facing one another; the faces of the cherubim are to be turned toward the mercy seat. You shall put the mercy seat on top of the ark, and in the ark you shall put the testimony which I will give to you."

After the ark was constructed according to God's pinpoint design, He granted the Presence that is still hard for fallen mankind to fathom. In Exodus 25:22 God promised, "There I will meet with you; and from above the mercy seat, from between the two cherubim which are upon the ark of the testimony, I will speak to you about all that I will give you in commandment for the sons of Israel." Even later when giving instructions about the particulars of the tabernacle, God again instructed and reminded, "You shall put this altar in front of the veil that is near the ark of the testimony, in front of the mercy seat that is over the ark of the testimony, where I will meet with you" (Exod. 30:6).

Even beyond the grace-given promise by God to meet with His people at His own tabernacle is one additional tremendous promise, although it is easy to miss this in a casual reading of Exodus 29:43-46:

"And I will meet there with the sons of Israel, and it shall be consecrated by My glory. And I will consecrate the tent of meeting and the altar; I will also consecrate Aaron and his sons to minister as priests to Me.

"And I will dwell among the sons of Israel and will be their God.

"And they shall know that I am the LORD their God who brought them out of the land of Egypt, that I might dwell among them; I am the LORD their God.

Even though Scripture later reveals, "The heavens are declaring the glory of God" (Ps. 19:1), and the seraphim of Isaiah 6:1-3, call out to one another, "Holy, Holy, Holy, is the LORD of hosts, the whole earth is full of His glory," the curse of Genesis 3 affected everyone—and every thing (Rom. 8:18-22). Centuries later the beloved Apostle John would write—even after Jesus had ascended into heaven—"the whole earth lies in the power of the evil one" (1 John 5:19). The putrid defilement of sins' effects did not begin at these passages such as Romans 8 or 1 John 5:19, or even the demonic hierarchy disclosed in Ephesians 6:12; they are simply revealed in these passages. They came into existence immediately as part of the consequences of the fall and the resulting curse.

This is why Exodus 29:43 ("And I will meet there with the sons of Israel, *and it shall be consecrated by My glory*") is so stunningly extraordinary. Since the expulsion of the newly defiled couple from God's garden and presence in Genesis 3, God Himself not only promised to dwell among His people—even beyond this—one particular place would be consecrated by His own glory. This is the first time is Scripture that God promised this; nowhere else on earth at any time after the fall did God display His special glory presence. If God revealed His glory in any special manifestation of it before the fall, He chose not to disclose in Scripture what that was (if it was any thing at all).

From this point, the remainder of the Book of Exodus leads to God's indwelling His own abode in the midst of His redeemed people. Even after the despicable worshiping of the golden calf of Exodus 32—which, ironically, was occurring at the same time Moses was receiving instructions for the tabernacle from God—God still kept His word. Eventually, Moses completed everything "just as the LORD commanded" (Exod. 40:32). God Himself—whose revealed creations range beyond what mortal minds can begin to imagine in both scope and majesty (let alone whatever else God has been doing in eternity past about which we have no disclosure)—chose to abide. *God Almighty* condescended to make His dwelling inside a tent, over the mercy seat—where He delights to meet with His own. In Exodus 40:34-38 God filled His dwelling with Himself:

> Then the cloud covered the tent of meeting, and the glory of the LORD filled the tabernacle. Moses was not able to enter the tent of meeting because the cloud had settled on it, and the glory of the LORD filled the tabernacle. Throughout all their journeys whenever the cloud was taken up from over the tabernacle, the sons of Israel would set out; but if the cloud was not taken up, then they did not set out until the day when it was taken up. For throughout all their journeys, the cloud of the LORD was on the tabernacle by day, and there was fire in it by night, in the sight of all the house of Israel.

God now dwelled in the very midst of His people. How reassuring it must have been for those of the wilderness generation who would awake at night, peer out from their tents and see the presence of God in visible fashion at the very center of the camp.

God Himself resided in His designated place of occupancy. But it would not be His last dwelling.

―――――――――――――

The Tabernacle could move; that was a major part of its purpose. It could cross ahead of the people, as when they crossed the flooded

Jordan River (Joshua 3:8-11), or go with them in battle, as during the Jericho campaign (Joshua 6:8). In the fuller revelation of God, this would change. Moriah, in Jerusalem—at the place where the Lord appeared to David—would become the permanent abode of God on earth.

By the time God gave instruction about the Temple, much had changed. The nation of Israel truly had become a nation. Centuries earlier they had taken possession of the Promised Land during the days of Joshua. Afterward, however, during the tumultuous times of the judges, the nation declined both spiritually and physically because they repeatedly rebelled against God. As the LORD had graphically forewarned in Leviticus 26 and Deuteronomy 28, physical enemies would invade and defeat Israel when the people abandoned Him. The pagan invaders were living object lessons that God used to chasten and to teach His rebellious nation that they must return to Him and to their covenant obligations. However, in further abandonment of God, the rebellious people reasoned that their problem was the lack of a suitable military leader; thus they demanded an earthly king so that they could become like the other nations (1 Sam. 8:1-4). God condescended by giving Israel what they asked for by raising up the non-spiritually qualified Saul as their first king. Later, God chose a man after His own heart, replacing Saul with young David (1 Sam. 13:11-14). King David solidified the kingdom and made Jerusalem his capital (2 Sam. 5:1-9). David wanted to build a house for God; however, God chose to build a "house" (i.e., a lineage or dynasty) for David (2 Sam. 7). God's dwelling house would eventually come—but not from David. Instead, David's son Solomon would build the Temple according to God's design—and equally as important, at God's specified place. Thus, as Second Chronicles 3:1 states, "Then Solomon began to build the house of the LORD in Jerusalem on Mount Moriah, where the LORD had appeared to his father David, at the place that David had prepared on the threshing floor of Ornan the Jebusite."

Construction of the Temple was considerably more elaborate than that of the tabernacle centuries earlier. Although David would not construct the Temple, he was instrumental in its preparation. The elder King gathered voluminous materials for the Temple so that his son would have everything that he needed. Solomon, then, would use his God-given mental abilities (2 Chron. 1:8-12) to construct the Lord's permanent abode according to God's precise instructions. When Solomon and the workers completed the Temple, the second demonstration of God's unique glory filling His designated dwelling place occurred. Second Chronicles 5:11-14 describes a scene reminiscent of God's taking residence in the tabernacle in Exodus 40:

> When the priests came forth from the holy place (for all the priests who were present had sanctified themselves, without regard to divisions), and all the Levitical singers, Asaph, Heman, Jeduthun, and their sons and kinsmen, clothed in fine linen, with cymbals, harps and lyres, standing east of the altar, and with them one hundred and twenty priests blowing trumpets in unison when the trumpeters and the singers were to make themselves heard with one voice to praise and to glorify the LORD, and when they lifted up their voice accompanied by trumpets and cymbals and instruments of music, and when they praised the LORD saying, "He indeed is good for His lovingkindness is everlasting," then the house, the house of the LORD, was filled with a cloud, so that the priests could not stand to minister because of the cloud, *for the glory of the LORD filled the house of God.*

Solomon then turned and faced the gathered assembly of Israel. In addressing the nation at the dedication of God's Temple, the King revealed more information than we have in the previous accounts. Solomon declared:

> "Blessed be the LORD, the God of Israel, who spoke with His mouth to my father David and has fulfilled it with His hands, saying, 'Since the day that I brought My people from the land of Egypt, I did not choose a city out of all the tribes of Israel in which to build a house that My name might be there, nor did I choose any man for a leader over My people Israel; but I have chosen Jerusalem that My name might be there, and I have chosen David to be over My people Israel.'
> "Now it was in the heart of my father David to build a house for the name of the LORD, the God of Israel. But the LORD said to my father David, 'Because it was in your heart to build a house for My name, you did well that it was in your heart. Nevertheless you shall not build the house, but your son who will be born to you, he shall build the house for My name.'
> "Now the LORD has fulfilled His word which He spoke; for I have risen in the place of my father David and sit on the throne of Israel, as the LORD promised, and have built the house for the name of the LORD, the God of Israel.
> "There I have set the ark in which is the covenant of the LORD, which He made with the sons of Israel" (2 Chron. 6:4-11).

From this we see that God actually honored David for the intentions of his heart with regard to building God's house. God considered it honorable that David would look at his own surroundings, compare them with the relative modest means that surrounded God Almighty, and desire to correct this discrepancy.

Solomon continued in prayer specifically about God's new Temple. "Then he stood before the altar of the LORD in the presence of all the assembly of Israel and spread out his hands. Now Solomon had made a bronze platform, five cubits long, five cubits wide and three cubits high, and had set it in the midst of the court; and he stood on it, knelt on his knees in the presence of all the assembly of Israel and spread out his hands toward heaven" (2 Chron. 6:12-13). Solomon prayed:

> "O LORD, the God of Israel, there is no god like You in heaven or on earth, keeping covenant and showing lovingkindness to Your servants who walk before You with all their heart; who has kept with Your servant David, my father, that which You have promised him; indeed You have spoken with Your mouth and have fulfilled it with Your hand, as it is this day.
> "Now therefore, O LORD, the God of Israel, keep with Your servant David, my father, that which You have promised him, saying, 'You shall not lack a man to sit on the throne of Israel, if only your sons take heed to their way, to walk in My law as you have walked before Me.'
> "Now therefore, O LORD, the God of Israel, let Your word be confirmed which You have spoken to Your servant David.
> "But will God indeed dwell with mankind on the earth? Behold, heaven and the highest heaven cannot contain You; how much less this house which I have built. Yet have regard to the prayer of Your servant and to his supplication, O LORD my God, to listen to the cry and to the prayer which Your servant prays before You; that Your eye may be open toward this house day and night, toward the place of which You have said that You would put Your name there, to listen to the prayer which Your servant shall pray toward this place" (2 Chron. 6:14-20).

King Solomon, who had been granted divine wisdom unrivaled by any other human, understood the vastness of space. While the extent of precisely what he knew is not disclosed, one thing the wise king understood to his core being: the utter folly to think that because "heaven and the highest heaven cannot contain You; how much less this house which I have built."

Solomon concluded his prayer by asking that God's attention be directed to His earthly home: "Now, O my God, I pray, let Your eyes be open and Your ears attentive to the prayer offered in this place.

Now therefore arise, O LORD God, to Your resting place, You and the ark of Your might; let Your priests, O LORD God, be clothed with salvation and let Your godly ones rejoice in what is good. O LORD God, do not turn away the face of Your anointed; remember Your lovingkindness to Your servant David" (2 Chron. 6:40-42).

As with the tabernacle centuries before, so then with His Temple:

> Now when Solomon had finished praying, fire came down from heaven and consumed the burnt offering and the sacrifices, and the glory of the LORD filled the house. The priests could not enter into the house of the LORD because the glory of the LORD filled the LORD'S house (2 Chron. 7:1-2).

God condescended by filling the finished Temple with a minuscule aspect of His glory; the full glory would immediately consume the universe and beyond. Yet, this minute demonstration of God's glory totally exceeded the composite riches and treasures of a billion earths.

While the accounts of God's filling both the tabernacle and the Temple with His glory are two of the more monumental occurrences in the entire Bible, most Christians would not consider them so. Nonetheless, they are when measured by God's standard, and that is the only means of evaluation that matters. Yet, as important as God's sending His glory to inhabit these places, equally important in its own way was God's taking back His glory from those to whom He had once given it.

The prophet Ezekiel was one of the Jewish captives exiled during the three deportations that Babylon inflicted on Israel. In 605 BC, Babylon, led by Nebuchadnezzar, completed the first deportation of a segment of Jewish people that included, among others, Daniel and his three friends. The Babylonians took Ezekiel among the second wave of deportees in 597 BC. The final segment of the exile occurred in 586 BC, which included the destruction of Jerusalem and the magnificent Temple that Solomon had built.

Ezekiel had arrived in Babylon when "the word of the LORD came to him" (Ezek. 1:1-3). His first chapter describes a vision of the glory of the LORD that he was allowed to witness. The prophet struggled to describe what he saw because there were no corresponding earthly counterparts or words that could aptly describe God's glory. He repeatedly wrote terms such as "something like" glowing metal (1:4) or "something like" an expanse (1:22). However, the primary reason that God displayed a small aspect of His glory to Ezekiel was not to frustrate the writer with an indescribable scene. God wanted the prophet to realize what he would later witness in chapters 8–11 when God removed His glory from Jerusalem. We know from the information given in Ezekiel 8:1 that this removal of God's glory occurred (using the modern calendar) on September 17, 592 B.C — six years before the Temple would be destroyed.

This is how Ezekiel 8 begins:

> It came about in the sixth year, on the fifth day of the sixth month, as I was sitting in my house with the elders of Judah sitting before me, that the hand of the LORD God fell on me there.
> Then I looked, and behold, a likeness as the appearance of a man; from His loins and downward there was the appearance of fire, and from His loins and upward the appearance of brightness, like the appearance of glowing metal.
> He stretched out the form of a hand and caught me by a lock of my head; and the Spirit lifted me up between earth and heaven and brought me in the visions of God to Jerusalem, to the entrance of the north gate of the inner court, where the seat of the idol of jealousy, which provokes to jealousy, was located (8:1-3).

Later Ezekiel made the proper connection with this new revelation by explaining in 8:4, "And behold, the glory of the God of Israel was there, like the appearance which I saw in the plain" — described in Ezekiel 1. The Lord then took His prophet in a vision to Jerusalem where abominations and idolatries were being performed in God's very own Temple — some even by His own priests. The remainder of Ezekiel 8 is a listing of some of the most heinous crimes against God that are recorded in the entire Bible: all done by His people, all done in His house, and all performed adjacent to His own glory.

But not for long.

God then began a three-step removal of His glory. The first step involved the glory of the Lord abandoning the Holy of Holies:

> Then I looked, and behold, in the expanse that was over the heads of the cherubim something like a sapphire stone, in appearance resembling a throne, appeared above them.
> And He spoke to the man clothed in linen and said, "Enter between the whirling wheels under the cherubim and fill your hands with coals of fire from between the cherubim and scatter them over the city." And he entered in my sight.

Now the cherubim were standing on the right side of the Temple when the man entered, and the cloud filled the inner court.

Then the glory of the LORD went up from the cherub to the threshold of the Temple, and the Temple was filled with the cloud and the court was filled with the brightness of the glory of the LORD (Ezek. 10:1-4).

The second phase of God's removal of His glory was from the threshold of the Temple to the east gate (Ezek. 10:18-19):

Then the glory of the LORD departed from the threshold of the Temple and stood over the cherubim. When the cherubim departed, they lifted their wings and rose up from the earth in my sight with the wheels beside them; and they stood still at the entrance of the east gate of the LORD'S house, and the glory of the God of Israel hovered over them.

God's glory departed in distinct stages, almost, it seems, reluctantly, sadly. It is as if anyone had called out, "Don't leave!" He would have stayed. But no one called. No one cared. No one noticed. No one knew. The glory of the Lord was leaving, but the people of Israel were so engrossed in their idolatry, fornications, and other acts of rebellion that they were spiritually senseless to the whole procedure. God's removal of His glory would make a difference to them only when the Babylonian captors began raping and pillaging the people and their city.

Before the final stage of removal, however, God promised a future restoration for Israel. In a lavish word of grace even unto a people who had blatantly rejected Him, God declared their future:

"Therefore say, 'Thus says the LORD God, "Though I had removed them far away among the nations and though I had scattered them among the countries, yet I was a sanctuary for them a little while in the countries where they had gone."'

"Therefore say, 'Thus says the LORD God, "I will gather you from the peoples and assemble you out of the countries among which you have been scattered, and I will give you the land of Israel."'

"When they come there, they will remove all its detestable things and all its abominations from it.

"And I will give them one heart, and put a new spirit within them. And I will take the heart of stone out of their flesh and give them a heart of flesh, that they may walk in My statutes and keep My ordinances and do them. Then they will be My people, and I shall be their God" (Ezek. 11:16-20).

In keeping with the promised judgment of the Mosaic Covenant, God would send His people into exile. However, in keeping with the promises of the Abrahamic Covenant, God would not completely abandon His people—ever.

Finally, the third step—the glory of God departed. The glory of God that the Lord had promised would dwell with His people is taken from where God had once resided. The glory that God had condescended to dwell in both the tabernacle and the Temple was no longer there. Instead, the glory departed to over the Mount of Olives, as Ezekiel 11 so sadly describes:

> Then the cherubim lifted up their wings with the wheels beside them, and the glory of the God of Israel hovered over them.
> The glory of the LORD went up from the midst of the city and stood over the mountain, which is east of the city.
> And the Spirit lifted me up and brought me in a vision by the Spirit of God to the exiles in Chaldea. So the vision that I had seen left me (Ezek. 11:22-24).

As Nebuchadnezzar's legions approached Jerusalem like picnic ants given free reign at an outdoors summer feast, God had long since abandoned His previous place of dwelling. Although the structure no doubt looked the same to the inhabitants of Jerusalem and to the Temple gatherers, it was then as different as a living human is from a dead human. Despite its majestic, ornate design and implements, and despite the regular sacrifices and rituals by a functioning priesthood, the Temple of God had now become desolate; God Himself had removed His glory and presence. It was a biblical necessity for God to remove His glory; otherwise, the combined forces of both the human and demonic worlds could never have entered into the Holy of Holies—let alone devour the Temple. If Moses or God's designated priests could not enter into the tabernacle or Temple because of God's glory, how much less could pagan barbarians putrefied in their own vileness approach the Holy One? God's glory had departed, and all that remained of the Temple was a vacant stone shrine of no lasting value. Long before the first Babylonian foot soldier approached the outermost sanctions of God's Temple, God had extracted every semblance and evidence of His previous abode—with one major exception. In spite of His absence, and in a mysterious way, God was uniquely present in His Temple.

After all, once God consecrated His Temple with His glory (2 Chron. 7:1-3), the LORD later made this promise to not only the young builder king, but also to His Jewish people and ultimately to the entire world:

> Then the LORD appeared to Solomon at night and said to him, "I have heard your prayer and have chosen this place for Myself as a house of sacrifice. If I shut up the heavens so that there is no rain, or if I command the locust to devour the land, or if I send pestilence among My people, and My people who are called by My name humble themselves and pray and seek My face and turn from their wicked ways, then I will hear from heaven, will forgive their sin and will heal their land.
> "Now My eyes will be open and My ears attentive to the prayer offered in this place.
> *"For now I have chosen and consecrated this house that My name may be there forever, and My eyes and My heart will be there perpetually (2 Chron. 7:12-16).*

Centuries later, when the at-that-time wicked King Manasseh sat on David's throne and led God's nation into deeper and deeper sin (2 Kings 21:1-18), Second Chronicles 33:7 states again the eternal importance of God's Temple, revealing that "which God had said to David and to Solomon his son, 'In this house and in Jerusalem, which I have chosen from all the tribes of Israel, *I will put My name forever.*'"

But this does not seem right. It only gives rise to numerous questions: how could God's presence still be in His Temple if He Himself had abandoned it? How could His holy name be there forever? How could God's presence be in the Temple and yet allow pagan Gentiles to desecrate the Holy of Holies?

Another inspired prophet of God had already revealed the answer in his prophecy almost a century and a half earlier.

As Scripture repeatedly indicates, God Himself had already placed His Stone in Zion, His holy mountain.

4

THE PLACEMENT

Before progressing to new matters on our own pilgrimage, we rest briefly in order to meditate on some of the important matters regarding God's house. We have seen that in Second Samuel 7 God condescended to have a temple built for Him. After David had made the offer to build God a house, and the prophet Nathan had instructed David to proceed as he desired, God commanded the prophet to return to the king with a different message. In the same night, the word of the Lord came to Nathan, saying, "Go and say to My servant David, 'Thus says the LORD, "Are you the one who should build Me a house to dwell in? For I have not dwelt in a house since the day I brought up the sons of Israel from Egypt, even to this day; but I have been moving about in a tent, even in a tabernacle. Wherever I have gone with all the sons of Israel, did I speak a word with one of the tribes of Israel, which I commanded to shepherd My people Israel, saying, 'Why have you not built Me a house of cedar?'"'" (2 Sam. 7:5-7). God ultimately permitted it. Thus Solomon built the Temple; thus God condescended to fill it with His glory.

If the Temple had been merely a clay pot instead of an ornate structure, the fact that God filled it with His glory made it unique to anything else within our solar system. The angels of God who minister before Him in the midst of heavenly glory likely would have gasped at the thought that God would fill any structure *on earth* with His glory. Defiled, fallen earth lay in the power of the evil one (1 John 5:19). Fallen earth—not the holy sanctity of heaven—constantly displayed its putrid effects of sin and evil. And yet, uniquely positioned in the midst of such spiritual darkness was the unmistakable glory of God. Neither angelic nor demonic realm had to inquire what it was; all in both realms knew. Why God chose to do it, they could not comprehend. First Peter 1:12

later revealed that angels "long [literally in the Greek, "lust after" in a good sense] to look" into the things relating to salvation. God's filling the Temple with His glory, as He previously had filled His tabernacle, would evoke many questions from the angels. For the demonic realm there would be intense interest: but interest always tempered with the hateful fear and defilement that evil always evokes whenever it encounters some aspect of God's revelatory holiness.

Although God's glory filling the Temple sparked angelic amazement, it would not spark amazement for long with the people of Israel. They soon spiraled downward deeper and deeper in sin. Finally in keeping with His word given back in the days of Moses, God eventually dispersed the nation because of their disobedience. In Deuteronomy 28:64-66, God warned that if the nation continued to sin and reject Him, "the LORD will scatter you among all peoples, from one end of the earth to the other end of the earth; and there you shall serve other gods, wood and stone, which you or your fathers have not known. Among those nations you shall find no rest, and there will be no resting place for the sole of your foot; but there the LORD will give you a trembling heart, failing of eyes, and despair of soul. So your life shall hang in doubt before you; and you will be in dread night and day, and shall have no assurance of your life." This predicted judgment of expelling the people from the land came about in two segments: first, the separated northern kingdom was dispersed to Assyria (722 BC); second, the southern kingdom was exiled to Babylon (586 BC). Also, as we will see in another chapter, a third aspect of equal importance that has both modern and future ramifications was the dispersion of the Jews from the land at the hands of the Roman Empire centuries later in AD 70.

Two crucial items made the Babylonian captivity unique. One item concerned the glory of God and His Temple. As we saw earlier, God purposely removed His glory before the Babylonians approached Jerusalem. Only then could the Temple be destroyed. The second unique item in the Babylonian captivity was that God specified a designated amount of time for the exile. In Daniel 9:1-2 the godly prophet explained, "In the first year of Darius the son of Ahasuerus, of Median descent, who was made king over the kingdom of the Chaldeans—in the first year of his reign, I, Daniel, observed in the books the number of the years which was revealed as the word of the LORD to Jeremiah the prophet for the completion of the desolations of Jerusalem, namely, seventy years." Daniel himself, taken in the first deportation in 605 BC, had read this passage: "'This whole land will be a desolation and a horror, and these nations will serve the king of Babylon seventy years. Then it will be when seventy years are completed I will punish the king of Babylon and that nation,' declares the LORD, 'for their iniquity, and the land of the Chaldeans; and I will make it an everlasting desolation'" (Jer. 25:11-12). Later when the Chronicler penned Judah's history, he too noted the divine limitation on the exile. Second Chronicles 36:19-21 gives this description of Jerusalem's fall, and a theological assessment:

> Then they burned the house of God and broke down the wall of Jerusalem, and burned all its fortified buildings with fire and destroyed all its valuable articles. Those who had escaped from the sword he carried away to Babylon; and they were servants to him and to his sons until the rule of the kingdom of Persia, to fulfill the word of the LORD by the mouth of Jeremiah, until the land had enjoyed its sabbaths. All the days of its desolation it kept sabbath until seventy years were complete.

Daniel, an elderly man by the time the events of Daniel 9 transpired, understood from God's Word that the seventy-year period was coming to its completion. *God Himself* would bring a remnant back to Jerusalem. He would use human governments and peoples, but it was God who had exiled the people, God who had determined the length of Jerusalem's desolation, and God who would bring them back into His land. Simply stated, nothing merely happened. Instead, God sovereignly worked in exact accordance with His Word, down to the smallest detail.

As would be expected, so much was different for the Jewish remnant that left Babylon and returned to Jerusalem. The land had been barren and desolate for decades. Grass and weeds and other plants grew where once commerce or legal debate had transpired. Two exceptional visual reminders, though, gave strong evidence of the severity of God's punishment. First was the destruction of the massive city walls that once protected the people from invaders; the rock fragments from its destruction were strewn all over the ancient city. Second, and more important than the first, the beautiful Temple of God no longer existed. Only the charred foundation offered evidence that a once glorious edifice had occupied this spot for over four hundred years. The competing composite emotions for those who returned from Babylon must have been hard to distinguish: relief for the end of the long journey; joy at being home again; deep grief for the desolation of Jerusalem — especially its centerpiece, the Temple; hopelessness that it would not return to the glory in man's eyes to which it once had laid claim.

A segment of Jews had returned home—but not really. They came back to something old, not to something new. They came back to a work in progress, and a hard and arduous work it would be. Everything was different—including them. Israel no longer had a functional kingdom because they had no Davidic Covenant king to reign over them. Humanly speaking, a Gentile world ruler had to grant this conquered remnant permission to return to their own land. When they did return, they were still subject to Gentile powers.

Whether audibly voiced or silently meditated was the likely ever-abiding question: *"Where was God in all this?"* — or perhaps shortened to its base level, *"Where was God?"* These people knew the prophecy of Ezekiel and how the glory of the Lord—and the Lord Himself—had abandoned His Temple. As Ezekiel 11:23 sadly describes, the third and last visible display of God's glory was its brief hovering over the Mount of Olives before disappearing to some place of His choosing. As this group either collectively or individually looked over to the mountain that marked God's exodus from them, would they not feel as orphans—strangers in a strange land that was once their own? Motivation to do anything other than exist must have been in short supply.

Yet, returning this people to the land was not the end of God's work. He already had so much more to accomplish already determined in His holy mind. In fact, an aspect of God's plan that He had revealed almost three centuries earlier had come about just as He had said it would. If the returning remnant had read God's Word carefully, they would have seen that God was in full control, predicting in minute details the exile, the return, and even the Gentile king who would be the human agent employed by God to bring this remnant back. Centuries earlier, the prophet Isaiah identified *by name* this king who would issue orders to rebuild Jerusalem. This prophecy is so precise. Of course, the fact that Cyrus would not be born for another one hundred and fifty years causes critics of the Bible to mock its accuracy. They conclude that because Isaiah's message is so clear—after all, no man can possibly know the future—that some Jewish historian must have written this *after* the fact. In other words, they have determined that it is only a historical account, not supernatural prophecy. For this group, Isaiah is considered only as biblical prophecy in some fraudulent manner.

God, however, disagrees. Note how He takes credit for the return and presents Himself in unique roles in Isaiah 44:24–45:7:

Thus says the LORD, your Redeemer, and the one who formed you from the womb, "I, the LORD, am the maker of all things, stretching out the heavens by Myself and spreading out the earth all alone, causing the omens of boasters to fail, making fools out of diviners, causing wise men to draw back and turning their knowledge into foolishness, confirming the word of His servant and performing the purpose of His messengers. It is I who says of Jerusalem, 'She shall be inhabited!' And of the cities of Judah, 'They shall be built.' And I will raise up her ruins again.

"It is I who says to the depth of the sea, 'Be dried up!' And I will make your rivers dry.

"It is I who says of Cyrus, 'He is My shepherd! And he will perform all My desire.' And He declares of Jerusalem, 'She will be built,' and of the Temple, 'Your foundation will be laid.'"

Thus says the LORD to Cyrus His anointed, whom I have taken by the right hand, to subdue nations before him and to loose the loins of kings; to open doors before him so that gates will not be shut: "I will go before you and make the rough places smooth; I will shatter the doors of bronze and cut through their iron bars. I will give you the treasures of darkness and hidden wealth of secret places, so that you may know that it is I, the LORD, the God of Israel, who calls you by your name. For the sake of Jacob My servant, and Israel My chosen one, I have also called you by your name; I have given you a title of honor though you have not known Me.

"I am the LORD, and there is no other; besides Me there is no God. I will gird you, though you have not known Me; that men may know from the rising to the setting of the sun that there is no one besides Me. I am the LORD, and there is no other, the One forming light and creating darkness, causing well-being and creating calamity; I am the LORD who does all these."

God remained in sovereign control. No mistakes had been made; the nation was precisely where God wanted them. Though a remnant, though not as strong, though divinely chastened for their sin, Israel had returned to the land because God Himself had sustained them and had brought them there. Read His Word; see His hand! He had not abandoned His people. There was an absence, but there was also a Presence—and it was time for God to move the people toward the Stone of Israel.

When David intended to build God a temple, a major reason for his desire was that it was ludicrous for him, a servant king, to "dwell in a house of cedar, but the ark of God dwells within tent curtains" (2 Sam. 7:2). But at the return from Babylonian exile, the mindsets of the people were considerably different. These often neglected books of Zechariah, Haggai, and Ezra reveal vital information—and vital promises—from God.

Wherein God condescended to have the first Temple built, He *demanded* that the second Temple be built. Once back in the land, the remnant directed their interests to their own homes, businesses and the affairs of everyday life. They decided that God's Temple would be built at some time in the future—but not now. There was no sense of urgency; other things seemed much more pressing.

God thought differently, responding in Haggai 1:1-2:

> In the second year of Darius the king, on the first day of the sixth month, the word of the LORD came by the prophet Haggai to Zerubbabel the son of Shealtiel, governor of Judah, and to Joshua the son of Jehozadak, the high priest, saying, "Thus says the LORD of hosts, 'This people says, "The time has not come, even the time for the house of the LORD to be rebuilt."'"

For God, this was the time—and that was all that mattered. Human delay would be no delay for Him. In fact, God promised He would punish the people until they responded as He intended for them to respond. Haggai presented this to the nation after the word of the Lord came to him:

> "Is it time for you yourselves to dwell in your paneled houses while this house lies desolate?"
>
> Now therefore, thus says the LORD of hosts, "Consider your ways! You have sown much, but harvest little; you eat, but there is not enough to be satisfied; you drink, but there is not enough to become drunk; you put on clothing, but no one is warm enough; and he who earns, earns wages to put into a purse with holes."
>
> Thus says the LORD of hosts, "Consider your ways! Go up to the mountains, bring wood and rebuild the Temple, that I may be pleased with it and be glorified," says the LORD.
>
> "You look for much, but behold, it comes to little; when you bring it home, I blow it away. Why?" declares the LORD of hosts, "Because of My house which lies desolate, while each of you runs to his own house.
>
> "Therefore, because of you the sky has withheld its dew and the earth has withheld its produce. I called for a drought on the land, on the mountains, on the grain, on the new wine, on the oil, on what the

ground produces, on men, on cattle, and on all the labor of your hands" (Hag. 1:4-11).

Again, contrast this with God's previous discourse with David in 2 Samuel 7. The first Temple God allowed—the rebuilt (or second one) He demanded. The Temple was important not only for the people and their relationship with God, but also because God Himself had already decreed eternal matters related to the world's salvation. Having the Temple rebuilt was not as much an option for the people as it was a necessary part of God's salvation story for the nations.

The Book of Ezra (1:1) begins, and Second Chronicles ends (32:22-23) with Cyrus' decree to rebuild the Temple, just as Isaiah had prophesied centuries earlier. Jeremiah had prophesied as to the exact time of the rebuilding:

> Now in the first year of Cyrus king of Persia, in order to fulfill the word of the LORD by the mouth of Jeremiah, the LORD stirred up the spirit of Cyrus king of Persia, so that he sent a proclamation throughout all his kingdom, and also put it in writing, saying: "Thus says Cyrus king of Persia, 'The LORD, the God of heaven, has given me all the kingdoms of the earth and He has appointed me to build Him a house in Jerusalem, which is in Judah. Whoever there is among you of all His people, may his God be with him! Let him go up to Jerusalem which is in Judah and rebuild the house of the LORD, the God of Israel; He is the God who is in Jerusalem. Every survivor, at whatever place he may live, let the men of that place support him with silver and gold, with goods and cattle, together with a freewill offering for the house of God which is in Jerusalem.'" (Ezra 1:1-4).

As before, nothing in this account merely happened. No world events simply took their normal course. God moved Cyrus as He had also "moved" Isaiah and Jeremiah (2 Pet. 1:20).

With the able leadership of Ezra and Zerubbabel—and at God's insistence—work finally began on the second Temple, starting with its foundation:

> Now in the second year of their coming to the house of God at Jerusalem in the second month, Zerubbabel the son of Shealtiel and Jeshua the son of Jozadak and the rest of their brothers the priests and the Levites, and all who came from the captivity to Jerusalem, began the work and appointed the Levites from twenty years and older to oversee the work of the house of the LORD.
> Then Jeshua with his sons and brothers stood united with Kadmiel

and his sons, the sons of Judah and the sons of Henadad with their sons and brothers the Levites, to oversee the workmen in the Temple of God.

Now when the builders had laid the foundation of the Temple of the LORD, the priests stood in their apparel with trumpets, and the Levites, the sons of Asaph, with cymbals, to praise the LORD according to the directions of King David of Israel. They sang, praising and giving thanks to the LORD, saying, "For He is good, for His lovingkindness is upon Israel forever." And all the people shouted with a great shout when they praised the LORD because the foundation of the house of the LORD was laid (Ezra 3:8-11).

Yet, as noted before, this dedication differed greatly from the previous Temple dedication—and many there knew it:

Yet many of the priests and Levites and heads of fathers' households, the old men who had seen the first Temple, wept with a loud voice when the foundation of this house was laid before their eyes, while many shouted aloud for joy, so that the people could not distinguish the sound of the shout of joy from the sound of the weeping of the people, for the people shouted with a loud shout, and the sound was heard far away (Ezra 3:12-13).

This was not the rebuilding of the Temple that Solomon had constructed; this was a Temple of lesser stature, a Temple of lesser structure. This was a Temple that evoked weeping from those who knew the splendor of the first Temple.

One quick note: enemies soon attempted to infiltrate the territory and sabotage the building of the Temple. Ezra 4:1-2 notes, "Now when the enemies of Judah and Benjamin heard that the people of the exile were building a Temple to the LORD God of Israel, they approached Zerubbabel and the heads of fathers' households, and said to them, 'Let us build with you, for we, like you, seek your God; and we have been sacrificing to Him since the days of Esarhaddon king of Assyria, who brought us up here.'" These people were the forefathers of the Samaritans—and of the Samaritan woman of John 4. Jesus, more intent on her spiritual needs, did not go into detail as He answered, "You worship what you do not know" (John 4:22). He could have quoted the answer given by Zerubbabel, Jeshua, and the heads of the households: "You have nothing in common with us in building a house to our God; but we ourselves will together build to the LORD God of Israel, as King Cyrus, the king of Persia has commanded us" (Ezra 4:3). Thus the rift between the Jews and Samaritans became even more greatly entrenched.

Even in the midst of enemies who attempted to short circuit the process, the second Temple was eventually completed. Ezra 6:13-15 records when this took place:

> Then Tattenai, the governor of the province beyond the River, Shethar-bozenai and their colleagues carried out the decree with all diligence, just as King Darius had sent. And the elders of the Jews were successful in building through the prophesying of Haggai the prophet and Zechariah the son of Iddo. And they finished building according to the command of the God of Israel and the decree of Cyrus, Darius, and Artaxerxes king of Persia.
> This Temple was completed on the third day of the month Adar; it was the sixth year of the reign of King Darius.

Years before, when the people wept over the puny comparison of the second Temple to the first, God intervened and encouraged them with majestic prophecies. Tucked away in a "distant" part of Scripture (for many) comes one of God's promises regarding His Temple and an incentive for the people to work diligently:

> On the twenty-first of the seventh month, the word of the LORD came by Haggai the prophet saying, "Speak now to Zerubbabel the son of Shealtiel, governor of Judah, and to Joshua the son of Jehozadak, the high priest, and to the remnant of the people saying, 'Who is left among you who saw this Temple in its former glory? And how do you see it now? Does it not seem to you like nothing in comparison? But now take courage, Zerubbabel,' declares the LORD, 'take courage also, Joshua son of Jehozadak, the high priest, and all you people of the land take courage,' declares the LORD, 'and work; for I am with you,' declares the LORD of hosts.
> "As for the promise which I made you when you came out of Egypt, My Spirit is abiding in your midst; do not fear!"
> For thus says the LORD of hosts, "Once more in a little while, I am going to shake the heavens and the earth, the sea also and the dry land. I will shake all the nations; and they will come with the wealth of all nations, and I will fill this house with glory," says the LORD of hosts. "The silver is Mine and the gold is Mine," declares the LORD of hosts. "The latter glory of this house will be greater than the former," says the LORD of hosts, "and in this place I will give peace," declares the LORD of hosts (Hag. 2:1-9).

These are divine promises—comforting promises: "I will fill this house with glory." "The latter glory of this house will be greater than the first." The concluding phrase "and in this place I will give peace" must have been wonderfully comforting to the older ones. After all, if they had seen the former glory of the temple that Solomon built, the elders also had seen the approaching Babylonian armies. They had witnessed the carnage and brutality of the pagan soldiers, and later as captives they had been marched a thousand miles away to a strange land. Yet, God Himself had declared: glory, wealth, and peace in this place.

So God's Word rejuvenated the spirit of the people. The returned remnant diligently worked and completed the Temple.

And then—God did not do what He had promised.

Everything is different. The Temple stands, but it lacks the grandeur of the one Solomon had built. The people are in the land, but they return as stewards to a Gentile ruler, not to Israel as a nation—certainly not as an independent national power. The Jews now lived in "the times of the Gentiles" (Luke 21:24).

Even with the Temple rebuilt in the same city on God's same designated location, two irreplaceable aspects are absent. First, just before the Temple was destroyed, the Ark of the Covenant disappeared. Many Jewish writers of the time indicate that Jeremiah and other faithful followers of God hid the Ark of the Covenant from the Babylonian invaders. We do not know if this is true or not. The ark simply disappears from Scripture without any accompanying information. However, this is more than merely Temple formality. The Ark of the Covenant is vital to God's original design. For instance, in Exodus 25:8 God stated, "Let them construct a sanctuary for Me, that I may dwell among them." The remaining chapter gives additional details, but ends with the same promise of God to the people that He will meet them from above the mercy seat:

> "You shall make a mercy seat of pure gold, two and a half cubits long and one and a half cubits wide. You shall make two cherubim of gold, make them of hammered work at the two ends of the mercy seat. Make one cherub at one end and one cherub at the other end; you shall make the cherubim of one piece with the mercy seat at its two ends. The cherubim shall have their wings spread upward, covering the mercy seat with their wings and facing one another; the faces of the cherubim are to be turned toward the mercy seat. You shall put the mercy seat on top of the ark, and in the ark you shall put the testimony which I will give to you.
> There I will meet with you; and from above the mercy seat, from between the two cherubim which are upon the ark of the testimony, I

will speak to you about all that I will give you in commandment for the sons of Israel" (Exod. 25:17-22).

God did just as He said regarding the tabernacle and later with His Temple that Solomon built. For the second Temple, however, there are significant problems. It would be most difficult to meet God above the cherubim because there was no ark in the Holy of Holies in the second Temple.

Second, an even bigger problem existed: God's glory never filled the second Temple. The people gathered, the Temple was dedicated, but God's glory never filled His holy place as He had with the tabernacle and later when Solomon dedicated the Temple. Exodus 29:43-45 reveals how great a quandary this presented. Regarding the sacrifice placed before God on the altar, He promised, "I will meet there with the sons of Israel, and it shall be consecrated by My glory. I will consecrate the tent of meeting and the altar; I will also consecrate Aaron and his sons to minister as priests to Me. I will dwell among the sons of Israel and will be their God."

A tent and later a stone structure were consecrated by God's own glory—"I will dwell among the sons of Israel and be their God." Wonderful promises from God—unless you are a participant at the second Temple.

Each element was true for the tabernacle and then for the first Temple. Not one element was true with the rebuilt Temple: no ark, no cherubim, no mercy seat, no dwelling, no Presence—and beyond these, no glory. How can God meet with His covenanted-people above the mercy seat if there is no ark and no such seat? How can the high priest of Israel enter into the Holy of Holies on the Day of Atonement and sprinkle blood on the ark to cleanse the nation from its sin if the mercy seat is absent? How can the high priest do what God Himself instructs for the Day of Atonement as outlined in Leviticus 16:11-17?

> Then Aaron shall offer the bull of the sin offering which is for himself and make atonement for himself and for his household, and he shall slaughter the bull of the sin offering which is for himself. He shall take a firepan full of coals of fire from upon the altar before the LORD and two handfuls of finely ground sweet incense, and bring it inside the veil. He shall put the incense on the fire before the LORD, that the cloud of incense may cover the mercy seat that is on the ark of the testimony, otherwise he will die.
> Moreover, he shall take some of the blood of the bull and sprinkle it with his finger on the mercy seat on the east side; also in front of the

mercy seat he shall sprinkle some of the blood with his finger seven times.

Then he shall slaughter the goat of the sin offering which is for the people, and bring its blood inside the veil and do with its blood as he did with the blood of the bull, and sprinkle it on the mercy seat and in front of the mercy seat.

He shall make atonement for the holy place, because of the impurities of the sons of Israel and because of their transgressions in regard to all their sins; and thus he shall do for the tent of meeting which abides with them in the midst of their impurities. When he goes in to make atonement in the holy place, no one shall be in the tent of meeting until he comes out, that he may make atonement for himself and for his household and for all the assembly of Israel.

For the rebuilt Temple, these divine instructions were virtually impossible. How could a high priest make atonement unless the mercy seat was there? Why even have a Temple if it cannot function as God Himself had prescribed?

This still funnels down to a core question: because the Ark of the Covenant and the glory of God were not present, exactly what was in the Holy of Holies in the second Temple?

Why the Stone of Israel, of course — just as God had already promised.

Isaiah ministered at the most significant turning point for the nation. Because of their blatant disobedience and repeated covenant violations, the ten northern tribes would fall to Assyria during this prophet's ministry. Isaiah would see God miraculously intervene to keep Judah from falling during Hezekiah's reign. God would grant the prophet vistas of the future — and of the future One — in amazing proportions. Isaiah's prophecy repeatedly points to the Messiah, both to His person and to His work.

Monumental chapters lead to the chapter of our immediate concern. In chapter six Isaiah saw the Lord, somewhat similar to what Ezekiel would later see:

In the year of King Uzziah's death I saw the Lord sitting on a throne, lofty and exalted, with the train of His robe filling the Temple. Seraphim stood above Him, each having six wings: with two he covered his face, and with two he covered his feet, and with two he flew. And one called out to another and said, "Holy, Holy, Holy, is the LORD of hosts, the whole earth is full of His glory."

And the foundations of the thresholds trembled at the voice of him who called out, while the Temple was filling with smoke.

Then I said, "Woe is me, for I am ruined! Because I am a man of unclean lips, and I live among a people of unclean lips; for my eyes have seen the King, the LORD of hosts" (Isa. 6:1-5).

Isaiah 7 contains the great prophecy of the virgin bearing a child: "Therefore the LORD Himself will give you a sign: behold, a virgin will be with child and bear a son, and she will call His name Immanuel" (Isa. 7:14). Although we might never make the connection on our own just from this account, Isaiah 7:14 was the basis for what the angel told Joseph in Matthew 1:22-23: "Now all this took place to fulfill what was spoken by the Lord through the prophet: 'Behold, the virgin shall be with child and shall bear a son, and they shall call His name Immanuel, which translated means, "God with us."'" More significant than the manifestation of God's glory in the ark or the Temple, "the Word became flesh and dwelt among us" (John 1:14). Immanuel—God with us—what a divine comfort in the midst of a sin-darkened world.

And then, in the midst of Isaiah 8 the first of two Stone prophecies was given to this holy prophet. Although we usually hurriedly read over them, these two prophecies are equally as important as Isaiah 7:14, although we generally do not consider them so. In the face of pending national judgment, Isaiah eternally recorded what Yahweh had revealed to him:

For thus the LORD spoke to me with mighty power and instructed me not to walk in the way of this people, saying, "You are not to say, 'It is a conspiracy!' In regard to all that this people call a conspiracy, and you are not to fear what they fear or be in dread of it. It is the LORD of hosts whom you should regard as holy. And He shall be your fear, and He shall be your dread.

"Then He shall become a sanctuary; but to both the houses of Israel, a stone to strike and a rock to stumble over, and a snare and a trap for the inhabitants of Jerusalem.

"Many will stumble over them, then they will fall and be broken; they will even be snared and caught" (Isa. 8:11-15).

God is to be the One whom the people must fear. Again, just because God gives His Word, it is no guarantee that people will readily receive it. Thus, a choice must be made: He will become something for them— either a sanctuary for those who fear Him or a stone to stumble over for those who disobey. This is an either/or scenario; God does not offer any other options.

Isaiah's second Stone prophecy came in the midst of further national apostasy. The original recipients complained of the simplicity of Isaiah's message of pending judgment for the nation's disobedience. They disdained him for the simple repetitive nature of his prophecy, insulted that he spoke to them as one would speak to a small child:

> "To whom would He teach knowledge, and to whom would He interpret the message? Those just weaned from milk? Those just taken from the breast?
> For He says, 'Order on order, order on order, line on line, line on line, a little here, a little there.'" Indeed, He will speak to this people through stammering lips and a foreign tongue, He who said to them, "Here is rest, give rest to the weary," and, "Here is repose," but they would not listen.
> So the word of the LORD to them will be, "Order on order, order on order, line on line, line on line, a little here, a little there," that they may go and stumble backward, be broken, snared and taken captive (Isa. 28:9-13).

In essence, God, through Isaiah, stated that the people would eventually believe this "baby talk" prophecy when they heard it from the foreign invaders who would overthrow the nation.

It was because of this willful rejection of God's Word that the prophecy continued. Notice the two-fold use of "therefore" in the next verses that links it with the previous section:

> Therefore, hear the word of the LORD, O scoffers, who rule this people who are in Jerusalem, because you have said, "We have made a covenant with death, and with Sheol we have made a pact. The overwhelming scourge will not reach us when it passes by, for we have made falsehood our refuge and we have concealed ourselves with deception."
> Therefore thus says the LORD God, "Behold, I am laying in Zion a stone, a tested stone, a costly cornerstone for the foundation, firmly placed. He who believes in it will not be disturbed" (Isa. 28:14-16).

In reaction to the scoffers who rejected His Word, God chose an additional means of revelation and prophetic judgment. In this case—a Stone.

These may not seem like monumental verses, but Isaiah 8:14 and 28:16 appear a surprising number of times elsewhere in Scripture. We will deal much more with these verses in upcoming chapters. However, perhaps if we break down the elements of Isaiah 28:16, we can see how loaded with content this is:

> Therefore, thus says the LORD God,
> "Behold! [Mark this! Pay attention!]
> I am laying in Zion [Jerusalem]
> a stone
> a tested stone
> a costly cornerstone
> for the foundation,
> firmly placed."

Somehow, faith must be exercised in this Stone, for God concludes by promising, "He who *believes* in it will not be disturbed."

Although we will get to the significance of this grand prophecy of God in other chapters, we should note the following truths this verse presents:

This is a pronouncement—not a command.

God places the stone—not someone else or some group of people.

God selects the place—Zion.

God selects the stone—singular—not stones.

This stone will be tested.

This stone is costly.

This stone is a cornerstone.

This stone will be for the foundation.

This stone will be firmly placed by God.

This stone—once placed by God—can be moved only by God, because after all, who else is strong enough to move what God Himself places?

This stone must be appropriated by faith.

Another prophecy in the Old Testament clarifies exactly where in Zion God will place this stone—even more importantly, why.

Zechariah the prophet was a contemporary of the prophet Haggai. He wrote his prophecy after the return from the exile and during Gentile domination when it seemed as though none of the promises of God would ever come true.

In his vision in Zechariah 3:1-2, God granted the prophet a divine behind-the-scenes view at one particular gathering. God was there—and surprisingly—so was Satan:

> Then he showed me Joshua the high priest standing before the angel of the LORD, and Satan standing at his right hand to accuse him. The LORD said to Satan, "The LORD rebuke you, Satan! Indeed, the LORD who has chosen Jerusalem rebuke you! Is this not a brand plucked from the fire?"

The subject of the gathering revolves around the matter of the priesthood, especially the high priest. Joshua (the one of Haggai and Ezra, not the one from the Book of Joshua) is clothed in filthy garments. Perhaps the filthiness was because the nation lacked purification while they were in exile. Perhaps, even more to the point, the filthiness may have been because the high priest was not able to make atonement for his own sins before making atonement for those of others:

> Now Joshua was clothed with filthy garments and standing before the angel. He spoke and said to those who were standing before him, saying, "Remove the filthy garments from him." Again he said to him, "See, I have taken your iniquity away from you and will clothe you with festal robes."
> Then I said, "Let them put a clean turban on his head." So they put a clean turban on his head and clothed him with garments, while the angel of the LORD was standing by.
> And the angel of the LORD admonished Joshua, saying, "Thus says the LORD of hosts, 'If you will walk in My ways and if you will perform My service, then you will also govern My house and also have charge of My courts, and I will grant you free access among these who are standing here" (Zech. 3:3-7).

Because the Temple had not yet been rebuilt, God graciously worked around the limitations and offered divine comfort and counsel regarding this. God thus offered this promise:

> "Now listen, Joshua the high priest, you and your friends who are sitting in front of you—indeed they are men who are a symbol, for behold, I am going to bring in My servant the Branch.
> "For behold, the stone that I have set before Joshua; on one stone are seven eyes. Behold, I will engrave an inscription on it," declares the LORD of hosts, "and I will remove the iniquity of that land in one day" (Zech. 3:8-9).

God marked the significance of what He said by using three instances of "Behold!"—easily translated as, "Mark this! Pay attention! Note this well!"

"Behold, I am going to send my servant the Branch."

"For behold, the stone that I have set before Joshua; on one stone are seven eyes."

"Behold, I will engrave an inscription on it, and I will remove the iniquity of that land in one day."

One Stone — set by God Himself.

One Stone — with attributes of God.

One Stone — with seven eyes, so it must be living.

One Stone — for the removal of iniquity of that land — in only one day!

One Stone — which, in order to remove sin, must accordingly have access to the Holy of Holies, which it does.

How could anyone ever explain — other than just by the sheer sovereignty of God — that the Jews chose a name for what was inside the Holy of Holies of the second Temple with which God Himself would agree? There was no ark, but there was a Stone. The name for this stone has never changed throughout the centuries. The Jews of Jesus' time called it by the same name. Even Old Testament believing Jews of modern times who hope soon to begin rebuilding the third Temple use the same name for the stone that alone had always resided inside the Holy of Holies on Moriah.

The Jews named this stone on which the ark once stood and later on which the blood was applied when no ark was present, *the Foundation Stone.*

God has too.

But He also named Him Jesus.

5

THE ONE

J ohn knew he was the one.

God's previous and last revelation had concluded with a promise. The final two verses in the English arrangement of the Old Testament, Malachi 4:5-6, reveal, "Behold, I am going to send you Elijah the prophet before the coming of the great and terrible day of the LORD. He will restore the hearts of the fathers to their children and the hearts of the children to their fathers, so that I will not come and smite the land with a curse."

A four-hundred-year segment of spiritual darkness followed during which God gave no additional revelation. Then, in the midst of the darkness, God sent an angelic messenger who began precisely where Malachi had ended. If we did not know from history of the four century lapse, it would seem that the chronology between the two accounts was simply a matter of days, not centuries. Luke 1:13-17 describes the divine encounter with the pronouncement of another birth to an older couple who long ago had given up any hope of ever bearing children. The elder priest Zacharias was ministering in the Temple of God:

> But the angel said to him, "Do not be afraid, Zacharias, for your petition has been heard, and your wife Elizabeth will bear you a son, and you will give him the name John. You will have joy and gladness, and many will rejoice at his birth. For he will be great in the sight of the Lord; and he will drink no wine or liquor, and he will be filled with the Holy Spirit while yet in his mother's womb.
> "And he will turn many of the sons of Israel back to the Lord their God. It is he who will go as a forerunner before Him in the spirit and power of Elijah, to turn the hearts of the fathers back to the children, and the disobedient to the attitude of the righteous, so as to make ready a people prepared for the Lord."

The angel Gabriel actually alluded to two Old Testament prophecies. This child would "turn the hearts of the fathers back to the children" which occurs in Malachi's prophecy (4:6). "To make ready a people prepared for the LORD" comes from the prophecy of the forerunner from Isaiah 40:3, as Matthew 3:1-3 would later reveal.

Zacharias inquired of the angel, "How will I know this for certain? For I am an old man and my wife is advanced in years" (Luke 1:18).

The angel could have responded to Zacharias in various ways, such as by asking how many angels he had conversed with in the past, in God's holy Temple or elsewhere. Instead, God's holy messenger was more to the point:

> The angel answered and said to him, "I am Gabriel, who stands in the presence of God, and I have been sent to speak to you and to bring you this good news.
> "And behold, you shall be silent and unable to speak until the day when these things take place, because you did not believe my words, which will be fulfilled in their proper time" (Luke 1:19-20).

"How shall I know this for certain?" —God would grant Zacharias a nine-month period of silent contemplation to consider the answer. The aged priest would not speak again until everything had happened exactly as the angel had said: "The people were waiting for Zacharias, and were wondering at his delay in the Temple. But when he came out, he was unable to speak to them; and they realized that he had seen a vision in the Temple; and he kept making signs to them, and remained mute" (Luke 1:21-22).

Then in fulfillment of God's Word, John—who would later be known as John the Baptist—was born:

> Now the time had come for Elizabeth to give birth, and she gave birth to a son. Her neighbors and her relatives heard that the Lord had displayed His great mercy toward her; and they were rejoicing with her. And it happened that on the eighth day they came to circumcise the child, and they were going to call him Zacharias, after his father. But his mother answered and said, "No indeed; but he shall be called John."
> And they said to her, "There is no one among your relatives who is called by that name." And they made signs to his father, as to what he wanted him called.
> And he asked for a tablet and wrote as follows, "His name is John." And they were all astonished. And at once his mouth was opened and his tongue loosed, and he began to speak in praise of God.

Fear came on all those living around them; and all these matters were being talked about in all the hill country of Judea. All who heard them kept them in mind, saying, "What then will this child turn out to be?" For the hand of the Lord was certainly with him (Luke 1:57-66).

"What then will this child turn out to be?" (Luke 1:66). Zacharias already knew part of the answer. Filled with the Holy Spirit, Zacharias later supplied additional details with virtually everything he stated based on previously disclosed divine promises, especially those found within the covenants of God. He first blessed God for His covenant faithfulness, for His mercy, and for His raising up a horn of salvation in Luke 1:67-75:

> And his father Zacharias was filled with the Holy Spirit, and prophesied, saying:
> "Blessed be the Lord God of Israel, for He has visited us and accomplished redemption for His people, and has raised up a horn of salvation for us in the house of David His servant—as He spoke by the mouth of His holy prophets from of old—salvation from our enemies, and from the hand of all who hate us.
> "To show mercy toward our fathers, and to remember His holy covenant, the oath which He swore to Abraham our father, to grant us that we, being rescued from the hand of our enemies, might serve Him without fear, in holiness and righteousness before Him all our days."

Zacharias addressed the child at hand and repeated the prophesies of the strategic role this child would have:

> "And you, child, will be called the prophet of the Most High; for you will go on before the Lord to prepare His ways, to give to His people the knowledge of salvation by the forgiveness of their sins, because of the tender mercy of our God, with which the Sunrise from on high will visit us, to shine upon those who sit in darkness and the shadow of death, to guide our feet into the way of peace" (Luke 1:76-79).

As noted before, almost everything Zacharias stated in regard to the child came from previous prophecies. "For you shall go to prepare his ways" (Luke 1:76)—Malachi 3:1. "The Sunrise from on high will visit us" (1:78)—Malachi 4:2. "To shine upon those in darkness" (1:79)—originates from Isaiah 9:1-2. A child whom God Himself had revealed in Scripture had been given to the nation. Luke 1:80 concludes the account stating, "And the child continued to grow and to become strong in spirit, and he lived in the deserts until the day of his public appearance to Israel."

Zacharias did not have to ask God anything else. He knew John was the one.

After so long a wait to have a child, Zacharias and Elizabeth no doubt delighted over John much in the same way that Abraham and Sarah previously had delighted over their long-awaited promise named Isaac. They would train the child, but with the exception of John's cousin Jesus, no other baby in the history of the world would be as easy to train as John. After all, God—who chose John and ordained his designated ministry long before the conception—filled the unborn child with His own Spirit before the birth (Luke 1:15). This baby arrived into the world with the unmistakable hallmark of God—and God did this with minute purpose and detail.

As the infant grew to toddler and then to young child, his wisdom would eventually surpass that of his parents. Soon thereafter, his biblical understanding would surpass the collective wisdom of all of the pious of Israel. Only one thing filled the void actually established by the Holy Spirit's indwelling: consumption of the Word of God. Nothing else in the world allured or attracted him except the constant feeding on the Word—a feeding in a sense that would never diminish or become satiated, but would grow only deeper as he matured. John's feeding was a communal consumption of fellowship, not the mere accumulation of information and knowledge from the double-lipped cup of God's Word abhorrently mingled with religious tradition or philosophy of man. That course was for others, including Saul the Pharisee before he became transformed into a child of God, and then into Paul the Apostle.

The Holy Spirit Himself created a passion and yearning filled only by the Word He Himself had inspired. John not only acquired biblical knowledge, he became—as all of God's true servants must become— transformed into the vessel of use that God intended.

No doubt, his parents informed John of the miraculous circumstances associated with his birth, and they probably would inform others. Having previously been prevented from talking, Zacharias eventually would have much to say—having conversed with the angel, having had his tongue bound, having waited nine months in silence for the birth of his aged wife's first baby. From the very first there were questions. Note in Luke 1:62, "And they made signs to his father, as to what he wanted him called," many assuming, as we sometimes assume, that because some people cannot speak, they also cannot hear. Then followed the birth, the naming, and the loosing of Zacharias' tongue—and what a loosing it was! Heaven alone knows the exact number of times old man Zacharias told about his encounter with the heavenly messenger and then proudly displayed the little answered prayer. If Zacharias was like many elderly people, he soon had to hunt for first-time listeners to hear his account. But then again, Zacharias had a message worth hearing.

Other Jewish faithful would have added their remembrances and encouragements to the young John. Many would no doubt quote the passages from the Word or from the angel. But more than anything else, the Holy Spirit affirmed him. The leaping inside his mother's womb in the presence of the One (Luke 1:41) was not a one-time leap for John. Long after his birth and throughout his life, the leaping within—or perhaps described better as a holy-flamed passion—erupted inside him. Surely Isaiah and Malachi became good friends with John through their writings—predictions that hundreds of years before specifically prophesied concerning him and his ministry. These passages, along with Gabriel's pronouncement, divinely verified who John was and what he was to accomplish in the spirit and power of Elijah.

And then, even much more powerful than in his previous walk, a major turning point occurred in John's life. Luke 3:1-2 records, "Now in the fifteenth year of the reign of Tiberius Caesar, when Pontius Pilate was governor of Judea, and Herod was tetrarch of Galilee, and his brother Philip was tetrarch of the region of Ituraea and Trachonitis, and Lysanias was tetrarch of Abilene, in the high priesthood of Annas and Caiaphas, *the word of God came to John*, the son of Zacharias, in the wilderness." Previously, John had read the Word; now he became a vessel by which God would present His Word to others. Before, the process was outside-in; read and consume. Now it was inside-out; the Word came to John, and he spoke God's holy Word to the nation. This is not some learned activity; this is the sovereign moving of the Mighty One of Israel within a prophetic vessel of His choosing.

Soon the messenger of God began his divinely-mandated ministry of the Word—and he immediately drew much attention. After all, it had been over four hundred years since God last sent a prophet to Israel, and both friend and foe alike would notice the advent of God's revelatory light. As with Jesus later, people (especially the religious leaders) wanted to know, "Who are you?" (John 1:19). John's first answer, quite simply, jumped ahead to the real issue at hand, "I am not the Christ" (John 1:20). A digression in dialogue followed:

> They asked him, "What then? Are you Elijah?" And he said, "I am not."
> "Are you the Prophet?" And he answered, "No."
> Then they said to him, "Who are you, so that we may give an answer to those who sent us? What do you say about yourself?"
> He said, "I am a voice of one crying in the wilderness, 'Make straight the way of the Lord,' as Isaiah the prophet said" (John 1:21-23).

Quoting Isaiah 40:3 in reference to his forerunner ministry, John knew he was the one.

Still, the questions about him persisted. Investigators had been sent to gain additional information and clarification:

> Now they had been sent from the Pharisees. They asked him, and said to him, "Why then are you baptizing, if you are not the Christ, nor Elijah, nor the Prophet?"
> John answered them saying, "I baptize in water, but among you stands One whom you do not know. It is He who comes after me, the thong of whose sandal I am not worthy to untie."
> These things took place in Bethany beyond the Jordan, where John was baptizing (John 1:24-28).

And then—Jesus arrived. Because John the baby leapt in the womb of his mother when Jesus approached in His mother's womb, one would think that recognizing Jesus would be somewhat simple for John. However, John 1:29-34 adds details that otherwise we would not know:

> The next day he saw Jesus coming to him and said, "Behold, the Lamb of God who takes away the sin of the world! This is He on behalf of whom I said, 'After me comes a Man who has a higher rank than I, for He existed before me.'
> "I did not recognize Him, but so that He might be manifested to Israel, I came baptizing in water."
> John testified saying, "I have seen the Spirit descending as a dove out of heaven, and He remained upon Him.
> "I did not recognize Him, but He who sent me to baptize in water said to me, 'He upon whom you see the Spirit descending and remaining upon Him, this is the One who baptizes in the Holy Spirit.'

"I myself have seen, and have testified that this is the Son of God."

John knew He was the One.

And the two of them ministered briefly for the same time, the messenger and the Message. But they did not do this as a team; forerunners run ahead, not beside:

> After these things Jesus and His disciples came into the land of Judea, and there He was spending time with them and baptizing. John also was baptizing in Aenon near Salim, because there was much water there; and people were coming and were being baptized — for John had not yet been thrown into prison.
> Therefore there arose a discussion on the part of John's disciples with a Jew about purification. And they came to John and said to him, "Rabbi, He who was with you beyond the Jordan, to whom you have testified, behold, He is baptizing and all are coming to Him."
> John answered and said, "A man can receive nothing unless it has been given him from heaven. You yourselves are my witnesses that I said, 'I am not the Christ,' but, 'I have been sent ahead of Him.'
> "He who has the bride is the bridegroom; but the friend of the bridegroom, who stands and hears him, rejoices greatly because of the bridegroom's voice. So this joy of mine has been made full.
> "He must increase, but I must decrease" (John 3:22-30).

And decrease he did.

Machaerus. A stone mountain east of the Dead Sea whose top had been leveled to provide a castle fortress and palace for its occupants who, at that time, happened to be King Herod and his ensemble. Here John stayed imprisoned for speaking the word of God to a most unwilling recipient. The name Machaerus does not occur in the New Testament, but the Jewish historian Josephus reports that John the Baptist was imprisoned and beheaded at Machaerus (Antiquities, 18.5.4). The sight sits high on a mountain that overlooks the Sea. The ruins remain there today in modern Jordan. But at the time of John the Baptist, they were anything but ruins.

Matthew 14:3-5 gives the reason for John's arrest: "For when Herod had John arrested, he bound him and put him in prison because of Herodias, the wife of his brother Philip. For John had been saying to him, 'It is not lawful for you to have her.' Although Herod wanted to put him to death, he feared the crowd because they regarded John as a prophet." The Bible does not tell exactly how long John was imprisoned at Machaerus, but it does not seem to have been an extended stay.

Now the Forerunner no longer runs. Instead, he sits in his prison cave carved out of the mountain stone. He could easily hear the merriment of parties only a few yards above his prison cell. If John's ridicule would in any way resemble the reception of the One of whom John spoke, he may have received the same type of audible barbs from those who so hated him.

"O Prophet! I know you are listening to me. Prophesy for me the day they shall remove your head from your shoulders!"

"O Prophet! O Herald of God! Where is your promised Christ? Why does He not come to rescue you? *Where is he?*"

The resounding echoes that emerged from the configuration of mountains and valleys would have danced before the imprisoned prophet like the hateful mockery games of children who gang up on a lesser.

"Where is he? . . . Where is he? . . . Where is he? . . ."

In spite of his bleak surroundings, no doubt whatsoever existed within John that he himself was the one of whom the prophets spoke. The holy fire of God within him repeatedly testified that he was the one as the Spirit affirmed him. But even in addition to this, he had witnessed the life-changing effects of God's Word on the masses. Multitudes upon multitudes repented; a people made ready for the advent of the Messiah who most assuredly would arrive soon.

Still, the very verses that John had committed to his soul and that had verified his own ministry caused him the greatest confusion:

"Comfort, O comfort My people," says your God.
"Speak kindly to Jerusalem; and call out to her, that her warfare has ended, that her iniquity has been removed, that she has received of the LORD'S hand double for all her sins."
A voice is calling, "Clear the way for the LORD in the wilderness; make smooth in the desert a highway for our God. Let every valley be lifted up, and every mountain and hill be made low; and let the rough ground become a plain, and the rugged terrain a broad valley;
"Then the glory of the LORD will be revealed, and all flesh will see it together; for the mouth of the LORD has spoken."
A voice says, "Call out." Then he answered, "What shall I call out?"
All flesh is grass, and all its loveliness is like the flower of the field.
The grass withers, the flower fades, when the breath of the LORD

blows upon it; surely the people are grass. The grass withers, the flower fades, but the word of our God stands forever.
Get yourself up on a high mountain, O Zion, bearer of good news; lift up your voice mightily, O Jerusalem, bearer of good news; lift it up, do not fear. Say to the cities of Judah, "Here is your God!"
Behold, the Lord God will come with might, with His arm ruling for Him. Behold, His reward is with Him and His recompense before Him. Like a shepherd He will tend His flock, in His arm He will gather the lambs, and carry them in His bosom; He will gently lead the nursing ewes (Isa. 40:1-11).

What divine promises of hope and comfort come from these mere eleven verses:

Then the glory of the LORD will be revealed — all flesh will see it together.
The grass withers, the flower fades, but the word of our God stands forever.

"Where is he? . . . Where is he? . . . Where is he? . . ."

Say to the cities of Judah, "Here is your God!"
Behold! (Mark this! Pay attention!) the LORD God will come with might!
Behold! (Mark this! Pay attention!) His reward is with Him and His recompense before Him.
Like a shepherd He will tend His flock.
In His arm He will gather the lambs, and carry them in His bosom.
He will gently lead the nursing ewes.

"Where is he? . . . Where is he? . . . Where is he? . . ."

The prophecy of Malachi 3:1 likewise befuddled him: "'Behold, I am going to send My messenger, and he will clear the way before Me. And the LORD, whom you seek, will suddenly come to His Temple; and the messenger of the covenant, in whom you delight, behold, He is coming,' says the LORD of hosts."

God had sent the messenger — John knew he himself was the one. But the Lord had not come suddenly to His Temple. Instead, He had departed and had turned in a direction *away* from the imprisoned prophet.

The Voice in the Wilderness finally sought answers from the Messiah. Matthew 11:1-3 records the account: "When Jesus had finished giving instructions to His own twelve disciples, He departed from there to teach and preach in their cities. Now when John, while imprisoned, heard of the works of Christ, he sent word by his disciples and said to Him, 'Are You the Expected One, or shall we look for someone else?'" Literally, John asked, "Are you the Coming One?" This expression, taken from Psalm 118:26 ("Blessed is he who comes in the name of the LORD") ultimately became a Jewish Messianic term. Another name for the Messiah is "the Coming One."

One point is essential: John's question concerned only Jesus — not himself.

John did not ask, "Am I really the messenger?"

He asked, "Are You the Coming One/Expected One?"

It may be strange to us that one who leapt in his Savior's presence before either was born, who witnessed the Holy Spirit descending on Jesus, who was told by God, in essence, "This is the One" — that John would later question His identity. Yet John was so set and secure in Scripture — as God intended — that he could not help but ask otherwise. In a true sense, Jesus had not done what was expected. Even more to the point, from John's understanding, Jesus had not done what was *required* of Him.

So John, who could not personally venture to the place where Jesus was, asks through his messengers, "Are You the Coming One?" This is not mockery. This is not brazen. Here was one of the tender lambs that the Shepherd of Isaiah 40 had promised to hold and to carry, one who was not being held or carried at that moment.

Jesus responded in a manner that perhaps no one else other than John could fully grasp. Knowing that the Holy Spirit had indwelt the prophet before his birth, Jesus appropriately answered him by means of John's lifeblood — namely, with Scripture.

Jesus answered and said to them, "Go and report to John what you hear and see: the blind receive sight and the lame walk, the lepers are cleansed and the deaf hear, the dead are raised up, and the poor have the Gospel preached to them" (Matt. 11:4-5). In this reply, Jesus quoted from one of John's favorite books, Isaiah (Isa. 35:5-6; 61:1). Point by point, John could go down this Messianic checklist.

The blind receive sight.

The lame walk.

The lepers are cleansed.

The deaf hear.

The dead are raised.

The poor have the Gospel preached to them.

"The lepers are cleansed" does not occur directly in the Isaiah prophecies, yet they could certainly qualify as those whom He would "bind up the brokenhearted" (Isa. 61:1). In addition to this, by the time John the Baptist questioned Jesus regarding His Messianic identity, Jesus had already cleansed at least one leper (Matt. 8:1-3). He further commissioned the Twelve He Himself had chosen to be His apostles for a short-term mission: "Jesus summoned His twelve disciples and gave them authority over unclean spirits, to cast them out, and to heal every kind of disease and every kind of sickness" (Matt. 10:1), authorizing them as One Who uniquely had such authority. He did not teach them *how* to do this; He gave them authority from Himself to do these miraculous deeds. Matthew 10:5-8 gives the marching orders about who they were to go to and what they were to do once there:

> These twelve Jesus sent out after instructing them, saying, "Do not go in the way of the Gentiles, and do not enter any city of the Samaritans; but rather go to the lost sheep of the house of Israel.
> "And as you go, preach, saying, 'The kingdom of heaven is at hand.'
> "Heal the sick, raise the dead, *cleanse the lepers*, cast out demons; freely you received, freely give.

John the Baptist would be fully aware of this and would need no additional substantiation on that point.

Then Jesus made one more allusion to another passage in Isaiah, but even beyond this, He also added a previously undisclosed earth-shattering revelation. The masses at large probably would not have understood His intention if they had heard Jesus' answer—but John would have, as Jesus knew he would.

Decades later in Scripture, the apostle Peter quoted the first "stone" prophecy of Isaiah 28:16: "Behold, I lay in Zion a choice stone, a precious corner stone, and he who believes in Him will not be disappointed" (1 Pet. 2:6). Peter would also use the second "stone" prophecy of Isaiah 8:14 in his first epistle, describing Jesus as "a stone of stumbling and a rock of offense." Peter employed the Greek word *skandalon*, which means "that which causes an offense." We get our modern word "scandal" from this. Peter made direct reference to Jesus as being the Stone of Stumbling—and the Rock of Offense.

Long before Peter penned these verses in his epistles, Jesus had employed them as well in answer to John the Baptist's question as whether He was the One: "And blessed is he who keeps from stumbling over Me" (Matt. 11:6) or "is not scandalized," employing the verb form of the same word *skandalon* that Peter would later write. In the same way that Peter would later be moved by the Holy Spirit to include these verses in his first epistle, Jesus had answered the imprisoned fore-runner by alluding to the same Isaiah 8:14-15 passage in reference to His identity: "Then He shall become a sanctuary; but to both the hous-es of Israel, a stone to strike and a rock to stumble over, and a snare and a trap for the inhabitants of Jerusalem. And many will stumble over them, then they will fall and be broken; they will even be snared and caught."

However, in answering John the Baptist, Jesus did something eter-nally monumental: He changed the Stone reference to Himself: "And blessed is he who does not take offense at *Me*" (Matt. 11:6). The Stone is present, but the Stone is a "*Me*," not an "*It*." How Jesus said this at the time with whatever accompanying hand gestures, if any, we do not know. But in the Greek the "Me" is in the emphatic form.

The rock that Moses struck, once in obedience (Ex. 17:7) and once in disobedience (Num. 20:18-21), symbolized or portrayed a type "of the shadow of the things to come, but the substance belongs to Christ [the Messiah]" (Col. 2:16-17). Whereas the New Testament so plainly discloses, especially in reference to the wilderness generation, "they were drinking from a spiritual rock that was following them, and the rock was Christ [the Messiah]" (1 Cor. 10:4), so also the original foun-dation stone inside the Holy of Holies — created by God — is a symbol, a foreshadowing, a temporary edifice until the true, living Foundation Stone arrives. Jewish groups past and present attempting to lay the foundation stone for the rebuilding of the pending third Temple com-pletely err, first, in who must establish it: God, *not* man and second, *who*, not what the Foundation Stone really is.

John the Baptist still had many questions. At this point, he still could not yet explain God's ways or reconcile Scripture. He would soon go to his grave without understanding the full details of God's design.

John did know this: he knew the Stone had arrived.

He knew Jesus was the One.

6

THE TESTED

*I*n order for Jesus to fulfill the "Me" — not "It" — for the Stone prophecies of Isaiah 8 and 28, He had to be tested. We know that Jesus was tested, as Hebrews 2:18 states, "For since He Himself was tempted in that which He has suffered, He is able to come to the aid of those who are tempted." We generally do not realize that God's Word necessitated this testing as part of His Messianic qualifications. Jesus was and is in essence the Stone, both in eternity past and in eternity future. The Tested Stone He would become.

As before, we must drop down into the world of the participants to see and hear what they saw and heard. As always, we must go to the source of Truth in order to understand with greater appreciation what the Stone of Israel accomplished in order to become the "tested stone, a costly cornerstone for the foundation" (Isa. 28:16).

A great connection exists between what people call the Old and New Testaments. Although these terms are found in Hebrews 8 as "old covenant" and "new covenant," the two-fold designation is a manmade device, especially as to where that division should begin and end. For instance, since Jesus was born "under the Law" (Gal. 4:4), that is, under the Mosaic Covenant, the Scripture from Matthew 1 to the point of Jesus' death is actually part of and describes the events in what people refer to as the Old Testament. In other words, although commonly called and referred to as such, Matthew 1 does not begin the New Testament/New Covenant. Luke 22:20 points to what would transpire the next day when Jesus would die on the cross: "And in the same way He took the cup after they had eaten, saying, 'This cup which is poured out for you is the new covenant in My blood.'" Simply put, the Gospel writers wrote of "Old Testament" events under which Mary and Joseph, John the Baptist, and Jesus lived—up until Jesus ratified the New Covenant in His blood on the cross. Stated differently, it was not the birth of Jesus that began the New Testament/New Covenant, but His death. Many people who read the Bible do not realize this, but it is crucial in understanding Scripture.

When viewed accordingly, and as a whole, and not separated by time into two distinct entities, an even greater continuity emerges between Malachi and Luke. Chronologically, the events of Luke 1 occur before the specific events related to Jesus' birth in Matthew 1. As we saw in previous chapters, God concluded what is called the Old Testament with (among other things) a prophecy regarding John the Baptist. Then over four hundred years of spiritual darkness followed in which God gave no more revelatory light. When God once again renewed His revelation, He picked up where Malachi ended—with the angel Gabriel using Malachi's prophecy as the basis of his divinely decreed announcement.

However, another continuity that we usually do not mark exists from what is called the Old Testament to the New Testament. To catch the fullness of this, we need to return to the Stone prophecy of Zechariah 3. One vital aspect of this account is the presence of Satan. Zechariah 3:1-2 begins describing a vision of heaven by stating, "Then he showed me Joshua the high priest standing before the angel of the LORD, and Satan standing at his right hand to accuse him. The LORD said to Satan, 'The LORD rebuke you, Satan! Indeed, the LORD who has chosen Jerusalem rebuke you! Is this not a brand plucked from the fire?'" Three times Satan is either noted or addressed in this passage. What is even more significant, this is the last time that Satan appears in what is called the Old Testament. Whereas God offered no additional divine revelation, we have no idea whether Satan had any other access to or dialogue with God during the time that follows—much in the same way we would not know that Satan was present or that this heavenly assembly revealed in Zechariah 3 even occurred unless He had revealed it. If God interacted in any way with Satan after this, He chose not to disclose it. The next time Satan appears in Scripture is in the Matthew 4/Mark 1/Luke 4 accounts where he tempts Jesus.

In Zechariah 3 Satan is present. But why? No dialogue exists between God and Satan such as that which occurred in Job 1-2. In Zechariah, God does not permit Satan to speak or even to reply to "The LORD rebuke you Satan!" But God does allow Satan to listen firsthand to the divine pronouncement of a coming One who would accomplish the most amazing acts in the future of Israel—and of the world. Observe carefully what God permitted—and even desired—Satan to hear:

> "Now listen, Joshua the high priest, you and your friends who are sitting in front of you—indeed they are men who are a symbol, for behold, I am going to bring in My servant the Branch.
> "For behold, the stone that I have set before Joshua; on one stone are seven eyes.
> "Behold, I will engrave an inscription on it," declares the LORD of hosts, "and I will remove the iniquity of that land in one day. In that day," declares the LORD of hosts, "every one of you will invite his neighbor to sit under his vine and under his fig tree" (Zech. 3:8-10).

God wanted Satan present to hear for himself this prophetic declaration. Each promise pointed to the One who would come. Each aspect meant the defeat and ruin of Satan and his kingdom. The prophets of God often did not understand the particulars about what they wrote (as 1 Pet. 1:10-12 indicates), but Satan immediately understood this prophecy when it was first uttered—every element of it. Three times "behold" marks a strategic statement by God.

> Behold! (Mark this! Pay careful attention!) I am going to bring in My servant the Branch.
> Behold! (Mark this! Pay careful attention!) The stone I have set before Joshua, on one stone are seven eyes.
> Behold! (Mark this! Pay careful attention!) I will engrave an inscription on it and I will remove the iniquity of that land in one day.

And Satan most assuredly did mark each divine pronouncement.

Since Satan later employed Scripture as a means of tempting Jesus, we know that he has access to and knowledge of the Bible. It is quite feasible to believe that he knows the entirety of God's verbal and written revelation verse-by-verse. Satan had access to similar prophecies already spoken and recorded. He understood that God was now expanding details to the prophecies of Isaiah over two hundred years earlier. Satan would especially catch the significance of the titles "Servant" and "Branch." He had good reason to pay careful attention. Isaiah 4:2-6 had already given a vivid prophecy concerning the One who would come with these credentials:

> In that day the Branch of the LORD will be beautiful and glorious, and the fruit of the earth will be the pride and the adornment of the

survivors of Israel.

It will come about that he who is left in Zion and remains in Jerusalem will be called holy—everyone who is recorded for life in Jerusalem. When the LORD has washed away the filth of the daughters of Zion and purged the bloodshed of Jerusalem from her midst, by the spirit of judgment and the spirit of burning, then the LORD will create over the whole area of Mount Zion and over her assemblies a cloud by day, even smoke, and the brightness of a flaming fire by night; for over all the glory will be a canopy. There will be a shelter to give shade from the heat by day, and refuge and protection from the storm and the rain.

Another prophecy, Isaiah 11:1-5, notes the Branch and His righteous character:

Then a shoot will spring from the stem of Jesse, and a branch from his roots will bear fruit. The Spirit of the LORD will rest on Him, the spirit of wisdom and understanding, the spirit of counsel and strength, the spirit of knowledge and the fear of the LORD.

And He will delight in the fear of the LORD, and He will not judge by what His eyes see, nor make a decision by what His ears hear; but with righteousness He will judge the poor, and decide with fairness for the afflicted of the earth; and He will strike the earth with the rod of His mouth, and with the breath of His lips He will slay the wicked. Also righteousness will be the belt about His loins, and faithfulness the belt about His waist.

The prophecy continues. When Messiah reigns, the benefits will accrue to every aspect of the earth (Isa. 11:6-10):

And the wolf will dwell with the lamb, and the leopard will lie down with the young goat, and the calf and the young lion and the fatling together; and a little boy will lead them. Also the cow and the bear will graze, their young will lie down together, and the lion will eat straw like the ox. The nursing child will play by the hole of the cobra, and the weaned child will put his hand on the viper's den. They will not hurt or destroy in all My holy mountain, for the earth will be full of the knowledge of the LORD as the waters cover the sea.

Then in that day the nations will resort to the root of Jesse, who will stand as a signal for the peoples; and His resting place will be glorious.

In addition to these prophecies, Satan would readily note the so-called "Servant Songs" of Isaiah (cf. 42:1-9; 49:1-13; 50:4-11; 52:13–53:12). Each "song" added additional details of the future Messiah's saving work, which included a crushing of the serpent's head and a restoration of the world. Just some samples of these texts include the following three passages, "Behold, My Servant, whom I uphold; My chosen one in whom My soul delights. I have put My Spirit upon Him; He will bring forth justice to the nations" (Isa. 42:1). The Servant will regather Israel and then reign over the entire world:

> "And now says the LORD, who formed Me from the womb to be His Servant, to bring Jacob back to Him, so that Israel might be gathered to Him (for I am honored in the sight of the LORD, and My God is My strength), He says, 'It is too small a thing that You should be My Servant to raise up the tribes of Jacob and to restore the preserved ones of Israel; I will also make You a light of the nations so that My salvation may reach to the end of the earth'" (Isa. 49:5-6).

The prophet thus offers an invitation in 50:10: "Who is among you that fears the LORD, that obeys the voice of His servant, that walks in darkness and has no light? Let him trust in the name of the LORD and rely on his God."

The Bible does not disclose whether or not Satan was present to hear any more of Zechariah's prophecy. However, the angelic explanation to the prophet concerning God's rebuilt Temple would not have surprised him:

> Also the word of the LORD came to me, saying, "The hands of Zerubbabel have laid the foundation of this house, and his hands will finish it. Then you will know that the LORD of hosts has sent me to you. For who has despised the day of small things? But these seven will be glad when they see the plumb line in the hand of Zerubbabel—these are the eyes of the LORD which range to and fro throughout the earth" (Zechariah 4:8-10).

In Zechariah 3:9 God described the Stone, stating, "For behold, the stone that I have set before Joshua; on one stone are seven eyes." The seven eyes are now described as, "the eyes of the LORD which range to and fro throughout the earth" (Zech. 4:10). If the human prophet did not understand the connection, Satan would—and did. As a previous holy cherub who walked in the midst of "the stones of fire" (Ezek. 28:12-14), Satan would at once recognize the Godhead attributes of the Stone that did not belong to any angel, and certainly not to any contaminated, fallen man. This Stone had "the eyes of the LORD." Satan immediately comprehended the significance of this prophecy. He did not need to wait until Revelation 5:6 pinpointed this divine attribute of Jesus: "And I saw between the throne (with the four living creatures) and the elders a Lamb standing, as if slain, having seven horns *and seven eyes, which are the seven Spirits of God, sent out into all the earth.*"

The Stone of Zechariah 3 was living. This Stone had eyes. This Stone possessed the attributes of God. The Stone would somehow be involved with having the iniquity of the land removed in only one day (Zech. 3:9).

In Zechariah's vision, Joshua, the *high* priest—not just Joshua the priest—was present. Both he and Satan would understand the imagery of engraving for the Stone from God's high priest requirements of Exodus 28. On the ephod (a sleeveless tunic) of the high priest, God required this:

> "You shall take two onyx stones and engrave on them the names of the sons of Israel, six of their names on the one stone and the names of the remaining six on the other stone, according to their birth.
> "As a jeweler engraves a signet, you shall engrave the two stones according to the names of the sons of Israel; you shall set them in filigree settings of gold.
> "You shall put the two stones on the shoulder pieces of the ephod, as stones of memorial for the sons of Israel, and Aaron shall bear their names before the LORD on his two shoulders for a memorial" (Exod. 28:9-12).

The breastplate worn by the high priest also required engraved stones:

> "You shall make a breastpiece of judgment, the work of a skillful workman; like the work of the ephod you shall make it: of gold, of blue and purple and scarlet material and fine twisted linen you shall make it. It shall be square and folded double, a span in length and a span in width.
> "You shall mount on it four rows of stones; the first row shall be a row of ruby, topaz and emerald; and the second row a turquoise, a sapphire and a diamond; and the third row a jacinth, an agate and an amethyst; and the fourth row a beryl and an onyx and a jasper; they shall be set in gold filigree.
> "The stones shall be according to the names of the sons of Israel: twelve, according to their names; they shall be like the engravings of a seal, each according to his name for the twelve tribes" (Exod. 28:15-21).

Also, the turban required an engraving:

"You shall also make a plate of pure gold and shall engrave on it, like the engravings of a seal, 'Holy to the LORD.' You shall fasten it on a blue cord, and it shall be on the turban; it shall be at the front of the turban. It shall be on Aaron's forehead, and Aaron shall take away the iniquity of the holy things which the sons of Israel consecrate, with regard to all their holy gifts; and it shall always be on his forehead, that they may be accepted before the LORD" (Exod. 28:36-38).

In addition to possessing the attributes of God, this Stone also possessed redemptive qualities. This Stone had not only High Priestly attire and engravings, but also function: the removal of the iniquity of others. In a capacity granted only to the high priest, this Stone had access to God Himself within the very Holy of Holies. We do not know whether or not Satan was still present to hear Zechariah 6:12-13, but he no doubt knew of this word when the prophet wrote it:

Then say to him, "Thus says the LORD of hosts, 'Behold, a man whose name is Branch, for He will branch out from where He is; and He will build the Temple of the LORD.
"Yes, it is He who will build the Temple of the LORD, and He who will bear the honor and sit and rule on His throne. Thus, He will be a priest on His throne, and the counsel of peace will be between the two offices.'"

Unique is this One of whom Zechariah wrote, "He will be a priest on His throne." Priests do not have thrones—kings do. But One coming Priest would have a throne. Furthermore, in the biblical accounts, Jewish kings were not priests; but One coming King would be. Unique to this coming One, He would be Priest and King—and Stone.

God emphasized the Stone prophecy of Zechariah 3 with three instances of Behold! Pay attention! Mark this!

Satan did; every part of it—he had good reason to do so. When—or if, in his mind—the Stone fulfilled these prophecies, Satan and his realm would be demolished. The Tempter had over four hundred years to plot his strategy before the Spirit led the Stone into the wilderness to be tempted by Satan (Matt. 4:1). Four centuries of strategizing and planning by Satan to defile the true High Priest, to short-circuit the King's coronation, to test and tempt Him beyond the entirety of Adam's lineage's testing. But this One was not only linked to Adam, He was the unique Son of God—and Jesus stepped into the arena of intense spiritual battle in order to qualify and to become the Tested Stone of Isaiah 28.

Matthew, Mark, and Luke all record Satan's temptation of Jesus, and each shows that the temptation was comprised of three areas. Matthew and Luke offer much more detail than Mark offers. Each writer had a different audience and a different purpose in his writing, which explains the different order of the temptation in Matthew 4:1-11 and Luke 4:1-13. Most commentators take the Matthew account to be the actual chronological sequence because the word "then" marks transitions in Matthew 3:13 ("then Jesus arrived from Galilee"), Matthew 4:1 ("then Jesus was led by the Spirit"), and 4:5 ("then the devil took Him into the holy city").

Why would Satan choose these three particular areas of temptation? After four hundred years to plot and plan, with the last reference to Satan in what is called the Old Testament has him hearing specific Stone prophecies, something remarkable takes place with the temptation: *Satan begins his temptation with something related to a stone!* This cannot be ignorance on Satan's part. He had so many years to prepare for this encounter that he knew would eventually come—with or without the Spirit's leading of the Messiah into the wilderness to be tempted (Matt. 4:1; Mark 1:12-13). Is this abject brazenness—or utter folly—to attempt to have Jesus command "these stones become bread" (Matt. 4:3)? Luke's account is even more specific: "Tell this stone [singular] to become bread" (Luke 4:3). It would seem that absolutely the *last* thing Satan would want would be a reminder to Jesus of the Stone prophecies—of the Stone role He would fulfill. Perhaps that was his main design: to have Jesus take His eyes away from Himself—the Stone—and to look to a lesser stone; to take His thoughts away from Who He is and think about a perceived need that He had. "Tell this . . . stone . . . to become bread." After all, the Stone had to "become" the Tested Stone. Why not, instead, make another stone become something it was not—namely bread? Yet, if Jesus had done this outside the Father's holy will, it would have been sinful.

The second aspect of Satan's temptation is equally surprising. Matthew 4:5-6 states, "Then the devil took Him into the holy city and had Him stand on the pinnacle of the Temple, and said to Him, 'If You are the Son of God, throw Yourself down; for it is written, "He will command his angels concerning You," and "on their hands they will bear you up, so that you will not strike your foot against *a stone*."'" How incredible that with thirty-nine Old Testament books from which to choose, the one passage that Satan selected had, as did the first temptation, a reference to a stone.

Satan quoted Psalm 91:11-12. Jesus could have responded another way, for instance, by quoting the next verse, Psalm 91:13, "You will tread upon the lion and cobra, the young lion and the serpent you will trample down." Each aspect would be true for Jesus; each aspect He would ultimately inflict on Satan. Yet—in some distant study for us—we will see that Jesus responded appropriately by how He answered. Time will not permit going in detail with this now, but He could have answered in several biblical ways and still have been correct. The short answer is He had to answer the way He did to be obedient to the Father—and to fulfill the Law.

Still, we miss something major in this account. Satan took Jesus to the pinnacle of *the Temple*. Of all places to take Jesus, this was the farthest from the best option for Satan. Some commentators foolishly write that Jesus would have swooned from the dizzying height. That describes us—not Him. Of all places—the pinnacle of the Temple. From there, even in the midst of Satan's temptation, Jesus could look over to Moriah, where He had once stopped Abraham from sacrificing Isaac; (note "the angel of the LORD" in Genesis 22:11, which is a reference to the preincarnate Jesus). To Moriah, where God would provide for Himself a Lamb. To Moriah, where He later appeared to David, designating the exact place where His own Temple would be built. To Moriah, where His own glory once indwelt the Temple—and then departed.

Depending on exactly where Calvary is, all that Jesus had to do was to shift His eyes to see the place where He would die. Perhaps He did, but if so, His eyes would go back to the Holy of Holies, where God Himself had set the Foundation Stone; the place where the Foundation Stone, with the attributes of God, ultimately would take away the iniquity of the land in only one day.

Before the next temptation, another shift of the eyes to the east would show the Mount of Olives, the last place where He had displayed His glory in Ezekiel 11:23. The Mount of Olives, where the same prophet Zechariah told of His victorious return:

> Behold, a day is coming for the LORD when the spoil taken from you will be divided among you. For I will gather all the nations against Jerusalem to battle, and the city will be captured, the houses plundered, the women ravished and half of the city exiled, but the rest of the people will not be cut off from the city.
>
> Then the LORD will go forth and fight against those nations, as when

He fights on a day of battle. In that day His feet will stand on the Mount of Olives, which is in front of Jerusalem on the east; and the Mount of Olives will be split in its middle from east to west by a very large valley, so that half of the mountain will move toward the north and the other half toward the south (Zech. 14:1-4).

Who knows exactly what Jesus focused on while the Tempter did his best to cause the Stone to stumble. Moriah. Holy of Holies. Foundation Stone. Calvary. Mount of Olives. All were readily seen from the pinnacle of the Temple if He chose to see them; each was vitally essential to the divine mission of the Stone.

Perhaps Jesus never took His holy gaze away from those places, even as the third enticement of the temptation came before Him. Matthew 4:8-9 shows, "Again, the devil took Him to a very high mountain and showed Him all the kingdoms of the world and their glory; and he said to Him, 'All these things I will give You, if You fall down and worship me.'"

"All the kingdoms of the world and their glory . . ." The first two temptations each had some reference to a stone. You would think that the third part would have had also—and you would be right.

———————

Daniel 2 occurred before the final fall of Jerusalem in 586 B.C. and the subsequent destruction of the Temple. How the Jews must have wrestled with the perception that their God had been defeated. His holy city—even the Holy of Holies—would be trampled under by pagan Gentile invaders in just a few years. What they would not know, unless they had received and believed the words of the prophets, was that pagan invaders had never driven out God Almighty. Rather, He Himself had removed His glory before the Babylonians arrived (Ezekiel 8-11). They did not drive Him out of His Temple; He left freely; He left unhurriedly; He left majestically. In God's chronology, the times of the Gentiles were about to begin (Luke 21:24).

In a time that seemed as though God was defeated—or soon would be—God revealed truths that demonstrated not only that was He in full control at that moment, but also that He has the entire world's future already laid out and established in His sovereign will. With Babylon at the height of its world prominence, God granted King Nebuchadnezzar a revelatory dream. The king awoke from his sleep in a disturbed state of mind. He knew that he had a monumental dream, but it frustrated him beyond measure that he could not recall it. He summoned the religious officials of the day and told them to relate his dream to him. They responded that the king should tell his dream to them, and then they would gladly interpret. Nebuchadnezzar, who it seems had a disregard for this group anyway, was far from comforted. In Daniel 2:8-9 the king replied, "I know for certain that you are bargaining for time, inasmuch as you have seen that the command from me is firm, that if you do not make the dream known to me, there is only one decree for you. For you have agreed together to speak lying and corrupt words before me until the situation is changed; therefore tell me the dream, that I may know that you can declare to me its interpretation."

The magicians attempted to show the king the preposterous nature of his command. They answered, "There is not a man on earth who could declare the matter for the king, inasmuch as no great king or ruler has ever asked anything like this of any magician, conjurer or Chaldean. Moreover, the thing which the king demands is difficult, and there is no one else who could declare it to the king except gods, whose dwelling place is not with mortal flesh" (2:10-11). If these verses were reworded to say, "there is no one who could declare it to the king but God" — you would have Bible-believing theology. If you said, "no one could declare it" — then you would have modern liberal theology.

With much rage and fury, the king ordered all the religious leaders to be killed at once — which would include Daniel and his friends. After hearing the news, the three young exiles convened a hurried but fervent prayer meeting, "so that they might request compassion from the God of heaven concerning this mystery, so that Daniel and his friends would not be destroyed with the rest of the wise men of Babylon" (Dan. 2:18). God revealed the mystery to Daniel in a night vision (2:19). Daniel blessed the true God of heaven saying:

> "Let the name of God be blessed forever and ever, for wisdom and power belong to Him. It is He who changes the times and the epochs; He removes kings and establishes kings; He gives wisdom to wise men and knowledge to men of understanding. It is He who reveals the profound and hidden things; He knows what is in the darkness, and the light dwells with Him.
>
> "To You, O God of my fathers, I give thanks and praise, for You have given me wisdom and power; even now You have made known to me what we requested of You, for You have made known to us the king's matter" (Dan. 2:20-23).

The king's attendant hurriedly brought Daniel before the still much enraged Nebuchadnezzar.

"Are you able to make known to me the dream which I have seen and its interpretation?" (2:26)

Daniel answered the king and said:

> "As for the mystery about which the king has inquired, neither wise men, conjurers, magicians nor diviners are able to declare it to the king. However, there is a God in heaven who reveals mysteries, and He has made known to King Nebuchadnezzar what will take place in the latter days. This was your dream and the visions in your mind while on your bed" (2:27-28).

Note the prophetic nature of Nebuchadnezzar's dream. Daniel made reference to "what will take place in the latter days" (2:28).

The description of the dream continued, as well as Daniel's testimony that God alone had revealed the dream to king and the interpretation to Daniel:

> "As for you, O king, while on your bed your thoughts turned to what would take place in the future; and He who reveals mysteries has made known to you what will take place.
> "But as for me, this mystery has not been revealed to me for any wisdom residing in me more than in any other living man, but for the purpose of making the interpretation known to the king, and that you may understand the thoughts of your mind" (Dan. 2:29-30).

King Nebuchadnezzar must have sat speechless as he listened. No dialogue occurred; the godly teenager did all of the talking. The king did not speak again until God's Word was fully proclaimed. Thus came the description of the king's dream in Daniel 2:31-35:

> "You, O king, were looking and behold, there was a single great statue; that statue, which was large and of extraordinary splendor, was standing in front of you, and its appearance was awesome. The head of that statue was made of fine gold, its breast and its arms of silver, its belly and its thighs of bronze, its legs of iron, its feet partly of iron and partly of clay.
> "You continued looking until a stone was cut out without hands, and it struck the statue on its feet of iron and clay and crushed them.
> "Then the iron, the clay, the bronze, the silver and the gold were crushed all at the same time and became like chaff from the summer threshing floors; and the wind carried them away so that not a trace of them was found. But the stone that struck the statue became a great mountain and filled the whole earth."

Then came the significance of the dream, Daniel 2:36-45:

> "This was the dream; now we will tell its interpretation before the king.
> "You, O king, are the king of kings, to whom the God of heaven has given the kingdom, the power, the strength and the glory; and wherever the sons of men dwell, or the beasts of the field, or the birds of the sky, He has given them into your hand and has caused you to rule over them all. You are the head of gold.
> "After you there will arise another kingdom inferior to you, then another third kingdom of bronze, which will rule over all the earth. Then there will be a fourth kingdom as strong as iron; inasmuch as iron crushes and shatters all things, so, like iron that breaks in pieces, it will crush and break all these in pieces. In that you saw the feet and toes, partly of potter's clay and partly of iron, it will be a divided kingdom; but it will have in it the toughness of iron, inasmuch as you saw the iron mixed with common clay. As the toes of the feet were partly of iron and partly of pottery, so some of the kingdom will be strong and part of it will be brittle. And in that you saw the iron mixed with common clay, they will combine with one another in the seed of men; but they will not adhere to one another, even as iron does not combine with pottery.
> "In the days of those kings the God of heaven will set up a kingdom which will never be destroyed, and that kingdom will not be left for another people; it will crush and put an end to all these kingdoms, but it will itself endure forever.
> "Inasmuch as you saw that a stone was cut out of the mountain without hands and that it crushed the iron, the bronze, the clay, the silver and the gold, the great God has made known to the king what will take place in the future; so the dream is true and its interpretation is trustworthy."

That last world kingdom that the Stone will strike will be the fierce fourth kingdom of Nebuchadnezzar's dream. It will also be the pinnacle of Satan's divinely-limited reign on earth, with his empowered Antichrist temporarily ruling as worldwide king (Rev. 13:1-10).

The Stone — cut out of the mountain without hands.

The Stone — whose feet will stand on the Mount of Olives.

The Stone . . .

"I will give You all this domain and its glory; for it has been handed over to me, and I give it to whomever I wish. Therefore if You worship before me, it shall all be Yours" (Luke 4:6-7).

"Begone, Satan!" (Matt. 4:10). Mark this to your core, beloved; *Jesus* ended the temptation—not Satan. Jesus decided when the contest was over. Actually, the devil had reached the zenith of his temptation, and of his base desire to have the Holy God worship the totally defiled Satan. The devil had nothing else to offer or to use as enticement.

Jesus could have responded in several ways to each of Satan's attacks, but chose, as one under the Law, the appropriate means. He would not have sinned, and would have been completely truthful, if He had responded accordingly:

"Turn this stone into bread."

"I AM the Stone—I AM also the Bread."

"Cast yourself down. He will give his angels charge over you lest you strike your foot against the stone."

"I AM the Stone. The Foundation Stone firmly placed by God Himself does not move until the Father moves Him. Once set, He does not cast Himself down. Others fall; others stumble—including you—over the Stone . . . over Me."

"All these kingdoms and their glory I will give you if you worship me."

"Begone, Satan. I AM the Stone cut out of the mountain, but not by human hands. Talk to me no more about world kingdoms and their glory. They all will end—including your beast of Daniel 9 who will come—when the Smiting Stone strikes."

Four hundred years of satanic plotting. Four hundred years of calculating the best approach. Where Satan was last seen in what is called the Old Testament, in the Stone prophecy of Zechariah 3, is where he began—and ended—his tempting of Jesus. Even with the centuries of preparation, even with the physically weakened Jesus, each element of the temptation could easily have been responded to with, "I AM the Stone." Satan knew He was—and that does not seem to have been the issue. The way he asked, "If you are the Son of God," has more of the inference in Greek of "since you are Son of God." From each element of Satan's temptation emerged another ray of refracted Light of perfection from God's Precious Stone. Each temptation segment by Satan ultimately revealed some additional aspect of Jesus' being and of His ministry. Each temptation actually gave additional credence to the fact that Jesus is the Stone. Jesus ended the temptation at His desired time—and He left the encounter with much more than when He entered.

The Stone He is, was, and always will be. The Tested Stone He had now become, at least to the degree necessary to this time of His life. Drinking His cup completely at Calvary would conclude the final and most grueling testing.

With so many references to the Stone throughout what is called the Old Testament, one would think that the Psalms would contain the most references because they contain so many Messianic prophecies. Actually, the Stone references occur only twice in the one hundred and fifty psalms recorded in Scripture. Satan quoted one in Psalm 91:11-12 when tempting Jesus in the wilderness. Jesus repeatedly quoted the other verse during the last week of His earthly life, beginning when the Stone rode from the Mount of Olives into Jerusalem.

7

THE LESSON:
PART ONE

hen writing his first epistle, Peter quoted Isaiah 28:16, a prophecy
concerning the future Messiah: "And he who believes in Him
shall not be disappointed" (1 Pet. 2:6). That Peter would cite an Old
Testament prophet is not particularly unusual; many other New
Testament authors often quoted from the Old Testament, as did Jesus
Himself in His teachings. Yet, all things considered, the truths from
Isaiah 28 did not match the circumstances of Peter's life. Here was a man
who faced imprisonment within weeks. He would suffer extensively for
his Lord, leaving this earthly realm only after experiencing the extreme
torture reserved for those crucified. Peter had attained no fortune, no
educational degrees, and no earthly inheritance to leave to his family—if
he had any family left. Perhaps they, too, had already died martyrs'
deaths for following Jesus.

Still, Peter confidently wrote, "he who believes in Him shall not be
disappointed." Peter's statement is emphatic, stressing his point with
the strongest manner possible in the Greek, and is translated, "by no
means whatsoever will one be disappointed." Peter knew what awaited
him, for Jesus had previously revealed the manner of death by which
Peter would glorify the Lord (John 21:18-19). As his prophesied death
approached, Peter neither shrank nor ran—he stood firmly. However, a
simple but compelling question remains: *Why?* Why this confidence?
Why this strong affirmation in the face of impending torture? Why this
evaluation of the worst circumstances of life, and yet he can confidently
state that one will by no means whatsoever be disappointed with Jesus?
Many people have been very disappointed with Jesus; many people still
are—from Judas up through modern times. If the truth be told, most of
us have experienced at one time or another—or will experience in the
future—some degree of disappointment with Jesus, especially when He

leads us into darkness that we do not understand.

A substantial base for Peter's confidence comes in the next verse of First Peter where he quoted Psalm 118:22: "The stone which the builders rejected, this became the very corner stone" (1 Pet. 2:7). This is a verse that Jesus had used in a personal lesson for Peter over thirty years before—a lesson that accompanied Peter for the rest of his life. It is a lesson that Jesus still intends for all of those who follow him—and for all who oppose Him.

So that we can understand why Peter regarded this verse as being so important, once again we must drop down into his life as recorded in the gospels to see with his eyes and to hear with his ears all that is happening, as much as we presently can.

If ever a time existed *not* to be disappointed with Jesus it is at His "Triumphal Entry" on what many people call Palm Sunday. The Triumphal Entry, however, is misnamed—and even more so, misunderstood. "The Preview of Jesus' Ultimate Triumphal Entry" or "The Prophetic Entry of the Humble Messiah" more accurately ascribes the event. But if you are among the confused disciples of Jesus, still argumentatively staking their claim as to which among them was the greatest (Luke 9:46; 22:24), then this is your day—especially since you "suppose that the kingdom of God is going to appear immediately" (Luke 19:11). Today is what you have waited and longed for, so desired to see, as Israel welcomes her Messiah. Jesus Himself has taught you that you will receive your promised thrones of authority when He sits on the throne of His glory (Matt. 19:28). Masses in Jerusalem are celebrating the advent of the Messiah. Biblical prophecies centuries old unfold before your own eyes. The multitudes respond as they should—*and* in accordance with Scripture. Especially Peter, James, and John could hardly contain their exuberance, since they have previewed the coming Kingdom power and glory months earlier at the Transfiguration (Matt. 17:1-8). They readily acknowledge what the multitudes do, but they cannot at this point disclose all that they know. The crowds have not beheld the glory of Jesus. At this point they view only His humanity and humility as Jesus silently rides through the human masses. These three of the inner circle understand that Jesus currently restrains Himself from displaying His glory. They are not exactly sure when He will manifest it to the entire world, but they know that He will—perhaps even this day.

Jesus rides into Jerusalem on a colt that is led, likely, by its mother—a donkey. He comes offering peace; He comes offering Himself. Matthew emphasized the biblical significance of Jesus' arrival by quoting Zechariah 9:9: "Now this took place that what was spoken through the prophet might be fulfilled, saying, 'Say to the daughter of Zion, "Behold your King is coming to you, gentle, and mounted upon a donkey, even upon a colt, the foal of a beast of burden"'" (Matt. 21:4-5). Jesus, in a meek manner, enters the city of David only days before the Passover meal. Many others prefer that He have a more regal entrance riding a white stallion, which indicates victory and triumph. A white horse does await Jesus, but one that is reserved for His true triumphal re-entry to His earth and to His city (Rev. 19:11-16).

Today, however, is not that day. Today's entry into Jerusalem fulfills the required prophecy and sets the course for the events of Passion Week. John recorded that he and the other disciples "did not understand at first [the significance of that day's events]; but when Jesus was glorified, then they remembered that these things were written of Him, and that they had done these things to Him" (John 12:16). The disciples' memories were of utmost importance to Jesus because, after all, memories are the fertile ground from which the greatest lessons often emerge. Even before there were any utterances during this Passover week, Jesus continually taught His disciples lessons that they would grasp only after the earth-shaking events of the next few days.

Movies and other accounts depicting Jesus' entry into Jerusalem that day usually do not capture the tumultuous nature of the event. Before computer animation, they simply did not have the necessary funds to present accurately the commotions that accompanied Jesus as He rode to Jerusalem. By a very conservative estimate, over 2,000,000 Jews were assembled around Jerusalem to celebrate the Passover week. Centuries earlier, when Israel was exiled because of her heinous covenant disobedience, God promised the ones whom He had just judged a future return to the Promised Land. When God desired to illustrate the glorious future repopulation of the nation that He Himself would perform, He used an illustration that would be familiar to the people: "Thus says the Lord GOD, 'This also I will let the house of Israel ask Me to do for them: I will increase their men like a flock. Like the flock for sacrifices, like the flock at Jerusalem during her appointed feasts, so will the waste cities be filled with flocks of men. Then they will know that I am the LORD'" (Ezek. 36:37-38). Obviously, "like the flock at Jerusalem during her appointed feasts" would be a massive number.

The Gospel writers stated that multitudes welcomed Jesus (Matt. 21:8-9; Luke 19:37); John described it as "the great multitude" (John 12:12). A multitude out of the ranks of two million is in the hundreds of thousands—not the dozens or a few hundreds that movies often show. Emotions run high. The electricity of so many people assembled in a festive mood is impressive. Yet, it is not merely Jesus the Man entering Jerusalem—Jesus the Messiah makes His way into the city of the King.

The crowd heralds Jesus with praise reserved only for the promised Coming One of Israel, although they misunderstand the mandatory salvific nature of Messiah's work. Many of the nation know that Israel's King has arrived; their exclamatory praise bears witness of their expectation. The masses shout Psalm 118:25-26, "Blessed is He who comes in the name of the Lord!" (Matt. 21:9), intermingled with other Messianic praise and expectation. "Hosanna!" which is interpreted. "save now!" becomes both praise and a prayer. "Blessed is the coming kingdom of our father David!" (Mark 11:10). "Blessed is the King who comes in the name of the Lord!" coupled with "peace in heaven and glory in the highest" (Luke 19:38), very similar to the angels' praise-filled worship at the birth of Jesus (Luke 2:13-14). Grandeur, excitement, joy, praise, unlimited expectation—all are associated with the advent of the Messiah King riding into His holy city.

However, not everyone rejoices at Jesus' arrival. The Pharisees also witness these events, chiding one another for their failed attempts to restrain Jesus and the masses. "You see that you are not doing any good; look, the world has gone after Him" (John 12:19)—which from their perspective gives another indication of the multitude's enormous size. About three months before Jesus arrived at Passover, as He was proceeding to Jerusalem (Luke 13:22), a group of Pharisees approach Jesus to warn Him about Herod wanting to kill Him (Luke 13:31). But these were no true friends of Jesus, and their motives were far from honorable. And instead of have Jesus thank them and flee in fright, He answers them—the group of Pharisees; He does not make a public proclamation at this point—and addresses how Herod will not thwart God's program or timing (Luke 13:31-33). But then Jesus gave a preview to them of what to expect:

> "O Jerusalem, Jerusalem, the city that kills the prophets and stones those sent to her! How often I wanted to gather your children together, just as a hen gathers her brood under her wings, and you would not have it!

"Behold, your house is left to you desolate; and I say to you, you shall not see Me until the time comes when you say, 'Blessed is He who comes in the name of the Lord!'" (Luke 13:34-35).

In Luke 13:35 Jesus quoted Psalm 118:26. He foretold the Pharisees what to expect when He entered Jerusalem, and the day He arrived, the multitudes have called out exactly as He said—and even more to point—the very words He said would occur. Instead of making them marvel and repent, this would only intensify the Pharisees' hatred for their Enemy.

Yet beyond what we have already seen lie two significant truths. First, Jesus' entry into Jerusalem begins the countdown to Calvary. Second—and of utmost importance—His entry established the foundation for much of Jesus' final teaching during the few days before His death. Although at this time, only He alone understands it, Jesus has already presented the first portion of His divine lesson: to Peter and John and the other disciples; to the hostile religious authorities; to Israel's collective masses. Today, Jesus initiates His lesson, but He has much more to teach them all regarding both Himself and His work.

The second segment of the lesson came two days later after Jesus had cleansed His Temple and had begun teaching in the newly purified edifice (Matt. 21:23ff.). While Jesus was teaching His followers, the chief priests and elders interrupted Him. They demanded to know by whose authority He did this—probably referring to both the cleansing of the Temple and to His right to teach, especially in God's house. Technically speaking, Jesus needed to give no explanation; He had committed no sin, not even by the holy standards of the Mosaic Law. Jesus had not defiled or profaned the Temple in any way. He had not entered into the restricted Holy of Holies. Instead, Jesus had expunged the foreign elements that had defiled God's house of prayer and had rendered it a bazaar of commerce (Matt. 21:12-13; Mark 11:15-18). If a Scripture passage existed that prohibited such cleansing, the opponents of Jesus would have readily cited it on the spot; but they could not. Consequently, His critics could ask only under whose authority Jesus had acted.

In good Jewish manner, Jesus responded to the question with a question. He would offer a full disclosure of the source of His authority if the religious leaders would answer one simple question from Him. Jesus asked, "The baptism of John was from what source, from heaven or from men?" (Matt. 21:25). Mark's account ends with the simple but clear injunction: "Answer Me!" (11:30). The crucial issue was the source of authority regarding both John the Baptist and Jesus—and the chief priests and elders immediately perceived the dilemma that Jesus had created for them. If they had answered that John was from God, Jesus could counter with, "Then why did you not believe him?" John the Baptist had previously said in reference to Jesus, "Behold, the Lamb of God who takes away the sin of the world" (John 1:29). He also had taught his followers about One who was coming after him who was greater than he was, *and*, even though Jesus was born after John, the forerunner testified that "He existed before me" (1:30). If the religious leaders had said that John was from God, then Jesus would have to be from God also because John had pronounced Him as such. On the other hand, if they had reasoned that John's authority was only from man, then "all the people will stone us to death, for they are convinced that John was a prophet" (Luke 20:6).

Trapped by this childishly simple question asked by Jesus, the leaders' external answer was, "We do not know" (in the Greek usually translated "to know intellectually; to understand"). As the blind man of John 8 had previously responded, "Herein is a wonderful [amazing] thing!", so the same could be said in response to the hardness of the chief priests and elders. The ones so devout and meticulously trained for decades in the very nuances of the Law could not view John's public ministry, the content of his message, the effect he had on the nation of Israel, his own attestation to their questions years earlier as to who he was, and then make a determination of whether or not he was a prophet sent by God. They had an "either/or" proposition set before them—but they had no "either/or" answer.

Jesus offered no additional discourse with the assembled religious leaders. At that time, it was senseless to continue. After all, if they could not judge correctly concerning the forerunner, then why bother interrogating the One of whom the prophet witnessed? The chief priests and elders, condemned by their own silence, stood before Jesus.

Jesus used the unwillingness of the response by the chief priests and elders as a transition to the Parable of the Two Sons, illustrating the religious leaders' utter unwillingness to repent at John the Baptist's teaching (Matt. 21:28-32). The parable that followed, that of the Landowner (21:33-44), depicted a pattern of rejecting the ones sent by God, culminating with the rejection and murder of the Son. The two parables combined to condemn the actions of Israel's religious authorities in not receiving the two select messengers sent by God Himself. One servant, the leaders had already rejected—the Other, they were in the process of rejecting—the Son sent by God the Father.

In the second parable, Jesus concluded by quoting Psalm 118:22—the same psalm which is the origin of the Hosannas that were repeatedly shouted by the crowds of the previous days. Peter and John would have witnessed this: "Jesus said to them, 'Did you never read in the Scriptures, "The Stone that the builders rejected, this became the Chief Cornerstone; this came about from the Lord, and it is marvelous in our eyes?"'" (Matt. 21:42).

The chief priests and elders understood that Jesus referred to them in both parables and responded to His teaching by seeking to kill Him (Matt. 21:45-46). They likely would have killed Him on the spot, as they would kill Stephen weeks later—if they could have. But they could not. Someone much greater than they controlled the events of this divinely predicted week.

Jesus mentioned no names in His parables. Why then did the chief priests and Pharisees react so violently? Simply put, the opponents of Jesus responded in wrath because they clearly understood what Jesus was claiming: *He Himself* was the cornerstone *placed by God*. This concerned Jesus' origin and mission and answered their initial question of, "By what authority are you doing these things?" (Matt. 21:23)—"by My Father who placed Me here."

Consider what Jesus said to them, "Did you never read in the Scriptures, 'The stone which the builders rejected, this became the chief corner stone?'" This question by Jesus contained many subsidiary implications that struck at the core of the Jewish leaders' tragically misguided and self-exalting theology.

Maybe the religious leaders did not know the psalm as did God's true worshipers who had shouted Psalm 118 two days before at the advent of Israel's Messiah.

Maybe they had read it, but it was merely a repeated ritual, a routine of no unusual significance: similar to having the right answer about where the Messiah would be born, but not by walking a few miles down the road to Bethlehem to investigate for themselves the heralded birth (Matt. 2:1-6).

Maybe Psalm 118 was merely an academic exercise without any personal relevance to them, and for some, certainly not the inspired holy word of God.

Maybe the religious leaders had mixed their tradition with the

Word of God so that the composite blend had become merely a form of godliness devoid of any true spiritual life.

But beyond these additional condemnations, one essential truth emerged above all the rest: Psalm 118 strongly supports the Messianic claims of Jesus of Who the Messiah of Israel is. Whoever the Messiah was, He *had to be initially rejected* before He would reign in order for Scripture to be fulfilled. Not only was the Messiah to be rejected, but also this rejection must come from those in places of religious authority and responsibility. This prophecy was being fulfilled from the very ones repudiating Jesus at that very moment. That hour was the Trinity-ordained time of Jesus' rejection—not His reign—as the Godhead had mandated in eternity past. Nevertheless, it still made those who rejected Him responsible for their actions (Matt. 21:44).

The chief priests and elders were not only the builders who rejected the Stone, but they were also the ones who opposed God the Father, because God Himself had placed the Stone. *They*—not the Stone—were the ones standing in direct opposition and hostility to God, and they collectively stood condemned by Scripture. Ironically, the rejection of the Stone by the religious leaders did not diminish the claims of Jesus: the stronger the hostile reaction by the leaders, the greater the Messianic substantiation. God's own Word predicted this would—and must—happen, just as it did, and predicted or not, they intended to add their intensified hostility against the Lamb of God who takes away the sins of the world (John 1:29).

The Stone was present, as were His rejecters. Jesus did not recite some ancient verse encumbered in some dusty scroll. The Incarnate Word brought forth the living and abiding Word of God that was being enacted before them, even with the most unwilling participants. For the second time in two days, Peter and John heard a portion of Psalm 118 recited as Jesus concluded the second segment of His lesson.

The continual instruction that Jesus intended required other elements to be set in place. Once again, events of the Passover week provided the appropriate classroom for such deep spiritual learning. In Matthew 22 Jesus answered multiple trick questions as various religious groups hopelessly tried to make Him stumble over some idle word that He spoke. But the Word of God (John 1:1; Rev. 19:13) had no idle words within Him, and their efforts to darken the sun would have rendered more possibility than the Word who became flesh (John 1:14) stumbling over His own Truth. Jesus concluded this interaction with a biblical substantiation of His Messiahship, as He pointed to His preexistent relationship with King David (Matt. 22:41-46). Quoting Psalm 110:1 ("the Lord said to my Lord, 'sit at My right hand'"), Jesus proved from Scripture that the Messiah was both David's son (physical heir) *and* David's God ("my LORD"). The result from the various responses that Jesus gave, and even from one simple question, was that "no one was able to answer Him a word, nor did anyone dare from that day on to ask Him another question" (Matt. 22:46).

Having shut the mouths of the stonehearted, Jesus then took the offensive. In Matthew 23 Jesus instructed the multitudes by rebuking the ways of the scribes and Pharisees. In concluding His denouncement of the religious leaders, Jesus promised pending judgment on that generation and other generations who had rejected or who would reject Him (23:34-36). Yet, even in the midst of His reproof, the deep love of the heartsick Messiah showed forth: "O Jerusalem, Jerusalem, who kills the prophets and stones those who are sent to her! How often I wanted to gather your children together, the way a hen gathers her chicks under her wings, and you were unwilling. Behold, your house is being left to you desolate" (Matt. 23:37-38).

Then Jesus said something totally unexpected—to the disciples, to the masses, and to His opponents. He quoted the *exact* phrase from Psalm 118 that many within the multitude had shouted only two days before at His unforgettable entry into Jerusalem: "For I say to you, from now on you shall not see Me *until* you say, 'Blessed is He who comes in the name of the LORD!'" (Matt.23:39).

When we consider them, Jesus' predictions must have greatly confused the vast majority of those who heard Him. Jesus' statements were made on the same day as the discourses of Matthew 21 and 22— and somewhere close to forty-eight hours after His, quote, "Triumphal Entry" into Jerusalem. His reasoning seems disjointed, as though two distinct conversations occurred simultaneously, each incongruous with the other. Jesus demanded future praise from Israel, praise that had previously been given Him only a few days earlier. The people had *already* publicly proclaimed what Jesus had told them was necessary for the nation to see Him, namely, "Blessed is He who comes in the name of the LORD" (Matt. 21:9; Ps. 118:26). One thing is certain; the answer that Jesus gave indicated that He did not view Psalm 118 as having had its fulfillment at the "Triumphal Entry."

Why did Jesus not accept Israel's praise at the advent of her

Messiah? Simply put, He could not have received the praise of Israel at that time because Psalm 118:22 ("the stone which the builders rejected") had not yet transpired, but would culminate in His crucifixion. The people sang and desired Psalm 118:25-26: "O LORD, do save [Hosanna!], we beseech You; O LORD, we beseech You, do send prosperity! Blessed is the one who comes in the name of the LORD!" But such prophesied days of blessing could not come without first having the builders reject the Stone placed there by God Himself. The times of blessing could not come unless the Lamb of God made proper atonement for the sin of the world (John 1:29). Most of those in Israel—especially the various religious groups—saw no need for such atonement; after all, they had the functioning Temple sacrifices. Jesus never permitted these basest of needs to leave His thoughts.

Jesus had not participated in the Triumphal Entry—only a preview. The true Triumphal Entry awaits Him.

"For I say to you, from now on you shall not *see* Me *until* you say, 'Blessed is He who comes in the name of the LORD'" (Matt. 23:39). Obviously, Jesus' declaration is not a total abandonment of the nation of Israel. One day God will pour out His Spirit on the Jewish people so that they will deeply mourn the One whom they rejected. One day Israel will see: "And it will come about in that day that I will set about to destroy all the nations that come against Jerusalem. And I will pour out on the house of David and on the inhabitants of Jerusalem the Spirit of grace and of supplication, so that they will *look on Me* whom they have pierced; and they will mourn for Him, as one mourns for an only son, and they will weep bitterly over Him, like the bitter weeping over a firstborn" (Zech. 12:9-10). One day, centuries yet in the future from Christ's days on earth, Israel will again sing Psalm 118 at the advent of Jesus. But next time, He will readily accept what has been rightfully His from the beginning. The next pouring forth of praise will be after the cleansing of the nation—and the cleansing of the nations. The next time, Jesus will enter Jerusalem in full Transfiguration glory (Matt. 25:31)—and on a white horse (Rev. 19:11).

Israel unwittingly wanted the glory without the cross. As Peter would reluctantly and slowly learn, Messiah's glory did not come without first the sufferings, as he later wrote in 1 Peter 1:10-11: "As to this salvation, the prophets who prophesied of the grace that would come to you made careful search and inquiry, seeking to know what person or time the Spirit of Christ within them was indicating as He predicted the sufferings of Christ and the glories to follow."

This was the third time in three days that a section of Psalm 118 had been publicly quoted. Even more importantly, this was the third time that Peter and John had heard for themselves this Messianic psalm during Passion Week, as the drama unfolded before their eyes.

But this was not the last time Psalm 118 occurred during Passover week. A most important segment, the fourth part of Jesus' lesson, was about to begin.

Luke 22:8 records that Jesus selected Peter and John to prepare the Passover that He and the disciples collectively would observe later that night. In view of the approaching trial and suffering of Jesus— approximately twenty-four hours of His incarnate life remained— sending two of the more prominent disciples to prepare the Passover meal seems at first to be an unwise choice. Let two other servants do this chore, or at least let two of the "lesser" disciples prepare the feast. So little time remained, and Jesus had much, much more to teach His disciples (John 16:12)—especially these two important members of His inner circle. Would Jesus not have greater lessons for them to learn than the physical activity of preparing the Passover? Actually, Jesus was teaching them—both then and in preparation for the future.

Taking the lamb to the Temple to be slain was the most critical element in the Passover preparation. Many thousands of participants representing their families or associates would proceed with their lambs to the Temple area at the prescribed afternoon just before the Passover Meal. But one could not arrive at the Temple and slaughter the lamb whenever one wanted to; all had to be done in proper order—and with the proper worshipful accompaniment. The sheer number of Passover lambs to be slain required the formation of three different groups who would enter the designated area when summoned by the priests and Levites.

As the multitudes assembled for the sacrificing of the lambs, the massive Levitical choir sang the Hallel, which consisted of Psalms 113-118. Eventually Psalms 113-118 began being called "The Egyptian Hallel," because of its use during the Passover observances. Each of these psalms reminded the participants of God's goodness, grace and provision for Israel. The congregation joined in the liturgy by repeating the first line of each psalm after the Levites sang it. They also chanted "Hallelu Yah" *(hallelujah – praise God!)* at the end of each line.

A very solemn procedure occurred at the actual sacrificing of the lamb. The participants — not the priests — killed their own lambs at the signal of the silver trumpets. Attending priests stood by in two rows waiting with bowls to catch the blood of the sacrifices. Each bowl would be passed down the line until the blood was finally poured out at the base of the altar.

When the Levitical choir came to Psalm 118, the entire congregation repeated verses 25-26 after them:

O LORD, do save, we beseech You;
O LORD, we beseech You, do send prosperity!
Blessed is the one who comes in the name of the LORD;

Many people who had just slain their lambs also had shouted and had sung these same verses at Jesus' entry into Jerusalem earlier in the week. These were the *exact* words Jesus had said that collective Israel would say before the next time they saw Him. Perhaps several looked around the Temple confines expecting to see Jesus make another dramatic entrance at that very moment, looking to see if some prophetic event accompanied this recitation of Psalm 118. Instead, all they saw were their sacrificial lambs before them — spotless and unblemished — having their life's blood poured out on an altar before the Lord. The significance of this threefold use of Psalm 118 for the masses no doubt caused much conversation and debate as the participants vacated the Temple area to prepare the final elements necessary for the Passover observance only a few hours away.

Peter and John also heard — and this time sang — Psalm 118 as they stood in the Temple court sacrificing their own Passover lamb. The two disciples may have understood some of what Jesus attempted to teach them. At this point, however, they fought to repress their growing fears that the real Lamb of God was about to be led to slaughter in similar manner. Did either one — or both — grasp the lesson that Jesus intended by specifically sending these two learners to prepare the Passover? Did they silently look at each other wondering if the other, too, understood the repeated use and significance of Psalm 118? Did Peter and John discuss this on the way back to where the Passover meal would be consumed, as they often had discussed among themselves the significance of Jesus' words? Or did they walk back in silence, each alone with his fearful expectations of what the night would bring forth? Both Peter and John had repeatedly heard Jesus predict His pending execution. The bounds of their love — coupled with their lack of understanding (Luke 9:44-45), especially on Peter's part—offered them false hope that somehow Jesus was not about to die this night or tomorrow. To them, one lamb slain that day for God sufficed; surely God would not call for the life of the Other.

This was the fourth time that Peter and John had heard Psalm 118 quoted that week, but there was one more essential usage in order for Jesus' lesson to be complete.

Although the nation of Israel sang the Egyptian Hallel (Ps. 113–118) at other prescribed Jewish feasts, these psalms particularly related to Passover. During the Passover meal, families recited or sang the Hallel in their homes in much the same way that the Levitical choir had sung them earlier that day while sacrificing their lambs. Before the Passover meal, the worshipers sang Psalms 113 and 114. After the meal, they sang Psalms 115-118, all done in accordance with the ancient prescribed order. This last psalm of the Hallel most certainly would have been what Jesus and His disciples sang at their "last supper" before leaving the room (Matt. 26:30). In any event, Psalm 118:22-29 would be one of the last things verbally communicated before the unspeakable suffering of Christ began:

> *The stone which the builders rejected has become the chief corner stone. This is the LORD'S doing; it is marvelous in our eyes.*
> *This is the day which the LORD has made; let us rejoice and be glad in it.*
> *O LORD, do save, we beseech You; O LORD, we beseech You, do send prosperity.*
> *Blessed is the one who comes in the name of the LORD.*
> *We have blessed you from the house of the LORD.*
> *The LORD is God, and He has given us light;*
> *Bind the festival sacrifice with cords to the horns of the altar.*
> *You are my God, and I give thanks to You; You are my God, I extol You.*
> *Give thanks to the LORD, for He is good; for His lovingkindness is everlasting.*

The lesson taught by God Incarnate—all week, even earlier that day, and now at Passover—resounded in tens of thousands of different homes and gatherings within crowded Jerusalem. Each service individually pointed to the One who had so stirred the city all week. Each service bore divine witness to God's Son—and to God's sacrifice.

Jesus and the Eleven sang Psalm 118 around the Lord's Table—and around the Lord's own Passover Lamb. Lost forever, except to only those present, were the hand gestures and voice inflections of the various words of Psalm 118 that Jesus may have applied specifically to

Himself. Did Jesus point toward Himself, by gesture or voice, as He said "stone . . . corner stone . . . blessed is He who comes in the name of the LORD . . . the LORD is God, and He has given us Light . . . bind the festival sacrifice . . ."? Perhaps He did. The words alone, especially in view of their repetitions during the week, may have spoken louder than they would have with any accompanying emphasis.

Would Peter and John make eye contact with each other as they struggled to join in the singing of this psalm? Could they do so without weeping as both realized, perhaps more than the others, what would take place next, having witnessed a graphic preview only hours before at God's Temple? Did Jesus slightly turn His face toward them, examining them with the holy soul-searching eyes of God to see if they understood, even in a child's limited manner, what He had been teaching them step-by-step?

Jesus and the disciples sing Psalm 118 — and leave the room for Gethsemane.

Throughout the city, and less than a mile from where Jesus promised His own, "I will not drink of the fruit of this vine from now on until that day when I drink it with you in My Father's kingdom" (Matt. 26:29), thousands upon thousands of Israel's religious establishment celebrated the same Passover meal, following the exact Passover procedure that Jesus and His disciples followed. Regardless of high rank or lowly status, all collectively or each individually recited Psalm 118; not one member was exempt. The religious authorities who celebrated the Passover that night repeated what they had heard and what they themselves had previously said. With varying degrees, some will be involved with the trial and sacrificial death of the Lamb. Each would offer his opinion — if any — as to the significance of the Psalm, especially regarding the multiple references to Jesus, that already had been made that week.

Multitudes of Jews in Jerusalem celebrated Passover that night, each reciting Psalm 118 — several, no doubt, were part of the multitude that had shouted "Hosanna!" days before when Jesus had entered Jerusalem. Some had shouted "Hosanna" that very day when sacrificing their Passover lambs, just as Peter and John had done. The repeated verses coupled with the events of the past week caused virtually every household to discuss fervently the significance of these verses, especially in relation to the identity and mission of Jesus. The person of Jesus had stirred tremendous debate for years, but it reached its zenith during this Passover. The finely orchestrated events and the multiple quotations of Psalm 118 only kindled the already white-hot debate concerning Jesus. No other topic of conversation would come remotely as close to the minds and lips of the Passover participants as that of the One who had come in the name of the Lord.

God bore testimony in His written Word to His Incarnate Word. He also bore testimony from collective Israel's own lips—from saddened disciples, to hostile foes, to confused masses. All—even the most blatant rejecters—bore witness to the Stone of Israel, the Son of God, placed there by God Himself. The whole nation awoke the next morning to see their sacrificial Lamb being slain before their eyes. Their Stone had been rejected by the builders, all in minute fulfillment of God's Holy Word:

> *"The stone which the builders rejected has become the chief cornerstone.*
>
> *"This is the LORD'S doing; it is marvelous in our eyes. This is the day which the LORD has made; let us rejoice and be glad in it.*
>
> *"O LORD, do save, we beseech You; O LORD, we beseech You, do send prosperity.*
>
> *"Blessed is He who comes in the name of the LORD."*
>
> *Psalm 118:22-26a*

8

THE LESSON:
PART TWO

From the original Passover to all subsequent ones, God Himself had given commands—not suggestions—regarding His Passover. And it is just that: His Passover, as the concluding verses regarding the first Passover instructions indicate, "it is the LORD's Passover" (Exod. 12:11). The previous verses of Exodus 12:1-6 gave precise directives regarding the Passover and its on-going importance for the nation of Israel, including precisely when the qualifying Passover lambs would be slain:

> Now the LORD said to Moses and Aaron in the land of Egypt, "This month shall be the beginning of months for you; it is to be the first month of the year to you.
> "Speak to all the congregation of Israel, saying, 'On the tenth of this month they are each one to take a lamb for themselves, according to their fathers' households, a lamb for each household. Now if the household is too small for a lamb, then he and his neighbor nearest to his house are to take one according to the number of persons in them; according to what each man should eat, you are to divide the lamb. Your lamb shall be an unblemished male a year old; you may take it from the sheep or from the goats. And you shall keep it until the fourteenth day of the same month, then the whole assembly of the congregation of Israel is to kill it at twilight.'"

Not only did God say what sacrifice He would accept, but He also told the entire assembly when to sacrifice: at twilight. The Hebrew rendering for "twilight" is literally translated, "between the two evenings."

Once God's tabernacle had been erected and an aspect of His glory had filled His own sanctuary (Exod. 40:34-38), while He was still at Mount Sinai, the LORD gave additional revelation regarding His Passover. The initial feast that began the nation's religious calendar became one of the many "appointed times of Yahweh," as Leviticus 23:1-5 shows:

> The LORD spoke again to Moses, saying, "Speak to the sons of Israel, and say to them, 'The LORD's appointed times which you shall proclaim as holy convocations—My appointed times are these: For six days work may be done; but on the seventh day there is a sabbath of complete rest, a holy convocation. You shall not do any work; it is a sabbath to the LORD in all your dwellings.
> "These are the appointed times of the LORD, holy convocations which you shall proclaim at the times appointed for them. In the first month, on the fourteenth day of the month at twilight is the LORD's Passover."

When the first anniversary of the original Passover was about to be observed, God reminded the nation about the importance of the continual celebration of this holy feast, and that it must be done in accordance with the strict word of God. As with the original instructions, this included when the Passover lambs were to be sacrificed. Obviously, many conditions were different for this second Passover, for the Hebrew nation was now in the wilderness of Sinai and was no longer enslaved in Egypt, as they had been during the previous year. Numbers 9:1-5 records the commands by Yahweh and the obedient response by the people:

> Thus the LORD spoke to Moses in the wilderness of Sinai, in the first month of the second year after they had come out of the land of Egypt, saying, "Now, let the sons of Israel observe the Passover at its appointed time. On the fourteenth day of this month, at twilight [as before, literally in the Hebrew, "between the two evenings"], you shall observe it at its appointed time; you shall observe it according to all its statutes and according to all its ordinances."
> So Moses told the sons of Israel to observe the Passover. And they observed the Passover in the first month, on the fourteenth day of the month, at twilight, in the wilderness of Sinai; according to all that the LORD had commanded Moses, so the sons of Israel did.

After the multiple sins of those who were physically redeemed out of Egypt, culminating with the evil report by the spies who were sent out to preview the Promised Land (Num. 13–14), God caused everyone except Joshua and Caleb to die in the wilderness during a forty-year timeframe. As the wilderness generation's children stood poised to enter the land that God had long promised them, the LORD gave an additional binding restriction regarding the place where the sacrifice was to be slain. In Deuteronomy 16:1-2 God decreed, "Observe the month of Abib and celebrate the Passover to the LORD your God, for in the month of Abib the LORD your God brought you out of Egypt by night. And you shall sacrifice the Passover to the LORD your God from the flock and the herd, in the place where the LORD chooses to establish His name." This first month, originally called Abib, ultimately took the name "Nisan." In the Jewish way of reckoning—by repeated holy command from God Himself—the Passover lambs were to be sacrificed on the fourteenth of Nisan/Abib.

Before this, the nation had been in a transient mode; ultimately, in the predetermined plan and foreknowledge of God, He would lead Israel to a fixed point of His creation where the Passover lambs would be slain—as well as His own Unblemished Lamb—because that was "the place where the LORD chooses to establish His name" (Deut. 16:2). Deuteronomy 16:5-6 is very clear regarding why the nation as a whole would ultimately journey to Jerusalem to sacrifice their lambs. Although He did not at that time specify the city, God maintained authority to lead the nation where He chose, stating, "You are not allowed to sacrifice the Passover in any of your towns which the LORD your God is giving you; but at the place where the LORD your God chooses to establish His name, you shall sacrifice the Passover in the evening at sunset, at the time that you came out of Egypt." From Deuteronomy 16 up until the ultimate arrival of the new heavens and the new earth—even in the Kingdom with the advent of the King (Ezek. 45:21-25)—a Passover lamb would be accepted by God only if sacrificed at the place *and* the time that He Himself had mandated. God would reject any less sacrifice, as He had previously rejected Cain's offering (Gen. 4:5).

We should mark one important question recorded in Scripture that occurred at the observance of the second Passover. Events arose that caused people to question what those who were ceremonially unclean should do. Should they miss the Passover completely? Moses did not know the answer to this, so he sought the LORD'S counsel. In Numbers 9:6-12 God gave His command that would be binding on all such affected Jewish participants from that day forward:

> But there were some men who were unclean because of [coming in contact with] the dead person, so that they could not observe Passover on that day; so they came before Moses and Aaron on that day. And those men said to him, "Though we are unclean because of

the dead person, why are we restrained from presenting the offering of the LORD at its appointed time among the sons of Israel?"

Moses therefore said to them, "Wait, and I will listen to what the LORD will command concerning you."

Then the LORD spoke to Moses, saying, "Speak to the sons of Israel, saying, 'If any one of you or of your generations becomes unclean because of a dead person, or is on a distant journey, he may, however, observe the Passover to the LORD. In the second month on the fourteenth day at twilight, they shall observe it; they shall eat it with unleavened bread and bitter herbs. They shall leave none of it until morning, nor break a bone of it; according to all the statute of the Passover they shall observe it.

Those who were ceremonially contaminated could observe a Passover that God would accept, but it had to be observed exactly one month later and precisely as the others were, at twilight. Scripture offers no additional information regarding what would happen if, for some reason, people had to miss the second Passover. From the silence of the account, it would seem that they would have to wait until the next Passover when the nation collectively celebrated it, namely, in the following spring on the 14th of Abib/Nisan.

However, Numbers 9:13 warned those in the present and those in the future of how severely God viewed the ones who had the opportunity to celebrate the Passover in accordance with His commands, but who may have considered not observing it: "But the man who is clean and is not on a journey, and yet neglects to observe the Passover, that person shall then be cut off from his people, for he did not present the offering of the LORD at its appointed time. That man shall bear his sin." All God-fearing Jews would take this holy warning most seriously. The observance of the Passover by Israel gave a reliable indication of whether or not they were living in covenant obedience to their covenanted LORD. For instance, both Kings Hezekiah (2 Chron. 30) and Josiah (2 Chron. 35) reinstituted the Passover after Israel had long failed to observe it. Not that the Passover was the only means of obedience, nor did it mean that partaking of the Passover was equated with holiness and obedience to God, but if the Jewish nation, often because of wicked leadership, did not observe God's Passover, they communally lived in direct disobedience to the commands of God—and as God plainly stated in Numbers 9:13, each one "shall bear his own sin."

This backdrop of the Passover helps to explain what many critics of the Bible have long pointed out what seems to be a great discrepancy in Scripture, namely, that Jesus sent James and John to sacrifice the

Passover lamb so that He could partake of the Passover meal with His disciples (Luke 22:7-9). Yet, during the trial of Jesus, which occurred *after* Jesus had eaten the Passover with His disciples, after Gethsemane, after the initial arrest of Jesus, and after Peter's denial, John 18:28 states, "They [the Jewish officials] led Jesus therefore from Caiaphas into the Praetorium, and it was early; and they themselves did not enter into the Praetorium in order that they might not be defiled, *but might eat the Passover*." John 19:14 is even more confusing, for it refers to the day Jesus was crucified as "the day of preparation for the Passover," something that Peter and John had already performed on the previous day when Jesus had beforehand partaken with His select disciples (Luke 22:7-20).

Fortunately, there is a good answer for this: the Jews used two distinct ways of calculating when a day began (three ways, if you include Roman time, which sometimes Scripture uses). [Those who are interested can read about this in *The MacArthur Bible Commentary*, p. 1420, or Robert Thomas and Stanley Gundry, *A Harmony of the Gospels*, pp. 321-22.] For the Galileans and the Pharisees, the day began at sunrise, and the new day began at the following sunrise. So for them, Thursday, Nisan 14 was from sunrise to sunrise. They would sacrifice the Passover lambs at the Temple from 3:00-5:00 PM ("between the twilights") and eat the meal only hours later that same night. If one had asked them when they sacrificed their Passover lambs, they would have responded, "Why on the 14th of Nisan, of course, as Scripture repeatedly commands us." By their way of reckoning, they would have been accurate and would have in no way violated the holy mandate of God.

Almost all of those who lived in Jerusalem, which would include the priests and Sadducees, used a sunset-to-sunset method of reckoning the days. So if one could have asked them on the day that Jesus was crucified what day it was, they would have answered it to be the Nisan 14—which began the previous sunset—and in order to be in compliance with the Torah, the Passover lambs must be sacrificed by sunset that day. The actual Passover meal would be eaten immediately after sunset, which closed the old day and began the new. These different means of reckoning time were not like King Jeroboam who had previously changed the God-ordained feast date that he had made "even in the month which he had devised in his own heart" (1Kings 12:33). These people had not changed. Both groups thought they were correct in how they told time; both thought they honored God, and depending on how they reckoned when a new day began, both groups (according to their own standard of measurement) actually sacrificed the Passover lambs on Nisan 14 between 3:00-5:00 PM ("between the twilights"), in accordance with the prescribed dictates of Passover, even though they did this separated by twenty-four hours from each other. Numbers 9:6-13 also helps explain the fear for those who had arrested Jesus. They "did not enter into the Praetorium *in order that they might not be defiled*, but might eat the Passover" (John 18:28). Many Jews of that time held to the presumption that abortions were commonly practiced within pagan Gentile homes. All fastidious holders of the Law could reason that they should not take the chance to enter within the home where they may — even unknowingly — come in contact with the dead fetus, and become ceremonially defiled according to Numbers 9:6-13, and consequently fail to qualify as a Passover participant.

As confusing as this may sound to the modern reader, having the actual sacrificing of the lambs occur on two distinct days became almost a necessity for those involved with this event. The sheer volume of Passover lambs that would be slain, if all were done on the actual same day, would have (almost) clogged the Temple. However, regardless of on which of the two days the Passover was done, all of its preparations were the same as before; no part of the ceremony could be missing or deleted. The Passover meal was also identical regardless of the day on which it was eaten, and the Hallel would be included (Psalms 113–118) as part of the ceremony that we saw in the previous chapter. The only difference was that the sacrifice of the lambs and the subsequent meals paralleled each other twenty-four hours apart.

Scholars are not sure when the two different days for sacrificing the lambs officially began. They are not sure who initially authorized it. But scholars do have a general idea about what percentage of the Jewish population used the Galilean sunrise-to-sunrise reckoning of when a day began, and they estimate this to have been about 70% of the people, which included the Pharisees (and as we have seen, would likewise have included Jesus and His disciples). If this is possibly the case, then roughly two out of every three Jews sacrificed their lambs and observed the Passover meal on the same day that Jesus and His disciples did. The remaining third did theirs the next day.

Long before the birth of Jesus, the side-by-side days of sacrificing Passover lambs became the normal part of the Jewish Passover celebration in God's chosen city of Jerusalem. How fitting that God's own Passover Lamb, who takes away the sin of the world (John 1:29), would die at approximately 3:00 PM when the other Passover lambs at the Temple were about to be slain. Multiplied streams of divine symbolism and parallelisms could be deduced.

Only, this day is different. The day when the true Lamb of God was sacrificed was unlike any previous Passover or any other day in history past or present.

As we have seen in previous studies, the darkness covered the land from about noon until about 3:00 PM (Matt. 27:45; Mark 15:33; Luke 23:44). Luke added the additional detail of "the sun being obscured" (23:45) — or literally in the Greek, "the sun failing." You can read more about this in "The Darkness" chapter of *The Darkness and the Glory*.

Think what pandemonium must have occurred once this totally unexpected darkness appeared and resided for three hours, especially for the remaining third of the population who had prepared for and had expected to gather at God's Temple and sacrifice their Passover lambs that day. Not only did they have no explanation for the reason the darkness was there in the first place, but also at that time they had no basis for knowing how long it would last. Especially for those who calculated the days from sunset to sunset and had not yet sacrificed their Passover lambs at the Temple, such astounding events would profoundly confuse them. These people told time daily by the sun, and yet such darkness had *never* happened before. They would not have seen the sun traveling its customary course to sunset, accompanied by the expected awe-inspiring sunset hues. The sun had been high in the sky, but then most unexpectedly it had become completely dark. Also, if literally in the Greek "the sun [was] failing" (Luke 23:45), it would certainly follow that the full moon of Passover was also hidden (if it could have been viewed at that time of the day), as were any subsequent stars. These who had always calculated the new day by the advent of sunset must have thought, "*What* day is it? Did we miss the Passover? *How* could we possibly have missed it?" Also, if it were now the "next day," then they *all* had missed the God-ordained sacrificing of the Passover lambs, and by God's Holy Law they would have to wait a month in order to participate in the next one. Furthermore, the extremely strong warning from God in Numbers 9:13 would weigh heavily on anyone who feared Yahweh: "But the man who is clean and is not on a journey, and yet neglects to observe the Passover, that person shall then be cut off from his people, for he did not present the offering of the LORD at its appointed time. That man shall bear his sin." Could it be possible that this promised curse resided on them? Were they to be cut off from God's people? Would they themselves bear the weight of their own sin?

What frantic scurrying there must have been as the remaining masses laboriously made their way in engulfing darkness to sacrifice their Passover lambs in the Temple. What agitation the priests and Levites must have experienced as they would have attempted to answer the countless questions they knew would come, while at the same time trying to execute everything in accordance with the Law. Yet, they, too, must have wondered why the darkness had occurred, and—since they calculated time by sunset—must have pondered whether this was the beginning of the new day. Had these who had been so thoroughly and meticulously trained in the Torah and who had been an active part of dozens of ritualistic slayings of previous years somehow have missed the Passover? Being strict observers of the Law, they would have known that God had set the requirement of where and when the Passover lambs were to be slaughtered, namely, "between the twilights." But at that time, there were no twilights like those on normal days. Many priests and Levites hastily convened, and heated discussions must have erupted about whether or not they should even attempt to fulfill their divinely-mandated priestly and Levitical duties—and they would not have had the option to debate this in the normal, leisurely academic manner. Two pressing questions obviously stood before them: first, what day was it, Passover or the day after it; and second, should they attempt to proceed with the ceremony in the dark? We will find out in heaven how they must have attempted to complete the most critical preparation of the Passover, namely, the designated sacrificing of the Passover lambs. Yet, not one time in history had they or any of their ancestors attempted to do that in the midst of total darkness. Even if the Levites had carried torches, they must have repeatedly bumped into one another and have been greatly hindered in their preparations, especially with something so delicate as the cutting of the sacrificial lambs' throats with the very sharp knives used by those attending.

But then—most unexpectedly—the answer to their dilemma came to them when the darkness departed and the light returned.

But then—most unexpectedly—a loud cry by a crucified Man not too many yards away from the Temple mount (Matt. 27:50).

But then—most unexpectedly—who knows the exact timing other

than God, as they either began the Passover preparation, or as they made things ready for preparation, Behold! Matthew 27:51-53 present six (aorist in the Greek) passive verbs in succession:

—The veil of the Temple was torn in two from top to bottom.
—The earth (was) shaken.
—The rocks were split (Matthew employed the exact verb he had just used for the Temple veil being torn).
—The tombs, made ready for Passover a month earlier by having them all painted white to keep people from defiling themselves by coming in contact with them, were opened. We do not know exactly how many tombs were opened; it may very well have been all of them; Matthew wrote only "the tombs," not "some of the tombs." When God shows us the full account when we are with Him in heaven, it will be interesting to see if it were the case that the preparatory white washing included what would eventually become the temporary tomb of Jesus, described later in Matthew 27:57-60. Even though it was Joseph of Arimathea's "own new tomb" (Matt. 27:60), it was a tomb, nonetheless, and may well have been included in the whitewashing preparation.
—The fifth and sixth (aorist) passive verbs that Matthew used did not take place until after Jesus had returned to life, and these would not readily be seen at the moment after Jesus' death: "and many bodies of the saints who had fallen asleep were raised; and coming out of the tombs after His resurrection they entered the holy city and appeared [literally, "were made to be manifest"] to many" (Matt. 27:52b-53).

The response of the centurion and his associates speaks for itself: "Now the centurion, and those who were with him keeping guard over Jesus, when they saw the earthquake and the things that were happening, became very frightened and said, 'Truly this was the Son of God!'" (Matt. 27:54). The soldiers would not have known about the Temple veil at that time, nor would they likely have cared if they had ever found out, but these seasoned veterans would have seen—and felt—and heard—everything else.

Similar to the time that the LORD passed by in 1 Kings 19:11 where the earth shook and the rocks were split, those at the Temple would have witnessed the same things that the Roman soldiers had—and more—and no doubt would have become extremely frightened as well, especially as they had a more established theological base by which to evaluate these events. What terror must have overcome them! All of the required Passover items, including the multiple golden censors used to catch the sacrificial blood of the slain lambs, would have been turned over at the Temple. Did the people get to sacrifice lambs that day? If some had even started the sacrifice, the blood would have spilled all over the place, all over them, and all over the priests in their previously clean festal attire. After God had shaken His earth when His only beloved Son had died, did *anything* or *anyone* remain that was not now considered ceremonially unclean?

If some of those who had gathered to worship in the Temple were able to sacrifice Passover lambs that day, they would have had to carry their lifeless lambs over the freshly strewn debris left from the earthquake back to their own homes—if their own homes still stood. As is true with any earthquake that shakes an inhabited city, no doubt many people had no homes to which they could return. The Levitical choir who had sung the Hallel the day before on the second floor of the Temple would have fled in fear during the earthquake. Not only this, but every other Passover element that normally would have been part of the standard Passover meal, if the house itself were not destroyed, would have received disastrous effects from the earthquake. Most or all of the Passover elements would have been overturned from their containers. Homes would have been partially or completely demolished. Cooking pots broken. Ovens destroyed. Wine containers damaged or ruined. Ceremonial wine cups crushed or dirtied. Were other Passover elements, such as the required bitter herbs, still usable? Jewish women of that particular time and onward—who took due pride in how they had so meticulously arranged their homes for this holy convocation that generally included beloved family members and friends—must have wailed in horror and mourning. For many, no doubt, all was ruined, and even if they could somehow find substitute Passover elements, not enough time existed to replace them in time for the scheduled feast.

We can reason that life went back to a relatively normal state rather quickly. John 19:31 states, "The Jews therefore, because it was the day of preparation, so that the bodies should not remain on the cross on the Sabbath (for that Sabbath was a high day), asked Pilate that their legs might be broken, and that they might be taken away." Interestingly, John just says, "The Jews," and does not mention whether they were Pharisees (who already had eaten the Passover meal the previous night and thus feared no defilement) or the chief priests and Sadducees (who previously had feared defilement, but may not have cared so much at this point since so many unexpected events had happened). Whichever group or groups they were, they, too, would have to make their way laboriously over the earthquake debris as they made their way to ask a pagan Gentile ruler to appease them with one small religious matter.

Just a quick note: Pilate, who wanted to release Jesus (Luke 23:20), who found no guilt in Him (John 19:6), who already was fearful of Jesus (John 19:7-9), who "while he was sitting on the judgment seat, his wife sent to him, saying, 'Have nothing to do with that righteous Man; for last night I suffered greatly in a dream because of Him'" (Matt. 27:19), who had granted permission for scourging and crucifixion of the one who was presented to him as "the Son of God," would have been tremendously affected by these events. Pilate and his wife would have witnessed a three-hour darkness that they had never experienced before, and could only have guessed what it was, and would have felt the earth shake, an event that Pilate would later find out had occurred immediately after Jesus had died. It would have been revealing to have been able to observe Pilate and his wife as they witnessed any of these events, or to have heard them converse about them afterward.

But let us consider the night at hand; the night immediately following a few hours after Jesus declared, "It is finished!" — and bowed His head, and gave up His spirit (John 19:30). We will have to wait until we are in heaven to find the answer to this simple question: *did the people get to eat the Passover meal the night Jesus was crucified, or did they have to wait until the next month or the next year as Scripture demanded?* They could not have eaten a "normal" Passover meal that night. Did they do the best they could do under the circumstances, or did these most serious and unexpected events dictate that if they could not do the feast properly, they would have to wait? We simply do not know because we do not have that information revealed in Scripture. Whether they somehow did observe the feast that night, or they were forced to wait until the following month or year, Jesus remained — even after His death — in total control, for His Word abides forever. No one was exempt from joining the collective chorus of Psalm 118 regardless of when the next Passover was celebrated: whether for those who were somehow able to celebrate it that very night, or for those who would wait the prescribed month to celebrate Passover, or for those who would return to their homes and not partake of the feast until the next year. Whenever they next observed God's Passover, the Hallel verses of Psalms 113–118 were required as a mandated part of God's Passover by the Stone that the builders had rejected.

If the obligatory Passover rituals were observed and said on the night that Jesus died, or if people were forced to wait until the following month or year, eventually *all* would say the words that Jesus said they would say. If they had done so that same night, a little over one hundred yards away from where Jesus had eaten the Passover with the eleven the night before, the high priestly family of Annas and Caiaphas would also have assembled to observe the Passover, as they had done for multiple decades. Each participant knew the ancient ritual by heart. Perhaps it went much slower on this night for the two who had been so intricately connected with Jesus' arrest and death. Annas and his son-in-law Caiaphas had unfinished business to attend in securing the grave of Jesus, but it would have to wait until the next day (Matt. 27:62-66). However, the prescribed procedure of the Passover feast restricted their movements. Did they have a Passover lamb to eat? As people of wealth, if any lambs were available, it would not be surprising if they had procured one, even in the midst of the chaos. If the Passover lamb were present, the ritual would have been precisely the same as it was on the previous night for Jesus and His disciples—and for the previous nights in generations past. As head of the household, Annas (the elder) would normally be the one officiating at the feast. Even if he looked upon the Passover as ancient history with no special spiritual significance, the specified dictates of the service—performed by the ex-high priest of Israel, no less—forced him to follow the procedure to the very letter. When the youngest member who partook of the feast asked the sacred question as an opening ritual, "Why is this night different?," a more teachable heart could have given testimony as to whether one was asking about "*this* night" as in "*this* day" when God's darkness had covered the land, the Temple veil had been torn from top to bottom, the earth was shaken, and the graves were opened. Of course, Annas would not have answered along these lines as part of the ceremony, but perhaps he would note the irony of the question.

Whether that same night, or whenever they eventually celebrated Passover, God still bore witness to these two hearts of stone, forcing them to recite the very words that Jesus had asked the authorities if they had ever read: "The stone which the builders rejected has become the chief corner stone. This is the LORD'S doing; it is marvelous in our sight" (Ps. 118:23). Annas and Caiaphas could not have failed to make the connection, for their intensely hated enemy Jesus had put His very own words in their mouths. How interesting it would have been to have watched their growing revulsion as those two of high priestly office further quoted what the multitudes had sung in the presence of Jesus, and what He said must be sung before the nation views Him again: "This is the day which the LORD has made; let us rejoice and be glad in it. O LORD, do save, we beseech You; O LORD, we beseech You, do send prosperity! Blessed is the one who comes in the name of the Lord" (Ps. 118:24-26a).

How revealing it would have been to have witnessed Annas and Caiaphas as they audibly voiced the very Scripture references that God used to attest to His beloved Son. Did they glance at each other, as every line of the psalm pointed to some previous encounter with Jesus during the week leading up to His crucifixion, attempting to detect if the other caught the significance of what they both recited? Did the eyes of the one reflect the spiritual barrenness of the other? Perhaps each was lost in his own thoughts. More probably, fomenting disgust overrode all other emotions and reactions that would have resided in a more fertile heart, as the two leaders of Israel sang divinely inspired Messianic truths.

Nothing indicates that they remotely understood that they had been an integral part of fulfilling Psalm 118:27: "Bind the festival sacrifice with cords to the horns of the altar." Indeed, they had done just that as John 18:12 indicates, "So the Roman cohort and the commander, and the officers of the Jews, arrested Jesus and *bound* Him." Every item was done in strict accordance with God's design, all performed as part of God's lesson — even to two so mired in dead-hearted disbelief.

At some point, Annas and Caiaphas recited Psalm 118, and did so after the arrest and death of Jesus. Nonetheless, they did so exactly as Jesus said the nation would do — including even these two — and did it as part of the Lord's own Passover from that night onward until each had observed his last Passover.

Throughout the city, and less than a mile from where Jesus had met with His disciples, thousands upon thousands of Israel's religious establishment usually celebrated the same Passover meal, following the exact Passover procedure. If somehow only a few, or even many, were still able to celebrate Passover the night that Jesus died — chief priests, lesser ranking priests, Levites, Pharisees, Sadducees and scribes — collectively and individually recited and sang Psalm 118; not one member was exempt. The religious authorities repeated what they had heard and what they themselves had previously said or sung. With varying degrees, some had even been involved with the trial and sacrificial death of the true Lamb of God. These who were accustomed to argument and debate would each offer his opinion as to the significance — if any — of Psalm 118, especially regarding the multiple uses in reference to Jesus and what had already occurred the week that He had entered Jerusalem.

Ultimately, for any Jew who was somehow able to eat the Passover when the sun set on the day that Jesus died, *everyone* was required to recite Psalm 118. No doubt, several had been part of the thunderous multitude that had shouted "Hosanna!" on the day that people call "The Triumphal Entry." The repeated verses coupled with the events of the past week caused virtually every household to discuss fervently the significance of these verses, especially in relation to Jesus — now including matters regarding the darkness, the earthquake, and the opening of the whitewashed tombs, something which Jesus, just days earlier, had used as an illustration of the spiritual deadness of the scribes and Pharisees (Matt. 23:27). The person of Jesus had stirred tremendous debate for years, but it reached its zenith during this Passover. The finely orchestrated events and the multiple quotations of Psalm 118 only kindled the already white-hot debate concerning His true identity and His mission. No other topic of conversation would come close to the minds and lips of the Passover participants as this of One who had come in the name of the Lord.

Even if because of the circumstances many were forced to wait until the next month or the next year — regardless of when they next partook of God's Passover — they still had to complete the prescribed feast exactly as laid out before them. God ultimately and repeatedly bore testimony in His written Word to His Incarnate Word. But He also bore testimony from collective Israel's own lips — from saddened disciples, to hostile foes, to confused masses. All — even the most blatant rejecters — bore witness to the Stone of Israel, the Son of God, placed there by God Himself, Whom Scripture requires must be rejected by the nation's leaders before He will be received as Messiah. The Galileans and Pharisees, who had celebrated the Passover meal on the same night that Jesus and His disciples had, awoke the next morning to see their sacrificial Lamb being slain. Their Stone had been rejected by the builders — all in minute fulfillment of God's Holy Word:

"The stone which the builders rejected has become the chief corner stone.

"This is the LORD's doing; it is marvelous in our eyes. This is the day which the LORD has made; let us rejoice and be glad in it.

"O LORD, do save, we beseech You; O LORD, we beseech You, do send prosperity.

"Blessed is the One who comes in the name of the LORD."

Psalm 118:22-26a

9

THE STUMBLE

*T*he Book of Exodus reveals God's design and desire to dwell among His redeemed people with a special manifestation of His glory (Exod. 25:8; 29:43-45). Although God had communed with the first couple in Genesis 2-3, the Fall had ruptured that fellowship. From the first sin onward, God would still communicate and appear in various ways and means—with each instance ultimately pointing to the person and work of Jesus—but after the Fall, communication was within a corrupted realm that necessitated restoration and release. Centuries later, after physically delivering the seed nation out of Egypt, God then established the means by which He Himself would reside in the very midst of His own people. As previously noted, the Book of Exodus ends with God's filling the tabernacle with His own glory, as He took up residence within His own Holy of Holies (Exod. 40:34-38).

To assist in Israel's worship of Himself, God devised a highly organized priesthood from the tribe of Levi. Not every male from the tribe of Levi qualified as a priest; the priests had to descend from Aaron's lineage (Exod. 28:1-2; Lev. 8). God used Levites in various ways with designated tasks and restrictions. God also assigned the priests various roles particularly related to the divinely mandated feasts and sacrifices. The Levites took care of physical matters related to either the tabernacle or Temple, and they taught the people God's Law. Within His choice of the tribe of Levi as the priestly line, God also commissioned the office of high priest. Thousands of priests functioned collectively at one time, but the position of the high priest was different. One high priest—many other priests. God designated only one functioning high priest at a time; never should two or more share the office. The position of high priest was to be held for life or until the one holding the office could not adequately function because of age or disability. A successor was determined who not only fit the ancestral requirement, but who also (ideally) epitomized the priesthood in genuine godly qualities.

Moses' brother Aaron was the first to hold this high and holy office. To distinguish the high priest's unique role among the people, God commanded him to wear clothing and accessories different from those worn by all the other priests. By God's own design, the high priest was to wear high priestly apparel "for glory and for beauty" (Exod. 28:2). This distinctive attire of the high priest was to be worn as long as he remained in office and was to be passed on at his death to his successor. In Exodus 29:29-30 God instructed, "The holy garments of Aaron shall be for his sons after him, that in them they may be anointed and ordained. For seven days the one of his sons who is priest in his stead shall put them on when he enters the tent of meeting to minister in the holy place." God's instruction included the passing on of the original raiment, not the making of new robes for each high priest.

No doubt existed among the people about when the high priest entered the tabernacle or Temple precincts when attired in his high priestly garb. No one had to ask who he was or why his clothes were different from those of all the other priests. By God's own intention the high priest stood out from among the rest of the nation. Not only did he have the garments common to all priests, but the high priest's wardrobe that he wore on special occasions also contained four aspects peculiar to his office. The first was a seamless blue robe worn under his other priestly attire. The hem of this blue skirt was ornamented according to God's instruction and purpose. Exodus 28:33-35 gives this description:

> "You shall make on its hem pomegranates of blue and purple and scarlet material, all around on its hem, and bells of gold between them all around: a golden bell and a pomegranate, a golden bell and a pomegranate, all around on the hem of the robe.
> "It shall be on Aaron when he ministers; and its tinkling shall be heard when he enters and leaves the holy place before the LORD, so that he will not die."

Jewish writings report that the pomegranate replicas and gold bells attached to the hem numbered seventy-two each, a total of one hundred forty-four. Not only would the high priest be seen, but whenever he moved he would also draw attention to the fact that he was present and active. Everyone knew that he was set apart by God.

For the installation of the first high priest, God further command-ed Moses to make "the ephod [the sleeveless outer garment] of gold, of blue and purple and scarlet material and fine twisted linen, the work of the skillful workman" (Exod. 28:6). This was to be crafted according to God's explicit instruction in Exodus 28:7-11:

> "It shall have two shoulder pieces joined to its two ends, that it may be joined. The skillfully woven band, which is on it, shall be like its workmanship, of the same material: of gold, of blue and purple and scarlet material and fine twisted linen.
> "You shall take two onyx stones and engrave on them the names of the sons of Israel, six of their names on the one stone and the names of the remaining six on the other stone, according to their birth. As a jeweler engraves a signet, you shall engrave the two stones according to the names of the sons of Israel; you shall set them in filigree settings of gold."

Beyond the dignity of the office, God also gave the reason—from His holy perspective—of what these stones signified: "You shall put the two stones on the shoulder pieces of the ephod, as stones of memorial for the sons of Israel, and Aaron shall bear their names before the LORD on his two shoulders for a memorial" (Exod. 28:12).

Another piece unique to the high priest's clothing was "the breast-plate of judgment." It was to be "the work of a skillful workman; like the work of the ephod you shall make it: of gold, of blue and purple and scarlet material and fine twisted linen you shall make it" (Exod. 28:15). The breastplate measured a "span" square (roughly six inches by six inches) and had twelve precious stones arranged in four rows of three. These stones also had engraved on them the names of the twelve tribes of Israel. Again God revealed that the purpose was more than just beauty for the high priest's costume. Somewhat similar to God's setting the rainbow in the sky for a memorial (Gen. 9:13-16), so, too, these stones served a spiritual function: "Aaron shall carry the names of the sons of Israel in the breastpiece of judgment over his heart when he enters the holy place, for a memorial before the LORD continually" (Exod. 28:29).

The fourth and final distinctive apparel was the "miter" or upper turban. This consisted of eight yards of linen coiled into a turban design. Attached to the front of the turban by a blue ribbon were God's instructions, "You shall also make a plate of pure gold and shall engrave on it, like the engravings of a seal, 'Holy to the LORD'" (Exod. 28:36). This was the turban of the high priest that was defiled in the midst of the heavenly assembly in Zechariah 3:3-5. Amazed at so visible a display of impurity for the high priest who stood in God's very presence, His prophet instinctively called out, "Let them put a clean turban on his head!" (3:5) After all, undefiled clothing is fitting only for one who would solely represent the entire nation in the very presence of God.

Although the high priest was involved in various other priestly functions, the pinnacle of his God-ordained work occurred on the Day of Atonement. Beginning with God's precise designated order and procedure in Leviticus 16, the high priest would actually enter into the otherwise off-limits Holy of Holies on the Day of Atonement. He could enter this area only once a year and only in meticulous obedience to the smallest instruction God had given.

Interestingly, although God had designated the design and ornamentation of the high priestly apparel, He also required something else. On the Day of Atonement, before entering the holy place, the high priest dressed in his high priestly splendor, adorned with the turban, the gold plate, the precious stones, and the jingling hem of his blue inner robe, appeared before the people. Then a curious thing happened. Turning away from the people, the high priest entered into the holy place of God. God had instructed that the high priest would then lay aside all of the high priestly raiment (Lev. 16:4, 23-24). For all but the last of the designated services, the high priest performed his official duties clothed only in linen garments, unique in that, unlike the other priests' attire, this attire was white, including the girdle he wore. No stones, no gold, no ornamentation—just linen. This was the same kind of fabric with which another High Priest would be wrapped at His burial (Matt. 27:59; Mark 15:46; Luke 23:53). Just before reappearing before the collective mass of worshipers, the high priest would again don his high priest's attire.

Thus this God-ordained festival continued each year for centuries. The Exile caused the holy ritual to cease for a while, but it resumed after the Jews rebuilt the Temple. The Torah contained the procedural details. The nation, well-versed in the particulars of this feast, would gather at God's Temple on the designated day. The week prior to the great day, the high priest would move his residence to within the Temple confines where he repeatedly rehearsed in detail the specified procedures. On the somber festive day itself, the high priest would appear before the masses in all the dignity and pomp of his divinely ordained office. The light reflecting on the stones and gold plate must have made a most striking impression on those present. In lowly contrast, the dumb animals required for the mandated blood sacrifice had long been secured by the attending priests and were prepared to be sacrifices. The huddled worshipers stood in reverence and respect as they waited for the beginning of the rituals that they knew by heart.

Only this time, everything was different. On this first Day of Atonement since the crucifixion six months earlier, the high priest of Israel began the service whereby he would step into the very Holy of Holies of God.

Everything Annas and Caiaphas did during Passover week, they did with a rushed urgency. Although they did not want to arrest Jesus during the Passover (Luke 22:1-2), by God's divine plan, the Passover was the time that God had designated that the Stone be rejected and the Lamb be bound. Beyond this immediate drama, the plot to kill Jesus had been brewing for some time. Surprisingly, though, efforts that had been thwarted for years unexpectedly fell into place earlier that week as one of Jesus' own apostles agreed to betray Jesus, their ultimate enemy, into their hands. Marshalling their forces to arrest Jesus, these two were not about to let this opportunity pass whether it be Passover or not.

While earthly enemies of Jesus had followed Him for most—if not all—of His ministry, their opposition to Jesus intensified as He drew nearer to Jerusalem. Of critical importance was that Jesus had raised Lazarus from the dead not many days before His own tumultuous entry into Jerusalem. The raising of Lazarus caused the entire nation to debate the identity of the One who might appear at the pending Passover. As always with any revelation concerning Jesus, the reaction was mixed. John 11:45-46 discloses two responses, "Therefore many of the Jews who came to Mary, and saw what He had done, believed in Him. But some of them went to the Pharisees and told them the things which Jesus had done." This report led to an association of two religious groups in Israel, neither that liked nor trusted the other. Yet, hatred against the One would make their common ground of depravity an appropriate basis for them to link arms:

> Therefore the chief priests and the Pharisees convened a council, and were saying, "What are we doing? For this man is performing many

signs. If we let Him go on like this, all men will believe in Him, and the Romans will come and take away both our place and our nation" (John 11:47-48).

The response by one of those present is most illuminating for many reasons:

> But one of them, Caiaphas, who was high priest that year, said to them, "You know nothing at all, nor do you take into account that it is expedient for you that one man die for the people, and that the whole nation not perish."
> Now he did not say this on his own initiative, but being high priest that year, he prophesied that Jesus was going to die for the nation, and not for the nation only, but in order that He might also gather together into one the children of God who are scattered abroad (John 11:49-52).

John's connective summary statement that follows is not surprising: "So from that day on they planned together to kill Him" (John 11:53).

Three factors within this account immediately stand out. One is God's behind-the-scenes total control of the entire scenario, including the most vehement enemies of His beloved Son. The second, and tied in with the first, is that God Himself produced what would be said by means of the inspiration of the Holy Spirit that He likewise used as the inspiration for His godly prophets. Much like Peter in Matthew 16, Caiaphas also spoke from a source beyond his own intuitive capacities; he prophesied from God. It should not be surprising that God can use an unbeliever to speak His truth whenever He so desires. Over a thousand years before, God had secured His own words inside the false prophet Balaam, in Numbers 22-24, who actually spoke inspired Messianic prophecies (Num. 24:17). A few weeks following John 11, God would again use the enemies of the Lamb by their reciting Psalm 118 at Passover. Every celebrant at Passover—including Annas and Caiaphas—eventually spoke the divine Stone prophecies. Before that, God had already placed a divine prophecy into the mouth of another enemy, the high priest of Israel—all to the glory and exaltation of His Son.

The third point is the most critical for our study. John 11:49 states that one member of the convened group was, "Caiaphas, who was high priest that year." Scripture adds additional details. We know Annas, "was father-in-law of Caiaphas, who was high priest that year" (John 18:13). John reminded us of the importance of Caiaphas' earlier statement in the next verse, "Now Caiaphas was the one who had advised the Jews that it was expedient for one man to die on behalf of the people" (John 18:14). On the night of the betrayal, after a brief interrogation of Jesus, "Annas sent Him bound to Caiaphas the high priest" (John 18:24).

"High priest that year" (John 11:49) is an interesting phrase that can be taken in two ways. "That year" may refer to that year of years that included Jesus' resurrection of Lazarus, the event that some people call "the Triumphal Entry," the encounters with the religious opponents of the Lamb of God, and the arrest and trial of Jesus. "That year" the beating, scourging, and crucifixion occurred. "That year" the Divine Darkness approached during the crucifixion. "That year" an earthquake rocked Jerusalem the day Jesus died (Matt. 27:54) "That year" a severe earthquake followed three days later at the resurrection (Matt. 28:2). Caiaphas was high priest "that year" when the Temple veil was ripped from top to bottom (Matt. 27:51). "That year" some Old Testament saints were resurrected and appeared to many in Jerusalem (Matt. 27:52-53). During "that year" the sound of a hurricane wind descended on Jerusalem. "That year" some fool upstart preacher preached a message with the three thousand responding (Acts 2). "That year" witnessed the continued growth of the Church—and countless other events Scripture does not record. Everyone who witnessed even one of these events would never forget "that year" when Caiaphas was high priest of Israel.

However, another way to consider the phrase "high priest that year" is to view it against how putridly defiled the office had become. As we saw, the high priest was originally supposed to hold his office for life. When he became too old, he would pass the office to his oldest son, the rightful heir to the office, if the son met the requirements for the priesthood. God's design was for one high priest—not many. But things changed. By New Testament times, the office of high priest had lost its Old Testament hereditary character. When Rome emerged as pagan occupier of the land, the practice eventually began of some pagan, high ranking Roman official granting this most prominent of positions in Israel to the one of his choosing—with the standard price being some political favor or monetary price. King Herod the Great continued the practice of appointing and dismissing the high priest, and he would always secure something costly before doing so. Choosing the one who would become the high priest was a most productive ransom used by those who ventured daily into the world of political intrigue. Thus not only did the office cease to be lifelong and hereditary, but it also became wholly dependent on the reigning political authority. Resulting cases of securing the position of high priest either by means of money or nepotism became the norm, especially nearing the birth of Jesus. The devout within Israel knew of the corrupted nature of the position, but they could do nothing about it. For those who knew the Law, they could see its mocking defilement even from afar.

With what we have seen, note how striking the statement is in Luke 3:2. The same Scripture that indicates, "the word of God came to John, the son of Zacharias, in the wilderness," also offers another perspective of the day. This verse also states that this occurred, "in the high priesthood of Annas and Caiaphas." High priesthood is singular in the text; it is not "the high *priesthoods*." Two high priests at once? A shared high priesthood? This is blatantly wrong and contrary to God's Law. Again, note how things had changed by the time Jesus would be betrayed almost thirty years later. Annas is no longer in power, at least in an official sense. The reference of John 11:49 shows, "Caiaphas, who was high priest that year." While Caiaphas was high priest when Jesus died, by the time Acts 4:6 occurs relatively shortly thereafter, yet another change has occurred: "and Annas the high priest was there, and Caiaphas." Annas and Caiaphas; Caiaphas and Annas. The temporary ping-pong possession of this highest religious office was by no means in keeping with God's holy dictates.

Some critics of the Bible mock Luke 3:2 and related verses saying that here is a prime indication that Luke erred by recording the existence of two high priests serving simultaneously. No, Luke—even more so, the Holy Spirit—was right. Rome erred. Herod the Great erred. Annas and Caiaphas were wrong. No dual high priesthood should have existed; but then again, adherence to God's Word had never been their strong suit. Annas and Caiaphas had a long history of total disregard for God and His Word, as did also their associates.

Although the high priest presided alone, he was part of a functional hierarchy of thousands of other priests and Levites. While the Day of Atonement was the pinnacle of his high priestly duties, he exercised authority over many other matters. Especially important was that the high priest presided over the Sanhedrin, which was the Jewish Supreme Court. The high priest accordingly officiated at the trials of Jesus (Mark 14:53, 60-64), of the early apostles (Acts 4:6; 5:17, 21, 27), and of the church's first martyr, Stephen (Acts 7:1). The authority of the high priesthood extended even to Jews outside the country. In Acts 9:1-2, "Now Saul, still breathing threats and murder against the disciples of the Lord, went to the high priest, and asked for letters from him to the synagogues at Damascus, so that if he found any belonging to the Way, both men and women, he might bring them bound to Jerusalem."

Next in rank and succession to the high priest was "the captain of the Temple," sometimes referred to as "the captain of the Temple guard" (Acts 4:1; 5:24). Vice-president to the high priest would be a good analogy. The captain of the Temple guard maintained order inside the Temple precinct and dispatched his guard to secure any potential Jewish blasphemer. After him, the chief priests followed in rank. Interestingly, "chief priests" is the same Greek word for "high priest" but occurs in the plural. The chief priests included the high priest and the captain of the Temple, but these two remained distinctive in their particular offices. The chief priests maintained control over all the Temple activities. While these priests had various administrative duties, of the utmost importance to them was their authority over all offerings and the Temple treasury. Coupled with this, the chief priests also held seats on the Sanhedrin. In fact, they exercised majority control of it. Very little official business took place in the Sanhedrin where the chief priests did not win the majority vote. Accordingly, no one would have been more incensed when Jesus twice cleansed God's Temple than the chief priests who nursed the Temple funds. Jesus had not only entered their domain of control, He potentially disrupted a most lucrative business. No matter what else Jesus did or said, nothing caused the collective seething of the chief priests as much as these acts caused. When the villain Jesus was eventually brought before them in trial, their verdict had long before been rendered. They simply had possessed no previous opportunity to employ it.

It is one thing to know what such chief priests did; by God's grace we are also permitted to know their theology. One verse in particular is most revealing about them. After the arrest of the Apostles, Luke notes in Acts 5:17, "But the high priest rose up, along with all his associates (that is the sect of the Sadducees), and they were filled with jealousy." Sadducees. What a horrendous sect to belong to—especially for, of all people, the high priest and chief priests of Israel.

Fortunately, historical writings present a considerable amount of information about the Sadducees. They began as a bona fide sect in approximately 166 BC and continually rose in dominance. Thus, by the time Jesus began His ministry, the Sadducees would have existed for about 200 years. Interestingly, similar to the Samaritans, the Sadducees accepted only the first five books of the Old Testament as authoritative. From the writings of Moses, they considered themselves very strict in the (outer) priestly purity detailed in the Book of Leviticus.

But Scripture gives more telling information about the beliefs of the Sadducees. Decades later in Acts 23, when Paul was on trial before the Sanhedrin, he appealed to his fellow Pharisees that he was on trial for the hope of the resurrection. A resulting vigorous argument erupted between the attending Pharisees and Sadducees. Luke added a most revealing verse that succinctly summarized the religion of the Sadducees: "For the Sadducees say that there is no resurrection, nor an angel, nor a spirit, but the Pharisees acknowledge them all" (Acts 23:8).

No resurrection. No angels. No spirit.

If the Sadducees were only a trade group or guild of varying relevance, they would have been a sect that would have rendered a great amount of damaging influence on the nation. But how much more—and how tragically sad for Israel—that for roughly the last two hundred years that the Temple had functioned, the high priest and his closest associates were all Sadducees. The High Priest of Israel—the one ordained by God's Word to enter the Holy of Holies once a year on the Day of Atonement—did not believe in the spiritual world. He and his associates would never accept Jesus' statement to the woman at the well, "God is spirit, and those who worship Him must worship in spirit and truth" (John 4:24). The truth to them was that the spiritual world did not exist. By claiming that angels do not exist, it logically follows that fallen angels and, ultimately, Satan are not real either. Not holding a belief in the resurrection would also require a lack of belief in either heaven or hell because, after all, the resurrected dead must have an abode in which to dwell.

The advent of John the Baptist would have caused the Sadducees to approach in cunning curiosity. Surprisingly, some came to be baptized, but John would not permit it. Instead he rebuked them, saying, "You brood of vipers, who warned you to flee from the wrath to come? Therefore bear fruit in keeping with repentance; and do not suppose that you can say to yourselves, 'We have Abraham for our father'; for I say to you that from these stones God is able to raise up children to Abraham" (Matt. 3:7-9). For the Sadducees, coming to John was not an act of repentance; it was merely a reconnaissance. Also, John the

Baptist knew them well enough to realize that their religious beliefs would not allow for any acceptance of him or his ministry. The Sadducees would never accept the story of the angel appearing to Zacharias—because, according to the Sadducees, angels do not exist. They would also reject the prophecies of Isaiah or Malachi, for these also were outside the Law of Moses. They especially would not accept John's pointing to Another, "As for me, I baptize you with water for repentance, but He who is coming after me is mightier than I, and I am not fit to remove His sandals; He will baptize you with the Holy Spirit and fire" (Matt. 3:11). Holy *Spirit?*—in a spiritual world that does not exist?

> How calamitous for the people of Israel that a Sadducee officiated as their high priest.
> A high priest who did not believe in the bondage of sin, since no future judgment from God awaited anyone.
> A high priest who did not believe in the spiritual world.
> A high priest who did not believe in angels—holy or fallen.
> A high priest who did not believe in Satan or his destructive power.
> A high priest who did not believe in the resurrection.

But elsewhere, another High Priest stands in total contrast to the others:

> The former priests, on the one hand, existed in greater numbers because they were prevented by death from continuing, but Jesus, on the other hand, because He continues forever, holds His priesthood permanently. Therefore, He is able also to save forever those who draw near to God through Him, since He always lives to make intercession for them.
> For it was fitting for us to have such a high priest, holy, innocent, undefiled, separated from sinners and exalted above the heavens; who does not need daily, like those high priests, to offer up sacrifices, first for His own sins and then for the sins of the people, because this He did once for all when He offered up Himself. For the Law appoints men as high priests who are weak, but the word of the oath, which came after the Law, appoints a Son, made perfect forever.
> Now the main point in what has been said is this: we have such a high priest, who has taken His seat at the right hand of the throne of the Majesty in the heavens, a minister in the sanctuary and in the true tabernacle, which the LORD pitched, not man (Heb. 7:23–8:2).

One final distinction of this group is worth noting. Scripture always presents the Sadducees negatively. Many others who were once enemies of Jesus ultimately repented and received Him as Lord and

Christ. For instance Acts 6:7 states, "a great many of the priests were becoming obedient to the faith." A great many priests became obedient—but not chief priests. Later beyond the conversion of the hyper-Pharisee Saul, Acts 15:5 adds the phrase, "some of the sect of the Pharisees who had believed." Such would never be written of the stone-hearted Sadducees. If even *one* Sadducee ever repented and received eternal life, it occurred outside of the report of Scripture. Appropriately, the Sadducees vanished into extinction with the fall of Jerusalem—and with the Temple—in AD 70. As God mandated, the Stone remains.

So in that year of Christ's death, the high priest of Israel—a Sadducee to his core—resided as high priest and prepared himself on the Day of Atonement to enter the Temple abode of God.

But before doing so, he had another unexpected encounter with the Stone that he had already rejected.

A teacher's work is best evident when a student becomes capable of reproducing on his own what he has learned. Five times in the five most memorable days of his life, Peter heard the Stone prophecy of Psalm 118:22 recited or quoted. He then became an eyewitness to a major aspect of this monumental fulfilled prophecy. Peter was a witness, and he had much to tell. Even when replacing the apostolic office that Judas had held, the qualification of a witness was necessary. In Acts 1:21-22 Peter explained, "Therefore it is necessary that of the men who have accompanied us all the time that the Lord Jesus went in and out among us—beginning with the baptism of John until the day that He was taken up from us—one of these must become a witness with us of His resurrection."

By this time, Jesus had already risen from the grave and had commissioned His disciples to make disciples throughout the entire world (Matt. 28:19-20). The earthly advent of Jesus concluded as the heavens received the glorified Jesus:

> And it came about that while He was blessing them, He parted from them. And they returned to Jerusalem with great joy, and were continually in the Temple, praising God (Luke 24:51-53).

With the Son ascended to the right hand of the Father (Ps. 110:1), a new phase in God's program began. Now by Divine ordination and Divine enablement, the Apostles become Jesus' primary mouthpieces. Following the first message that Peter preached on Pentecost in Acts 2, about three thousand souls were saved (Acts 2:41). It is most likely that many of the new believers had participated in the events of the Passover week, as God's Word was already bearing fruit from seeds the Messiah Himself had planted only weeks before.

The healing of a lame man in the Temple confines and the subsequent excitement prompted Peter's second message in Acts 3. Glimmers of what Christ taught immediately show in Peter's discourse, including Acts 3:18: "But the things which God announced beforehand by the mouth of the prophets, that His Christ should suffer, He has thus fulfilled." Peter now understood the components of the lesson that Jesus so patiently had taught him. Christ's suffering was God's design, God's divine plan—and Jesus had fulfilled it in minute detail, repeatedly bearing witness and instructing followers and opponents alike.

We do not know the exact timeframe between the Pentecost message of Acts 2 and Peter's next message in Acts 3. Acts 2:46-47 indicates, "Day by day continuing with one mind in the Temple, and breaking bread from house to house, they were taking their meals together with gladness and sincerity of heart, praising God and having favor with all the people. And the Lord was adding to their number day by day those who were being saved." We do not know how long the double use of "day by day" took place before Acts 3 occurred, but most likely it would not have been too long. Acts 4:4 indicates that following the message recorded in Acts 3, "the number of the men came to be about five thousand," which is not a massive jump from the three thousand reported in Acts 2.

The timeframe between Acts 2 and 3 is important because the Apostles were arrested in the midst of this second sermon. Acts 4:1-3 explains:

> As they were speaking to the people, the priests and the captain of the Temple guard and the Sadducees came up to them, being greatly disturbed because they were teaching the people and proclaiming in Jesus the resurrection from the dead. And they laid hands on them and put them in jail until the next day, for it was already evening.

Notice that the teaching about the resurrection of the dead is what really prompted the Sadducees to act because such teaching stood directly at odds with their own beliefs. Luke next identified the attending officials and disclosed the change in the high priesthood:

> On the next day, their rulers and elders and scribes were gathered together in Jerusalem; and Annas the high priest was there, and

Caiaphas and John and Alexander, and all who were of high-priestly descent (Acts 4:5-6).

The previous reference to "Caiaphas, who was high priest that year" (John 11:49) gives no doubt that Caiaphas held the office when they crucified Jesus. Yet, by the time of the arrest in Acts 4, the order is "Annas, the high priest, and Caiaphas." Exactly when the transition occurred is unclear, but there are two distinct possibilities. Annas was most pragmatic. One could not survive the realm of political cannibalism for so long without being cunningly adept in positioning himself for his own benefit. Annas was a survivor; he was adroitly good at what he did. Therefore, Annas may have retaken the office for himself immediately after the crucifixion in an attempt to give some stability to a menace that was quickly growing out of control. Not only had Jesus been crucified, but now came repeated reports that the dead One now lived. Annas by no means believed such nonsense, but the nuisance of this so-called Messiah's followers not only increased in intensity, they also increased in numbers. Fearing an uprising, Annas somehow gained permission from the authorities to replace Caiaphas and to begin residing once more as high priest. This change could have occurred at any time, but no doubt the commotion associated with the Day of Pentecost would have pushed him to action if he had lingered in any hesitancy. Regardless of the exact day, by the time Acts 4 occurs, Annas had retaken the position of high priest.

Another possibility also exists. Passover occurred during the Jewish month of Nisan, somewhere during our present March-April. Pentecost followed fifty days later in the third month, our May-June. On the tenth month, our September-October, the Feast of Trumpets took place. Two aspects of this yearly autumn feast were important. First, it set the stage for the next feast, the holy and vital Day of Atonement. Second, the Feast of Trumpets marked the beginning of the Jewish New Year. In the Jewish way of thinking, "that year" of Caiaphas could have ended with the Feast of Trumpets. Perhaps mildly wanting to "abide by the Law" — or stated better, abide so as not to bring any unwanted interference from those who kept the Law — Annas waited until the year was officially over. If Annas waited until the Feast of Trumpets, he probably incorporated the switch in priesthood as part of the New Year festivities, receiving back the high priestly clothing from his son-in-law Caiaphas as part of the festival.

The importance of this is that the Day of Atonement followed only ten days after the Jewish New Year. If that is when Annas regained the office, he would have been the one to officiate at the Jewish holy day, which is probably what happened. Yet either way — whether Annas or Caiaphas — not much difference existed between the two. Both were mirror images; both mimicked outer holiness that temporarily enshrouded hearts of stone.

However, Acts 3-4 makes no reference to any Jewish feast occurring. Coupled with the growth in the Church from three thousand to five thousand, most likely Annas took back the office from his son-in-law Caiaphas, probably right after either the Passover frenzy or the commotion caused at Pentecost. Shrewdly political and self-preserving all of his life, he would not likely linger in any vacillation — Law or no Law. Public opinion or perception had never haunted or restrained him, and it most certainly was not going to begin doing so now.

With Annas presiding over the Sanhedrin, a re-enactment of the Passover week was about to play out again. The issue at hand was identical to what this same group had asked Jesus, only weeks before, after He had cleansed the Temple: "By what authority are You doing these things, and who gave You this authority?" (Matt. 21:23) Now the same people would ask Jesus' followers the same thing. "By what power, or in what name have you done this?" (Acts 4:7), in reference to the healing of the man who had been born lame (Acts 3:1-10).

Although Jesus was not physically present, the Holy Spirit manifested Himself by filling Peter and bringing about once more the exact words that God intended for the renewing of His lesson (Acts 4:8a). The disciple repeated to the same people what they collectively had heard from the Lord Jesus only a few months earlier. Acts 4 continues the account:

> "Rulers and elders of the people, if we are on trial today for a benefit done to a sick man, as to how this man has been made well, let it be known to all of you, and to all the people of Israel, that by the name of Jesus Christ the Nazarene, whom you crucified, whom God raised from the dead — by this name this man stands here before you in good health.
> *"He is the stone which was rejected by you, the builders, but which became the very corner stone.* And there is salvation in no one else; for there is no other name given among men, by which we must be saved" (Acts 4:8-12).

The following verse describes the reaction of those who were once more confronted face-to-face with this message that they long assumed had died. Luke noted the shocked reaction of the gathered religious leaders, detailing that "they were marveling, and began to recognize that they had been with Jesus" (4:13). Their amazement probably resulted as much as anything from hearing afresh the quotation of Psalm 118:22. Their heads must have snapped up in unison when they heard this Messianic Psalm for at least the sixth time. Try as they might, the rejecters could not rid themselves of the Stone. Though absent from view, the Stone continually encountered them. Everywhere they went—both physically and spiritually—the Foundation Stone awaited them. Everywhere they went, they still stumbled over the Stumbling Stone.

It would not be the last time they stumbled—especially for the high priest. After all, the Stone—the Foundation Stone, placed inside the holy of holies by God Himself—awaited the high priest's entrance in just a few days.

How different was this first Day of Atonement after the resurrection of Messiah. How spiritually dead this stone-hearted one was who represented the people before a God that he did not know or believe existed.

Yet, with clock-like precision the high and holy day began. The high priest appeared before the people wearing the ornamentation of his "holy" office. After a few ritual confessions, he turned from the people to enter into the holy place of the Temple that eventually led into the holy of holies. Left alone with thoughts known only to him and God, he went about the prescribed procedure. While stoic about Levitical purity, other parts of this ritualistic routine must have seemed ridiculously absurd to one who would not accept the possibility of the resurrection. Why apply the blood for atonement when, after all, the absence or presence of atonement has no eternal consequence? Why have forgiveness of sins if there is no judgment in the afterlife? By what would the sins be removed? Even more important, by whom would they be removed? But the high priest continued, and by the jingling of his steps—caused by the God-ordained design of the hem of his garment—was heard by many outside who stood closest to the sanctuary.

Once inside and removed from the people's sight, the high priest was supposed to remove his high priestly attire. Would Annas? In virtually every respect he was in his heart a practicing atheist; a religious atheist, to be sure, but, nonetheless, one who denied the essentials of the faith. Why show reverence for a God that you are not sure exists? Perhaps, except for the prescribed bells and pomegranates attached to his hem, he would have skipped the designated undressing. But then again, perhaps not. After all, the Sadducees were known for their strict adherence to Levitical purity — outward purity anyway. Annas would be careful not to defile himself, such as when his associates would not enter the Roman Praetorium fearing they would defile themselves and be unable to celebrate the feast (John 18:28). The fact that they themselves were already putridly defiled would not enter into consciences that had long since ceased functioning as any safeguard.

From the holy place, the high priest made his way toward the holy of holies. He would approach the Temple veil that was torn at the death of Christ. As one of the chief priests who had charge of the Temple, the high priest would have known immediately that it had been torn. He would also have known that once torn, the veil that covered the entrance to the holy of holies could never be repaired. Contrary to many people's idea of this being somewhat similar to a bridal veil, the writings of the time present the veil to the holy of holies as being 60 feet by 30 feet and as thick as a palm of the hand — about four inches thick. They further report that the veil was originally constructed of three hundred squares assembled together in a quilted fashion. Though possibly somewhat embellished, the writings of the time also say it took three hundred men to manipulate the veil in place when it was first hung at the entrance into the holy of holies. After God tore the veil, there was no way it could ever be sown again — as God no doubt intended. Matthew 27:51 discloses, "And behold, the veil of the Temple was torn in two from top to bottom." Possibly, God left a small piece of the veil connected at the very bottom to give testimony that indeed the tearing had been from the top down; otherwise, how would other priests who ministered in the holy place and encountered the two separated pieces know from which direction the tearing began? We will find out for sure when we get to heaven.

Walking through — or perhaps stepping over — the irreparably torn veil, the high priest entered into the very holy of holies. Many years had passed since Annas had last officiated at the Day of Atonement. Even before entering, he knew what awaited him. Firmly placed before him was the immovable Foundation Stone. In spiritual-death coldness Annas heard only his own shallow breath — and piercing silence.

He stands in the presence of God.

He stands in the absence of God.

What he thought as he stood there, God alone knows. Would the events of the past year play back in his mind's eye? What about the multiple references to Jesus as being the Stone of Psalm 118, voiced even by the high priest on all previous Passovers that he had attended and officiated—would any come to mind? Would the "Stone Message" of Peter in Acts 4 that he had heard perhaps only a few days before echo inside him? Would Annas begin the atonement procedure of applying the sacrificial blood directly on—of all things—the Foundation Stone?

> Behold! I place in Zion
> The Stone that the builders rejected
> Foundation Stone
> Chief corner Stone
> A Stone of Stumbling and
> A Rock of offense

Who knows what the high priest thought or did; one dead stone before the Living Stone leaves few clues.

Whether or not he punctiliously carried out his mandated duties, when Annas turned to leave, the high priest of Israel stumbled. If not physically, he certainly stumbled spiritually—and that is far more disastrous. It still happens today. People still stumble over the Stumbling Stone placed by God Himself.

Many scholars believe the Book of Romans to be a masterpiece of logic. Paul wrote to the church at Rome, hoping, among other things, that it would become his missionary base as he traveled onward to Spain (Rom. 15:24). Having received opposition in virtually every place that he had traveled before, Paul often wrote to correct problems inside existing churches. When Paul wrote Romans, he had just finished a most trying segment with the church at Corinth. Hoping to fend off a repeat episode with other churches, the apostle disclosed the core of his gospel to the Roman churches before he had ever visited them.

While we cannot delve into even a broad exposition of the book at the present time, one segment is most appropriate for our study. Having presented in logical format both the necessity and the means of salvation, Paul changed subjects beginning in chapter nine. Having argued for salvation through faith based on the finished work of Christ and the faithfulness of God, he had to consider questions that he most likely would encounter. For instance, why should one trust God's Word since He had made hundreds of promises to the Jews in the Old

Testament that had not yet come true? Also, from a Gentile standpoint, how strong can this God be, Paul, who cannot even save His own chosen people? How great a salvation can this actually be if most of those who originally were offered it refused to accept it?

So Paul wrote Romans 9–11 to explain God's sovereignty in choosing Israel (most of chapter 9), Israel's responsibility and failure to accept by faith God's offer (chapter 10), and how God will save the Gentiles and ultimately fulfill His word to the Jews (chapter 11). So in first explaining why the nation did not receive Jesus, Paul explains in Romans 9:30-33:

> What shall we say then? That Gentiles, who did not pursue righteousness, attained righteousness, even the righteousness which is by faith; but Israel, pursuing a law of righteousness, did not arrive at that law. Why? Because they did not pursue it by faith, but as though it were by works. They stumbled over the stumbling stone, just as it is written, "Behold, I lay in Zion a stone of stumbling and a rock of offense, and he who believes in Him will not be disappointed."

Paul incorporated the two Stone prophecies of Isaiah 8:14 and 28:16. What happened to Annas and his associates also has taken place with the majority of the Jews up through the present time. Note also that just as Jesus had proclaimed years before, the Stone for Paul is a "Him" — not an "it."

A chapter later, in emphasizing the responsibility of the one to receive God's salvation offer by faith, Paul again wrote in Romans 10:8-10:

> But what does it say? "The word is near you, in your mouth and in your heart" — that is, the word of faith which we are preaching, that if you confess with your mouth Jesus as Lord, and believe in your heart that God raised Him from the dead, you will be saved; for with the heart a person believes, resulting in righteousness, and with the mouth he confesses, resulting in salvation.

Noting the Old Testament requirement of faith, Paul continued by again quoting the last part of the Stone prophecy of Isaiah 28:16 in the next verse: "For the Scripture says, 'Whoever believes in Him will not be disappointed'" (Rom. 10:11).

Stated in its simplest form: the Stone remains always; individuals will either believe and not be disappointed, or they will stumble over the Stone of Stumbling and the Rock of Offense to utter damnation, unless they repent and receive God's Gospel and are redeemed by the blood of the Lamb of God before they die.

While Paul wrote particularly about the nation of Israel, Peter employed the same teaching to encompass the world at large. As before, the issue is either acceptance or rejection of the Stone. As Paul had done earlier in Romans, Peter also drew from the two Stone prophecies of Isaiah. In First Peter 2:6, Peter gives the basis for his injunction, quoting Isaiah 28:16.

> For this is contained in Scripture: "Behold, I lay in Zion a choice stone, a precious corner stone, and he who believes in Him will not be disappointed."

Fittingly, Peter chose to draw from one more Old Testament quote. After all, not only had he repeatedly heard it from the lips of his Savior, but he had witnessed firsthand its fulfillment. Memories were as vivid to Peter as though they had occurred that day. In writing decades later, Peter recalled that Passover night when Jesus and the disciples had sung or had quoted Psalm 118 together—the day he and John had chanted or had sung it earlier at the Temple with the slaying of the lamb. That was the night he himself would deny knowing the One he loved so dearly. As an old man, could he ever say or write Psalm 118:22 without seeing the look on his Master's face?

> This precious value, then, is for you who believe; but for those who disbelieve, "The stone which the builders rejected, this became the very corner stone" (1 Pet. 2:7).

And as Peter had witnessed, he likewise quoted Isaiah 8:14: and "A 'stone of stumbling and a rock of offense,' for they stumble because they are disobedient to the word, and to this doom they were also appointed" (1 Pet. 2:8; cf. Isa. 8:14).

The Stumbling Stone, however, awaits everyone, not merely a handful of Jewish leaders who lived and died almost two thousand years ago. Everyone who is ever born must encounter the Stone—God has so mandated this. The Stone is too big to remove, step over, or leisurely walk around—also as God had intended all along. God placed the Stone there Himself; nothing indicates He has removed Him. Same issues—same claims by Jesus. For those who believe, He is a Stone of Foundation, the Solid Rock Himself. A Stone, when once received, will ultimately by no means whatsoever be disappointing. The same required belief and acceptance—or the same stumbling by those who reject Him. As Peter wrote, unbelief is not some isolated mental condition or description. Instead, a spiritual status results: "disobedient to the word." Not mere unbelieving, as some people delight to say, "I'm an atheist," or "I'm an agnostic"—as though that once and for all settles the issue. No, you are unbelieving and, therefore, disobedient to the Word Himself—the Stone you will eventually encounter, one way or the other.

People do not change His essence or identity by their belief or unbelief. The Stone remains the same—it is your own relationship to the Stone that changes.

He is the Cornerstone.

He is the Foundation Stone.

And for many, He is the Stumbling Stone and the Rock of Offense.

What He is—and eternally will stay—funnels down to what you accept and receive Him to be.

He is the Stone alive and firmly placed. He is the Stone that soon will return to this world—as God has repeatedly promised (Matt. 24:32-33).

10

THE TWO

O ne of the most consistent and repeated themes throughout the Bible is that God is the God who not only keeps His Word, but is able to and will bring about "every jot and tittle" of what He states will be (Matt. 5:18; 24:35). This is true regarding the original sin of the first couple in Genesis 3 up through the bringing in of the New Heavens and New Earth (Rev. 21–22), which includes the Great White Throne judgment of Revelation 20 and the casting into the lake of fire the human and satanic enemies of God.

God is long-suffering, patient and merciful, but He also promises that He will not sit idly by as sin proliferates without ultimately responding either in this life or the next—or in both. In the simplest terms possible comes this repeated divine promise: God will bless obedience to Him and His Word and will punish those who live in disobedience.

No casual reader of the Old Testament should miss this. After redeeming the nation of Israel out of physical bondage and bringing them to Mount Sinai, God gave forth His Word to His newly redeemed people. As those who were just brought into a different covenant relationship in what most scholars call the Mosaic Covenant or the Mosaic Law (or simply "The Law") in Exodus 24, Yahweh instructed the people in the way that they were to live before Him. Even before the ratification of the Mosaic Covenant, God had given Moses the Ten Commandments (Exod. 20:1-17); the first four commandments addressed how the people were to worship and serve the one true God alone, and the next six commandments gave commands of how those of the Jewish nation were to live with others. In essence, the remainder of the Law from Exodus through Deuteronomy would flow forth from these simple Ten Commandments (also known as the Decalogue).

Leviticus 26 is one of those chapters that very specifically set forth for the Jewish people the consequences of their own actions. While still at Mount Sinai, and before the spies would be sent out and would return with an evil report to rebel against Yahweh, and before His condemning that generation to die in the wilderness (Num. 13–14), God promised, "Obey Me, and I will bless you" (Lev. 26:1-13), or "Disobey me, and I will curse you" (Lev. 26:14-46). Part of the specific curses named by God concerned the Promised Land that the young nation was about to enter. If Israel broke their covenant commands and remained in rebellion, Yahweh would remove them from it, as Leviticus 26:31-35 clearly states:

> "I will lay waste your cities as well, and will make your sanctuaries desolate; and I will not smell your soothing aromas. And I will make the land desolate so that your enemies who settle in it shall be appalled over it. You, however, I will scatter among the nations and will draw out a sword after you, as your land becomes desolate and your cities become waste.
> "Then the land will enjoy its sabbaths all the days of the desolation, while you are in your enemies' land; then the land will rest and enjoy its sabbaths. All the days of its desolation it will observe the rest which it did not observe on your sabbaths, while you were living on it.

However, immediately following this promise of exile, God gave far-reaching promises regarding His greater future work, and He reminded the people of His specific eternal land promises that He had already sworn in the Abrahamic Covenant. Leviticus 26:40-45 gives the account of the covenant-keeping God who always keeps His Word:

> "If they confess their iniquity and the iniquity of their forefathers, in their unfaithfulness which they committed against Me, and also in their acting with hostility against Me—I also was acting with hostility against them, to bring them into the land of their enemies—or if their uncircumcised heart becomes humbled so that they then make amends for their iniquity, then I will remember My covenant with Jacob, and I will remember also My covenant with Isaac, and My covenant with Abraham as well, and I will remember the land.
> "For the land shall be abandoned by them, and shall make up for its sabbaths while it is made desolate without them. They, meanwhile, shall be making amends for their iniquity, because they rejected My ordinances and their soul abhorred My statutes. Yet in spite of this, when they are in the land of their enemies, I will not reject them, nor will I so abhor them as to destroy them, breaking My covenant with them; for I am the LORD their God.

"But I will remember for them the covenant with their ancestors, whom I brought out of the land of Egypt in the sight of the nations, that I might be their God. I am the LORD."

After the wilderness generation had died for the multiple brazen covenant violations and spiritually dead hearts, their children and grandchildren stood poised and ready to enter into the land that God had given them. However, before Israel went in to take possession of what God had promised them, Yahweh set forth the same offer — the same promise — that He had given before: "Obey Me, and I will bless you" (Deut. 28:1-14), and "Disobey Me, and I will curse you" (Deut. 28:15-68). In the midst of the long and specific list of covenant curses, one of the curses that God promised was exile out of the land, found in Deuteronomy 28:64-67:

"Moreover, the LORD will scatter you among all peoples, from one end of the earth to the other end of the earth; and there you shall serve other gods, wood and stone, which you or your fathers have not known. And among those nations you shall find no rest, and there shall be no resting place for the sole of your foot; but there the LORD will give you a trembling heart, failing of eyes, and despair of soul. So your life shall hang in doubt before you; and you shall be in dread night and day, and shall have no assurance of your life. In the morning you shall say, 'Would that it were evening!' And at evening you shall say, 'Would that it were morning!' because of the dread of your heart which you dread, and for the sight of your eyes which you shall see."

As is true so many times in Scripture, God offers only two options: life or death, obedience or disobedience, the blessing or the curse, sheep or goats — heaven or hell. Such was and still is true for the Jewish people from that day forward, and many of the same truths apply to every person who has ever lived or who will ever live.

Each generation of the Jewish people knew exactly what awaited them — or at least should have known. When godly Joshua led the people to victory, it was because of the nation collectively being in covenant obedience that resulted in the covenant promise of victory that God had given (e.g. Deut. 28:7). When Joshua and his generation died (Judges 1-2), the people quickly fell into spiritual sin, and just exactly as God had promised, *He* raised up multiple enemies in the times of the Judges. The Moabites and other invaders did not ravage the country by their own design; God raised them up to punish His disobedient people just as He had said He would. Read what is called the Old Testament and you will find His raising up of enemies occurring time and time again. In fact, the Mosaic Law became somewhat of a "spiritual barometer" for how the nation of Israel lived. If they were victorious in war, they were in covenant obedience to Yahweh; if they lost, the true problem did not indicate a lack of military capacity as much as it indicated that they were in covenant disobedience to Yahweh. The same is true for their crops, rain, drought—all were contingent on whether they lived in obedience to God or not.

As we fast-forward to the building of God's Temple by means of Solomon, it should not be surprising that Yahweh reiterated and elaborated many of the same truths as He had done with previous Jewish generations, only this time they were more specific because His holy Temple was being dedicated. The account of 1 Kings 8:10-11 shows that God filled His own Temple with a manifestation of His glory just as He had previously done with the tabernacle in Exodus 40. King Solomon noted some of the significance of what occurred in 1 Kings 8:12-21:

> Then Solomon said, "The LORD has said that He would dwell in the thick cloud. I have surely built You a lofty house, a place for Your dwelling forever."
> Then the king faced about and blessed all the assembly of Israel, while all the assembly of Israel was standing. And he said, "Blessed be the LORD, the God of Israel, who spoke with His mouth to my father David and has fulfilled it with His hand, saying, 'Since the day that I brought My people Israel from Egypt, I did not choose a city out of all the tribes of Israel in which to build a house that My name might be there, but I chose David to be over My people Israel.'
> "Now it was in the heart of my father David to build a house for the name of the LORD, the God of Israel. But the LORD said to my father David, 'Because it was in your heart to build a house for My name, you did well that it was in your heart. Nevertheless you shall not build the house, but your son who shall be born to you, he shall build the house for My name.'
> "Now the LORD has fulfilled His word which He spoke; for I have risen in place of my father David and sit on the throne of Israel, as the LORD promised, and have built the house for the name of the LORD, the God of Israel. And there I have set a place for the ark, in which is the covenant of the LORD, which He made with our fathers when He brought them from the land of Egypt."

As part of the dedication, Solomon understood that God considered this "a place for [His] dwelling forever" (8:12). It should also be noted that the account repeatedly indicates that particular house would be specifically for the name of God. Having explained to the assembled people why the Temple existed, Solomon continued with a prayer of dedication (1 Kings 8:22-30):

> Then Solomon stood before the altar of the LORD in the presence of all the assembly of Israel and spread out his hands toward heaven.
> And he said, "O LORD, the God of Israel, there is no God like You in heaven above or on earth beneath, keeping covenant and showing lovingkindness to Your servants who walk before You with all their heart, who have kept with Your servant, my father David, that which You have promised him; indeed, You have spoken with Your mouth and have fulfilled it with Your hand as it is this day.
> "Now therefore, O LORD, the God of Israel, keep with Your servant David my father that which You have promised him, saying, 'You shall not lack a man to sit on the throne of Israel, if only your sons take heed to their way to walk before Me as you have walked.' Now therefore, O God of Israel, let Your word, I pray Thee, be confirmed which You have spoken to Your servant, my father David.
> "But will God indeed dwell on the earth? Behold, heaven and the highest heaven cannot contain You, how much less this house which I have built!
> "Yet have regard to the prayer of Your servant and to his supplication, O LORD my God, to listen to the cry and to the prayer which Your servant prays before You today; that Your eyes may be open toward this house night and day, toward the place of which You have said, 'My name shall be there,' to listen to the prayer which Your servant shall pray toward this place. And listen to the supplication of Your servant and of Your people Israel, when they pray toward this place; hear in heaven Your dwelling place; hear and forgive.

Solomon continued his dedication prayer (1 Kings 8:31-43):

> "If a man sins against his neighbor and is made to take an oath, and he comes and takes an oath before Your altar in this house, then hear in heaven and act and judge Your servants, condemning the wicked by bringing his way on his own head and justifying the righteous by giving him according to his righteousness.
> "When Your people Israel are defeated before an enemy, because they have sinned against You, if they turn to You again and confess Your name and pray and make supplication to You in this house, then hear in heaven, and forgive the sin of Your people Israel, and bring them back to the land which You gave to their fathers.
> "When the heavens are shut up and there is no rain, because they

have sinned against You, and they pray toward this place and confess Your name and turn from their sin when You afflict them, then hear in heaven and forgive the sin of Your servants and of Your people Israel, indeed, teach them the good way in which they should walk. And send rain on Your land, which You have given Your people for an inheritance.

"If there is famine in the land, if there is pestilence, if there is blight or mildew, locust or grasshopper, if their enemy besieges them in the land of their cities, whatever plague, whatever sickness there is, whatever prayer or supplication is made by any man or by all Your people Israel, each knowing the affliction of his own heart, and spreading his hands toward this house; then hear in heaven Your dwelling place, and forgive and act and render to each according to all his ways, whose heart You know, for You alone know the hearts of all the sons of men, that they may fear You all the days that they live in the land which You have given to our fathers.

"Also concerning the foreigner who is not of Your people Israel, when he comes from a far country for Your name's sake (for they will hear of Your great name and Your mighty hand, and of Your outstretched arm); when he comes and prays toward this house, hear in heaven Your dwelling place, and do according to all for which the foreigner calls to You, in order that all the peoples of the earth may know Your name, to fear You, as do Your people Israel, and that they may know that this house which I have built is called by Your name.

Solomon's prayer shows that he foresaw, to a degree, some of the sins of the people and the very specific consequences that God had already decreed would occur if the people rejected Him (1 Kings 8:44-53):

"When Your people go out to battle against their enemy, by whatever way You shall send them, and they pray to the LORD toward the city which You have chosen and the house which I have built for Your name, then hear in heaven their prayer and their supplication, and maintain their cause.

"When they sin against You (for there is no man who does not sin) and You are angry with them and deliver them to an enemy, so that they take them away captive to the land of the enemy, far off or near; if they take thought in the land where they have been taken captive, and repent and make supplication to You in the land of those who have taken them captive, saying, 'We have sinned and have committed iniquity, we have acted wickedly'; if they return to You with all their heart and with all their soul in the land of their enemies who have taken them captive, and pray to You toward their land which You have given to their fathers, the city which You have chosen, and the house which I have built for Your name; then hear their prayer and their supplication in heaven Your dwelling place, and maintain their cause, and forgive Your people who have sinned against You and all their transgressions which they have transgressed against You, and make them objects of compassion before those who have taken them captive, that they may have compassion on them (for they are Your people and Your inheritance which You have brought forth from Egypt, from the midst of the iron furnace), that Your eyes may be open to the supplication of Your servant and to the supplication of Your people Israel, to listen to them whenever they call to Thee.

"For You have separated them from all the peoples of the earth as Your inheritance, as You spoke through Moses Your servant, when You brought our fathers forth from Egypt, O Lord GOD."

Elements of the blessing and the curse of Deuteronomy 28 are seen throughout Solomon's prayer at the Temple dedication. If the people were removed from the land, and ultimately from God's Temple, it would be because they had greatly sinned against Yahweh.

In the next chapter, 1 Kings 9:1-9, God gave His reply to Solomon's prayer and very specific promises regarding His own house:

Now it came about when Solomon had finished building the house of the LORD, and the king's house, and all that Solomon desired to do, that the LORD appeared to Solomon a second time, as He had appeared to him at Gibeon.

The LORD said to him, "I have heard your prayer and your supplication, which you have made before Me; I have consecrated this house which you have built by putting My name there forever, and My eyes and My heart will be there perpetually. As for you, if you will walk before Me as your father David walked, in integrity of heart and uprightness, doing according to all that I have commanded you and will keep My statutes and My ordinances, then I will establish the throne of your kingdom over Israel forever, just as I promised to your father David, saying, 'You shall not lack a man on the throne of Israel.'

"But if you or your sons indeed turn away from following Me, and do not keep My commandments and My statutes which I have set before you, and go and serve other gods and worship them, then I will cut off Israel from the land which I have given them, and the house which I have consecrated for My name, I will cast out of My sight. So Israel will become a proverb and a byword among all peoples.

"And this house will become a heap of ruins; everyone who passes by will be astonished and hiss and say, 'Why has the LORD done thus to this land and to this house?' "And they will say, 'Because they forsook the LORD their God, who brought their fathers out of the land of Egypt, and adopted other gods and worshiped them and served them, therefore the LORD has brought all this adversity on them.'"

Of special importance are the truths that go beyond Solomon's time. God promised in 1 Kings 9:3, "I have consecrated this house which you have built by putting My name there *forever*, and My eyes and My heart will be there *perpetually*." From the original day that God's Temple was dedicated onward, at all times His name in someway will be there, and His eyes will look upon His holy mountain. Technically speaking, as long as there is an earth, God's name and God's special look will always be there: even during the times of the Gentiles (Luke 21:24); even when Messiah was born, even when there is a pagan shrine on the site where the Holy of Holies was; these do not change anything: God has put His name there *forever*; God has placed His eyes there *perpetually*. However, Yahweh also promised that if the people were disobedient, He Himself would make His own house "a heap of ruins" so that everyone would be astounded. Ironically, all will know that the Lord did this and why: because His people were not faithful to Him.

Then, most amazing and most frightening for anyone who loves the Lord, Solomon did exactly what God had warned against. He forsook the Lord to follow other gods (1Kings 11:1-13). While God in His grace and sovereignty did not immediately destroy His Temple (which He could have done immediately and would have been true to His Word), He did bring about the promised curses of Leviticus 26 and Deuteronomy 28 as multiple enemies arose against the Jews during Solomon's days and the decades that followed.

Centuries passed, and while there were pockets of obedience in the land, most of the people rejected God and lived in blatant covenant disobedience before Him. God raised up prophet after prophet who called His people to repent. Consequently, much of what is called the Old Testament points to the coming judgment on God's people – and on God's Temple – just as He had repeatedly promised (2 Chron. 36:15-16). Over a hundred years before Jerusalem would fall, the prophet Isaiah looked to the Babylonian invasion and plunder; not just plunder of the treasury, which would occur, but plunder of even the young men and women (Isa. 38–39). Habakkuk lived in the days just a few decades before Jerusalem would fall and called out to ask God why He allowed such wickedness to go rampant among His people (Hab. 1). God in turn promised to judge His people by raising up the

Chaldeans/Babylonians (Hab. 2) which caused God's prophet even more consternation: we are wicked, but they are even more wicked. Ezekiel was deported to Babylon, and he was given a vision of the heinous sins that were being committed in God's own Temple, and by those, supposedly, who were to serve Him (Ezek. 8). (We should note that the account of God's removing his glory from His Temple takes place in the subsequent chapters of Ezekiel 9–11).

Jeremiah prophesied in the days immediately before and after the fall of Jerusalem. He repeatedly denounced the sins of the people — including those of the kings — and prophesied God's promised judgment that would surely come. In the midst of other condemnatory messages, the Book of Jeremiah contains what are called two "Temple Messages" (Jer. 7–10 and 26:1-6). Space does not permit the total text, so you can go back and read these on your own, but here is a sample of what God promised:

> The word that came to Jeremiah from the LORD, saying, "Stand in the gate of the LORD's house and proclaim there this word, and say, 'Hear the word of the LORD, all you of Judah, who enter by these gates to worship the LORD!'"
> Thus says the LORD of hosts, the God of Israel, "Amend your ways and your deeds, and I will let you dwell in this place. Do not trust in deceptive words, saying, 'This is the Temple of the LORD, the Temple of the LORD, the Temple of the LORD.'
> "For if you truly amend your ways and your deeds, if you truly practice justice between a man and his neighbor, if you do not oppress the alien, the orphan, or the widow, and do not shed innocent blood in this place, nor walk after other gods to your own ruin, then I will let you dwell in this place, in the land that I gave to your fathers forever and ever.
> "Behold, you are trusting in deceptive words to no avail. Will you steal, murder, and commit adultery and swear falsely, and offer sacrifices to Baal and walk after other gods that you have not known, then come and stand before Me in this house, which is called by My name, and say, 'We are delivered!' — that you may do all these abominations?
> "Has this house, which is called by My name, become a den of robbers in your sight? Behold, I, even I, have seen it," declares the LORD (Jer. 7:1-11).

God instructed Jeremiah to tell the people to go and see the desolation of a previous place where God had once dwelt in the tabernacle. The same desolation would come true for Jerusalem, as Jeremiah 7:12-14 shows:

165

"But go now to My place which was in Shiloh, where I made My name dwell at the first, and see what I did to it because of the wickedness of My people Israel.

"And now, because you have done all these things," declares the LORD, "and I spoke to you, rising up early and speaking, but you did not hear, and I called you but you did not answer, therefore, I will do to the house which is called by My name, in which you trust, and to the place which I gave you and your fathers, as I did to Shiloh."

Jeremiah 7:23-27 gives clear evidence that the people did not sin out of ignorance as to what God required of them in the same context:

"But this is what I commanded them, saying, 'Obey My voice, and I will be your God, and you will be My people; and you will walk in all the way which I command you, that it may be well with you.'

"Yet they did not obey or incline their ear, but walked in their own counsels and in the stubbornness of their evil heart, and went backward and not forward. Since the day that your fathers came out of the land of Egypt until this day, I have sent you all My servants the prophets, daily rising early and sending them. Yet they did not listen to Me or incline their ear, but stiffened their neck; they did more evil than their fathers.

"You shall speak all these words to them, but they will not listen to you; and you shall call to them, but they will not answer you."

Jeremiah 9:11-16 gives another "judgment is coming because of the multitude of your sins" warning:

"I will make Jerusalem a heap of ruins, a haunt of jackals; and I will make the cities of Judah a desolation, without inhabitant."

Who is the wise man that may understand this? And who is he to whom the mouth of the LORD has spoken, that he may declare it? Why is the land ruined, laid waste like a desert, so that no one passes through?

The LORD said, "Because they have forsaken My law which I set before them, and have not obeyed My voice nor walked according to it, but have walked after the stubbornness of their heart and after the Baals, as their fathers taught them,"

Therefore thus says the LORD of hosts, the God of Israel, "behold, I will feed them, this people, with wormwood and give them poisoned water to drink.

"And I will scatter them among the nations, whom neither they nor their fathers have known; and I will send the sword after them until I have annihilated them."

God made it abundantly clear in Jeremiah 10:17-18 that God Himself was the one who was casting out the people from the land:

> "Pick up your bundle from the ground, you who dwell under siege! For thus says the LORD, "Behold, I am slinging out the inhabitants of the land at this time, and will cause them distress, that they may be found."

The second Temple message is more precise, for the judgment of God stood right at their door, as Jeremiah 26:1-6 indicates:

> In the beginning of the reign of Jehoiakim the son of Josiah, king of Judah, this word came from the LORD, saying, "Thus says the LORD, stand in the court of the LORD's house, and speak to all the cities of Judah who have come to worship in the LORD's house all the words that I have commanded you to speak to them. Do not omit a word! Perhaps they will listen and everyone will turn from his evil way, that I may repent of the calamity which I am planning to do to them because of the evil of their deeds."
>
> "And you will say to them, 'Thus says the LORD, "If you will not listen to Me, to walk in My law which I have set before you, to listen to the words of My servants the prophets, whom I have been sending to you again and again, but you have not listened; then I will make this house like Shiloh, and this city I will make a curse to all the nations of the earth."'"

Note that "all the cities of Judah" are mentioned, which meant that this warning occurred probably during one of the three national feasts where the people would collectively assemble.

The entire Book of Lamentations "laments" the fall of God's Temple. Hebrew scholars tell us that it is written in somewhat of a "funeral dirge march:" slowly, sadly, accompanied by much weeping. You can read the entire five chapters to get the full flow, but again, just some samples of the verses show what happened and why. Lamentations 1:12-14 gives this summary:

> "Is it nothing to all you who pass this way? Look and see if there is any pain like my pain which was severely dealt out to me, which the LORD inflicted on the day of His fierce anger. From on high He sent fire into my bones, and it prevailed over them; He has spread a net for my feet; He has turned me back; He has made me desolate, faint all day long.
>
> "The yoke of my transgressions is bound; by His hand they are knit together; they have come upon my neck; He has made my strength

fail; the Lord has given me into the hands of those against whom I am not able to stand."

Lamentations 2:1-7 shows God acting in wrath against His people and His dwelling:

> How the Lord has covered the daughter of Zion with a cloud in His anger! He has cast from heaven to earth the glory of Israel, and has not remembered His footstool in the day of His anger. The Lord has swallowed up; He has not spared all the habitations of Jacob. In His wrath He has thrown down the strongholds of the daughter of Judah; He has brought them down to the ground; He has profaned the kingdom and its princes. In fierce anger He has cut off all the strength of Israel; He has drawn back His right hand from before the enemy. And He has burned in Jacob like a flaming fire consuming round about. He has bent His bow like an enemy, He has set His right hand like an adversary and slain all that were pleasant to the eye; in the tent of the daughter of Zion He has poured out His wrath like fire.
> The Lord has become like an enemy. He has swallowed up Israel; He has swallowed up all its palaces; He has destroyed its strongholds and multiplied in the daughter of Judah mourning and moaning.
> And He has violently treated His tabernacle like a garden booth; He has destroyed His appointed meeting place; the LORD has caused to be forgotten the appointed feast and Sabbath in Zion, and He has despised king and priest in the indignation of His anger.
> The Lord has rejected His altar, He has abandoned His sanctuary; He has delivered into the hand of the enemy the walls of her palaces. They have made a noise in the house of the LORD as in the day of an appointed feast.

These are samples from the Book of Lamentation as Jeremiah (and in a sense God Himself) "laments" the fall of God's Temple. Yet, for anyone who reads God's Word and accepts it for what it is, this should not be surprising: the LORD has kept His promise of judgment because of the nation's repeated rejection of both Him and His Word.

Even without the inspiration of the Holy Spirit, I think many people who love God and read His Word could have written the summary statement in 2 Chronicles 36:15-21 of why Jerusalem and the Temple fell:

> The LORD, the God of their fathers, sent word to them again and again by His messengers, because He had compassion on His people and on His dwelling place; but they continually mocked the messengers of God, despised His words and scoffed at His prophets, until the wrath of the LORD arose against His people, until there was no remedy.

Therefore He brought up against them the king of the Chaldeans who slew their young men with the sword in the house of their sanctuary, and had no compassion on young man or virgin, old man or infirm; He gave them all into his hand. All the articles of the house of God, great and small, and the treasures of the house of the LORD, and the treasures of the king and of his officers, he brought them all to Babylon.

Then they burned the house of God and broke down the wall of Jerusalem, and burned all its fortified buildings with fire and destroyed all its valuable articles.

And those who had escaped from the sword he carried away to Babylon; and they were servants to him and to his sons until the rule of the kingdom of Persia, to fulfill the word of the LORD by the mouth of Jeremiah, until the land had enjoyed its sabbaths. All the days of its desolation it kept sabbath until seventy years were complete.

One who had lived in Jerusalem and was exiled to Babylon as part of God's prophetic word read the prophetic Word of God and understood that God was by no means finished. He had many other promises to keep.

The godly prophet Daniel was an old man by the time he wrote Daniel 9. In this extensive prayer, God's Word gives the time frame and content of Daniel's prayer:

In the first year of Darius the son of Ahasuerus, of Median descent, who was made king over the kingdom of the Chaldeans—in the first year of his reign I, Daniel, observed in the books the number of the years which was revealed as the word of the LORD to Jeremiah the prophet for the completion of the desolations of Jerusalem, namely, seventy years.

So I gave my attention to the Lord God to seek Him by prayer and supplications, with fasting, sackcloth, and ashes. I prayed to the LORD my God and confessed and said, "Alas, O Lord, the great and awesome God, who keeps His covenant and lovingkindness for those who love Him and keep His commandments, we have sinned, committed iniquity, acted wickedly and rebelled, even turning aside from Your commandments and ordinances.

"Moreover, we have not listened to Your servants the prophets, who spoke in Your name to our kings, our princes, our fathers and all the people of the land. Righteousness belongs to You, O Lord, but to us open shame, as it is this day—to the men of Judah, the inhabitants of Jerusalem and all Israel, those who are nearby and those who are far away in all the countries to which You have driven them, because of their unfaithful deeds which they have committed against Thee.

"Open shame belongs to us, O Lord, to our kings, our princes, and our fathers, because we have sinned against You. To the Lord our God belong compassion and forgiveness, for we have rebelled against Him; nor have we obeyed the voice of the LORD our God, to walk in His teachings which He set before us through His servants the prophets.

"Indeed all Israel has transgressed Your law and turned aside, not obeying Your voice; so the curse has been poured out on us, along with the oath which is written in the law of Moses the servant of God, for we have sinned against Him. Thus He has confirmed His words which He had spoken against us and against our rulers who ruled us, to bring on us great calamity; for under the whole heaven there has not been done anything like what was done to Jerusalem.

"As it is written in the law of Moses, all this calamity has come on us; yet we have not sought the favor of the LORD our God by turning from our iniquity and giving attention to Your truth.

Daniel continued his prayer as he repeatedly contrasted God's faithfulness with the people's unfaithfulness and prayed toward God's future faithfulness in being merciful, as Daniel 9:14-19 shows:

"Therefore, the LORD has kept the calamity in store and brought it on us; for the LORD our God is righteous with respect to all His deeds which He has done, but we have not obeyed His voice. And now, O Lord our God, who have brought Your people out of the land of Egypt with a mighty hand and have made a name for Yourself, as it is this day—we have sinned, we have been wicked.

"O Lord, in accordance with all Your righteous acts, let now Your anger and Your wrath turn away from Your city Jerusalem, Your holy mountain; for because of our sins and the iniquities of our fathers, Jerusalem and Your people have become a reproach to all those around us.

"So now, our God, listen to the prayer of Your servant and to his supplications, and for Your sake, O Lord, let Your face shine on Your desolate sanctuary.

"O my God, incline Your ear and hear! Open Your eyes and see our desolations and the city which is called by Your name; for we are not presenting our supplications before You on account of any merits of our own, but on account of Your great compassion.

"O Lord, hear! O Lord, forgive! O Lord, listen and take action! For Your own sake, O my God, do not delay, because Your city and Your people are called by Your name."

If the Jewish people as a whole had prayed Daniel's prayer, instead of this prayer by only a singular godly prophet, God would have been merciful to the repentant nation (Lev. 26:40-46). One day in the future, God's promise of mercy will come true, but that time was not during Daniel's life.

Often when we go over such verses in the Bible classes that I teach (and I assure you this is about one one-hundredth of such verses teaching the same thing), it may seem like an overkill of information; actually more verses have been left out than have been put in this chapter. God presented *so* many witnesses through prophets' verbal preaching and their writings who told of the coming downfall of God's Temple in Jerusalem that it seems almost "ridiculous" to have so much recorded about the fall of the Temple. Consider the voluminous amount of material about the fall of Jerusalem and God's Temple contained in the following books:

Isaiah
Habakkuk
Jeremiah
Ezekiel
Lamentations
Daniel
Second Kings
Second Chronicles

An incredible amount of biblical information is directly related to the fall of God's Temple. Every major prophet dealt with the fall. Virtually everything in the book of Jeremiah ultimately is related to the time before the Temple fell and then for a brief time afterward. All of Lamentations mourns the fall of Jerusalem and God's Temple as a direct result of the repeated and heinous sins of the people of Israel.

So here is the question before us: with the abundance of material given about the fall of God's Temple in 586 BC, how many gave warning about the fall of the Temple in 70 AD?

Only the Two.

Let us return briefly to 1 Kings 9 where God appeared to Solomon after the first Temple had been dedicated and filled with the Glory of God. First Kings 9 is just as true when the Temple was rebuilt after the exile; just as true during the earthly life of Jesus: "I have consecrated this house which you have built by putting My name there forever, and My eyes and My heart will be there perpetually" (9:3). Perhaps a reminder is in order about God's original and far-reaching dictates concerning His house as shown in 1 Kings 9:6-9:

> "But if you or your sons shall indeed turn away from following Me, and shall not keep My commandments and My statutes which I have set before you and shall go and serve other gods and worship them, then I will cut off Israel from the land which I have given them, and the house which I have consecrated for My name, I will cast out of My sight. So Israel will become a proverb and a byword among all peoples.
> "And this house will become a heap of ruins; everyone who passes by will be astonished and hiss and say, 'Why has the LORD done thus to this land and to this house?'
> "And they will say, 'Because they forsook the LORD their God, who brought their fathers out of the land of Egypt, and adopted other gods and worshiped them and served them, therefore the LORD has brought all this adversity on them.' "

God did not need to reiterate this blessing or curse scenario; it already was in place, and since it was previously consecrated by His name forever, it did not need to be done again. In the same way, if the people lived in disobedience before Yahweh, He Himself would destroy His own Temple. He did it the first time — and repeatedly bore witness that the destruction originated from Him and not merely from human invaders.

Any Bible-believing Jew who at this point does not believe that the Messiah has already come, and thus currently has rejected Jesus, would readily acknowledge what is *so* evident in the Holy Word because it is repeated so many times: the only way possible that God's own Temple would or could ever be destroyed was if God Himself did it, and that being said, the only way that God would destroy His Temple was if the nation was living in blatant covenant disobedience before Him.

But that is exactly the problem. For an "Old Testament" believing Jew (not a Christian), an orthodox Jew, there is no good, logical explanation for the second destruction of God's Temple in 70 AD by the Romans on the exact same day of the year that God's first Temple was destroyed. With the first Temple, idolatry proliferated in the land (Ezek. 8); with the second Temple, there were no idols, no high places, no Baal worship. The Temple functioned; rabbis, Pharisees, Sadducees, priests; sacred days, fastidiously observed traditions, practices and sacrifices.

A currently unsaved Torah-believing Jew can explain the fall of the first Temple as easily as Daniel could in the prayer of Daniel 9. God gave a great number of warnings from His Word of what was to come as prophet after prophet bore witness.

How many bore witness about the fall of the second Temple accomplished by the Romans in 70 AD? Only the Two: the written Word of God (1 Kings 9) where God the Father is quoted, and the Incarnate Word of God, Jesus. The Second Member of the Godhead said this as He approached Jerusalem at what many call "The Triumphal Entry," stating in Luke 19:41-44:

> And when He approached, He saw the city and wept over it, saying, "If you had known in this day, even you, the things which make for peace! But now they have been hidden from your eyes. For the days shall come upon you when your enemies will throw up a bank before you, and surround you, and hem you in on every side, and will level you to the ground and your children within you, and they will not leave in you one stone upon another, because you did not recognize the time of your visitation."

Luke wrote his Gospel to a primarily Gentile audience who may not have known anything about God's Temple, its history, or its significance. Jesus did not specifically say at this point that the Temple would be destroyed, although "they will not leave one stone upon another" in reference to the city certainly could include the destruction of God's Temple. This was early in the Passion Week, and the Master had much to teach — and to denounce — to His own nation.

After Jesus had taught daily in the Temple at Passover and rebuked the hypocrisy of the religious leaders, He concluded His teaching in His last public appearance before Israel, bemoaning the hardness of the nation — both past and present (Mark 12:35). In Matthew 23:37-39 are the *last* recorded words of Jesus to the nation publically before He went to Gethsemane, to trial and to His cross, and He made them in His very own Temple:

> "O Jerusalem, Jerusalem, who kills the prophets and stones those who are sent to her! How often I wanted to gather your children together, the way a hen gathers her chicks under her wings, and you were unwilling.
> "Behold, your house is being left to you desolate!
> "For I say to you, from now on you will not see Me until you say, 'Blessed is He who comes in the name of the Lord !' "

Continuing from there, the Second of the Two, who is One with the Father, gave this simple, profound and binding divine revelation in Matthew 24:1-2:

> Jesus came out from the Temple and was going away when His disciples came up to point out the Temple buildings to Him.
> And He answered and said to them, "Do you not see all these things? Truly I say to you, not one stone here will be left upon another, which will not be torn down."

In the entire Bible, this is the only specific divine promise that the second Temple would be destroyed as the first one had been. (Revelation 11 later reveals that God's Temple during the Tribulation will be given over to the Gentiles, but does not reveal that this necessitates the Temple to be destroyed).

So what great sin did the nation of Israel commit that was so bad that God responded by destroying His own Temple the second time? In its shortest form, this was their grievous sin: "This is My beloved Son in whom I am well pleased; hear Him." Some did, but most did not. Consequently, other than a remnant of the redeemed who are currently part of the body of Christ, the Jewish people as a whole have continuously lived in covenant violation just as much as their ancestors had in the wilderness generation of Numbers 13–14, or the time when the first Temple fell.

"Not one stone will be left upon another," said the Shepherd, the Stone of Israel, whom the builders had already rejected, but who would also become the Chief Cornerstone, a stone of stumbling and a rock of offense.

11

THE RETURN

*T*he prophet Ezekiel recorded the threefold exodus of God's glory departing from His Temple (Ezek. 8–11). Stage by stage, accompanied by angelic beings beyond the capacity of any human writer to convey in an accurate description, God removed His glory. The light of God's glory was not only abandoning His Temple; in a sense the glory of God was leaving the earth. How dark the Temple—and the entire planet—must have appeared to angelic beings who have witnessed different aspects of God's glory throughout large portions of eternity. The glory always produced dazzling amazement in God's angels whenever He manifested it—especially on sinfully defiled earth, of all places. It is one thing for God to show forth His glory in the pure and undefiled heavens of His abode; it is another for Him to do so in the midst of sin's pollution. Both are displays of divine majesty, but the latter particularly manifests grace upon grace. This would be part of God's work on earth that so intrigues the angels of God (1 Pet. 1:12).

As much as the angels marveled whenever God displayed His glory on fallen earth, even more amazed were they when God retracted His glory (unless God chose ahead of time to inform them that He was going to remove His glory). What caused God's angels to ponder was not that His glory departed; what might have left them aghast would have been the relatively little effect that the departure had on the inhabitants of earth, especially on the ones who lived in Jerusalem. To those deeply enshrouded in caverns of spiritual darkness, there would be no immediately perceptible change. Life would—very temporally—go on as always. Yet, the angels knew firsthand that whatever earthly pursuits and pleasures its residents sought, the glory of God completely surpassed their sum because His glory vastly surpasses the expanse of His creation—let alone a microscopic planet such as earth. In all of God's creations, in all of the billions of galaxies and solar systems, God designated one—one solar system, one planet, one country, one city, one tabernacle, one Temple—in which His own glory would reside.

And then—God's glory departed.

Roughly six centuries transpired without any visible display of God's glory on earth. Six hundred years of judgment, exile, regathering, plus the rebuilding of the Temple—but no glory. Gentile kingdoms rose and fell: Medo-Persia, Greece, Rome—but no glory. After returning from the Babylonian Exile, mandated Jewish festivals and sacrifices once more began their yearly cycles, being carried out according to the Mosaic Law—but with no glory. The devout sought God and prayed for the Messiah to come—but no glory inhabited the house where they prayed. Long centuries had passed since anyone had lived who had actually encountered or witnessed any aspect of God's specific, revelatory glory. If you could have asked any inhabitants of Jerusalem about the glory of God, they would have replied that for unexplained reasons this was part of the ancient biblical record; something true for the nation's history, but not for the present. Rabbis have debated this bewildering predicament for centuries.

And then, the most amazing development: without any warning or expectation from a prophetic passage of Scripture, God's glory suddenly reappeared to a most unlikely assemblage:

> In the same region there were some shepherds staying out in the fields and keeping watch over their flock by night. And an angel of the Lord suddenly stood before them, and the glory of the Lord shone around them; and they were terribly frightened (Luke 2:8-9).

The mere sight of an angel of God would have frightened these sheep herders on any occasion, for angels always have frightened humans who have viewed them exhibiting any of their great power. Immeasurably beyond this, the glory of God shining round about these watchers would greatly have compounded their fear. They had no point of reference as to what it was. These were field workers, not scholars or theologians. They tended sheep, many of which would become Passover lambs at nearby Jerusalem. Even without the presence of an angel, they knew they were witnessing something that transcended anything on earth. The most majestic sunrise or sunset that they had ever joyously witnessed paled in comparison. So would have any manmade structure or art. As the Law required, these Jewish men had often gathered at Jerusalem, about seven miles away, for the national feasts and for other occasions. Yet, what they now beheld brilliantly outshone the grandeur of the city, including the most majestic edifice of that age—God's Temple.

If only the glory of the Lord had appeared without the angel, the shepherds would not have known what it was any more than Ezekiel did in the first chapter of his prophecy. In the same way, even if they had known what they were beholding, they would have had no answer as to why they—simple folk smudgened from the demands of their occupation who were deemed ceremonially unclean according to the strict tradition of the Pharisees—would be the recipients of God's presence. They had no status, no refinement, no fame. Nothing regarding their daily routine would make others envious of their humble place in society.

Accordingly, the heavenly messenger offered this quick explanation:

> But the angel said to them, "Do not be afraid; for behold, I bring you good news of great joy which will be for all the people; for today in the city of David there has been born for you a Savior, who is Christ the Lord.
> "This will be a sign for you: you will find a baby wrapped in cloths and lying in a manger" (Luke 2:10-12).

Before the shepherds had time to discuss the meaning of this, or to question the angel, another unexpected exhibition took place before this mesmerized gathering:

> And suddenly there appeared with the angel a multitude of the heavenly host praising God and saying, "Glory to God in the highest, and on earth peace among men with whom He is pleased" (Luke 2:13-14).

What an indescribable contrast between myriads of angels of light praising God in abject worship and the stark humility of the Word becoming lowly flesh to dwell among the race He Himself had created. Glory to God in the highest! And on earth? The Grace of God is born in a barn, asleep in a feeding trough.

How appropriately these faithful ones who heard and believed responded to the angelic report (Luke 2:15-18):

> When the angels had gone away from them into heaven, the shepherds began saying to one another, "Let us go straight to Bethlehem then, and see this thing that has happened which the Lord has made known to us."

> So they came in a hurry and found their way to Mary and Joseph, and the baby as He lay in the manger.
>
> When they had seen this, they made known the statement which had been told them about this Child. And all who heard it wondered at the things which were told them by the shepherds.

Simple men received a simple message in content, and responded in simplistic faith and obedience. As was fitting with those who witnessed the glory of God — in the sky and in the manger — they, too, could not help but join in heartfelt praise to God: "The shepherds went back, glorifying and praising God for all that they had heard and seen, just as had been told them" (Luke 2:20). As always, the Father delights in those who worship Him in spirit and truth — angels and shepherds.

Thus God's glory returned to earth, but, then again, not exactly; at least not as Scripture requires. What transpired was simply a preview and proclamation. For the first time in approximately six hundred years, the glory of God became visible again, at least for a little while; however, this was not the return of the glory to earth that the prophets had written of centuries before. Especially pertinent is that the glory did not return to the Temple where God's glory had previously resided. The glory seems to have shone above the earth — not on it — especially since this display was from heaven downward, not from earth upward. What the shepherds witnessed was not remotely a full display of God's glory on earth. The Greek text contains no article, reading literally, "and glory of God shone" — not "the glory of God." It was an appropriate display; a divine pronouncement, but God had much more glory to reveal in His grand design.

So God's glory appeared for a brief instance and then departed again. But this time, the departure was different. Previously, God had removed His glory before the pending judgment on the sinful nation. This time the glory became visible as a harbinger of grace — and especially, as with all the previous biblical instances — to mark the unique presence of God. Similar to the filling of His Tabernacle while in the wilderness, and later with His Temple built by Solomon, the glory of God once again resided on earth — and appropriately, even in the Temple He Himself had selected.

Thirty years later, and early in His ministry, Jesus temporarily cleansed God's Temple of its putrid defilements. John 2:13-16 describes the event:

> The Passover of the Jews was near, and Jesus went up to Jerusalem.
> And He found in the Temple those who were selling oxen and sheep

and doves, and the money changers seated at their tables. And He made a scourge of cords, and drove them all out of the Temple, with the sheep and the oxen; and He poured out the coins of the money changers and overturned their tables; and to those who were selling the doves He said, "Take these things away; stop making My Father's house a place of business."

The outraged opponents — particularly the Sadducees and chief priests who had control over the profit-intense Temple markets — demanded from Jesus an answer to the question that would face Him many times throughout His life:

The Jews then said to Him, "What sign do You show us as Your authority for doing these things?"
Jesus answered them, "Destroy this Temple, and in three days I will raise it up."
The Jews then said, "It took forty-six years to build this Temple, and will You raise it up in three days?" (John 2:18-20)

Even at this early encounter, Jesus spoke beyond the limitations of the physical — and infinitely deeper than His opponents perceived. As He later would draw the Samaritan woman at the well into deeper truths, He likewise did so at times with His enemies. John explained Jesus' use of the Temple metaphor, stating, "But He was speaking of the Temple of His body" (John 2:21). These stone-hearted ones so saturated in hate did not perceive His intent, but they most certainly remembered His words. When these same ones eventually arrested Jesus, "those who had seized Jesus led Him away to Caiaphas, the high priest, where the scribes and the elders were gathered together" (Matt. 26:57). The nature of the trial, as well as the words spoken by Jesus three years before, became clearly evident:

Now the chief priests and the whole Council kept trying to obtain false testimony against Jesus, so that they might put Him to death. They did not find any, even though many false witnesses came forward. But later on two came forward, and said, "This man stated, 'I am able to destroy the temple of God and to rebuild it in three days' " (Matt. 26:59-61).

In a way quite similar to the Tabernacle and the Temple containing God's glory centuries before, so it was with Jesus: in a way, yet infinitely distinct, God's glory inhabited the Son. Sometime nearly thirty years after His birth, Jesus merely showed what was His in essence and by nature at the Transfiguration (Matt. 17:1-9; Mark 9:2-8; Luke 9:29-36). To enter earth's domain, Jesus had willingly laid aside equality with God and had taken on the form of a bondservant (Phil. 2:5-11). If the Trinity had so determined, Jesus could have revealed the glory that was His anytime He wanted, to whom He wanted, and in the degree He wanted—even when being spat upon, scourged, and crucified. For the most part, Jesus chose not to reveal His glory, leaving that display instead to His pending return to earth, as dozens of prophecies bear divine promise.

So on the night that Jesus was born, it would not be fitting to have the glory of God reside in the heavens when the Glory of God had been born on earth. And in a real sense, the body of Jesus was the Temple that the glory of God inhabited. Jesus was the means by which God would dwell (or "tabernacle") among His people (John 1:14). God's majestic glory, greater than all His creations, became temporarily encased in the body of Jesus. That God's glory would inhabit a place so small should not be surprising. Even the Ark of the Covenant built during the Exodus generation is about the size of a coffin. It must have caused the devout in Israel to ponder: *You mean the glory of God can take up residence in something about the size of a human body?*

Of course. God did so with the Ark. He did so in Jesus.

But it would not be the last place for God's glory to inhabit. God had something much more astounding in mind to accomplish—even then, with you and me in mind.

They come there alone. A country man and his country wife approached with their newborn boy: a Son partly theirs, partly not. Unto them a Child is born; unto them a Son is given—but given even more unto the world. Even at His early stage, they would learn that their Son was theirs; they would learn in an ever-expanding way that He was also God's—as well as God's gift to the world. Mary and Joseph would grow in their understanding of this by the various ones they encountered who in some way had expected the arrival of this Promised One.

The first to arrive were the shepherds from Bethlehem (Luke 2:8-16). Having found the parents and baby just as the angel had said, these recipients of the Word excitedly would have told of their angelic encounter—and yet who at the same time, due to their lowly status in life and the custom of the day, likely would have apologized for the intrusion on one who had just given birth. Joseph and Mary listened. Each had heard similar words from a similar source. Each could have looked into the other's eyes, remembering the nine months before when each had a revelatory episode with God's messenger angels. Did Joseph reveal this to the shepherds, or did he merely nod understandingly? The shepherds had no need to try to persuade the couple of the truthfulness of their testimony. Joseph knew the reliability of their account. He would have very few—if any—questions for the shepherds, as one whose spiritual experience so similarly resembled their own.

Eventually, in the reverence of the moment, there would be nothing else to say. Worshipful silence and wonder in the presence of God is always appropriate. Besides, these seekers did not come to discuss angelology—they came to behold their King. Somewhat similar to Jacob's dream of the ladder that reached to heaven, these shepherds likewise received progressive divine revelation that they would ponder for the rest of their lives: an angel, glory, angels—God—and it changed them eternally. Huddled around the One whom the prophets had foretold, what words could be added in the presence of the Promised Child—God Incarnate born as a baby? As Paul would later write in Romans 8:26, deep-heart expressions before God so often clumsily trip over any attempt at words.

Mary probably would not have said much. Out of innate modesty, out of recuperation from the arduous travel and then the labor, out of the norms of her culture, she would have deferred any discourse to her God-given soul mate with her. Besides, Mary was a heart-ponderer (Luke 2:19), as she would be all of her life. Heart-ponderers rarely engage strangers about their treasures stored within their soul's confine. But she would eventually. Decades later, Mary would confide to a kindred spirit, the gentle Gentile Dr. Luke, who would end his chapter in poetic description: "and His mother treasured all these things in her heart" (Luke 2:51). A gentle teacher of her Son she would be; a gentle disciple of her Savior she would become.

Her Baby was "born of a woman, born under the Law" (Gal. 4:4), and the Law had much to say about mothers and their newborns. In keeping with the God-ordained procedure, a little over a week would elapse before this One would receive His divinely-revealed name that is both a description and a promise, as the angel had declared nine months earlier in Matthew 1:21: "and you shall name Him Jesus, for it is He who will save His people from their sins." Luke 2:21 records accordingly, "And when eight days had passed, before His circumcision, His name was then called Jesus, the name given by the angel before He was conceived in the womb."

Luke added other revealing aspects of what the Law required. In Luke 2:22 he wrote, "And when the days for their purification according to the Law of Moses were completed, they brought Him up to Jerusalem to present Him to the Lord."

What a sight this young couple and Child must have been, and yet how they must have blended in completely with the masses who surrounded them. Like anything else concerning God's truth, if you apprehended the significance of the revelation, this event was earth-shaking. If you did not, they were merely another couple from the country who were lost in the whirring busyness of the big city. Hailing from tiny Nazareth in Galilee, Joseph and Mary probably never would have felt at home in the bustle of Jerusalem. Besides, parents of their first newborn rarely marvel at their physical trappings wherever they are. It usually takes a lot of effort to remove their eyes from this miracle of life. Protecting, fearing failure as parents, sensing far too much activity and noise surrounding them that was not good for a baby, God's couple would, nonetheless, obey His word and proceed to the Temple precincts as required by the Law.

Such designated ceremonies for firstborns had occurred for over fourteen hundred years. Leviticus 12:1-7 describes the procedure Mary and Joseph would follow:

> Then the LORD spoke to Moses, saying, "Speak to the sons of Israel, saying: 'When a woman gives birth and bears a male child, then she shall be unclean for seven days, as in the days of her menstruation she shall be unclean.
> 'On the eighth day the flesh of his foreskin shall be circumcised.
> 'Then she shall remain in the blood of her purification for thirty-three days; she shall not touch any consecrated thing, nor enter the sanctuary until the days of her purification are completed. But if she bears a female child, then she shall be unclean for two weeks, as in her menstruation; and she shall remain in the blood of her purification for sixty-six days.
> 'When the days of her purification are completed, for a son or for a daughter, she shall bring to the priest at the doorway of the tent of meeting a one year old lamb for a burnt offering and a young pigeon or a turtledove for a sin offering. Then he shall offer it before the LORD and make atonement for her, and she shall be cleansed from the flow of her blood. This is the law for her who bears a child, whether a male or a female.'"

The following verse adds a touch of grace for the poor — including Mary and Joseph — and what they were to offer:

> "But if she cannot afford a lamb, then she shall take two turtledoves or two young pigeons, the one for a burnt offering and the other for a sin offering; and the priest shall make atonement for her, and she will be clean" (Lev. 12:8).

Luke 2:24 states that Mary came "to offer a sacrifice according to what was said in the Law of the Lord, 'A pair of turtledoves or two young pigeons.'" This shows, among other things, that the divinely-chosen couple was poor — very poor. The wise men would come eventually and bring their costly gifts, but that would be many days after Jesus was born. The poverty that would follow the humble Servant of Yahweh His entire life (2 Cor. 8:9) began with His earthly caretakers.

God could have written — and actually did write scattered throughout His unfolding Word: "But if she cannot afford a lamb for a burnt offering (Lev. 12:8) . . . God will provide for Himself the lamb for the burnt offering" (Gen. 22:8). On Moriah, where "Abraham called that place The LORD Will Provide, as it is said to this day, 'In the mount of the LORD it will be provided'" (Gen. 22:14). Moriah — the place to see God. Moriah — the place where God will appear. Moriah — where the present Temple stood. Moriah — where the Baby Jesus was presented before His Father. Mary, too poor to afford a lamb for the burnt offering, brings the Lamb of God whom God Himself had provided into His very own Temple where God had chosen for His name to dwell there forever.

He comes alone. No masses accompany him. Neither does a group such as the shepherds of Bethlehem join him. In the midst of an apostate high priesthood and a nation not yet prepared by the Forerunner, he still comes. He, however, needs no preparation. He is Simeon, a man "righteous and devout, looking for the consolation of Israel" (Luke 2:25). He arrives early, waiting, and anticipating what he knows will surely follow. In the midst of the thousands associated with the hectic Temple activities and rituals, there is One who will come — and he knows this deep within his soul.

The couple entered the Temple, dressed in humble garb of their economic status. Nothing about them called any attention to themselves whatsoever — not even the Baby in her arms. Hundreds of parents; hundreds of babies. Nothing different about these, unless you had been told who He was—and Simeon had.

Simeon did not seek the high priest; he awaited the Messiah. He would not have marveled at the dazzling attire of the high priest; he longed for One—and he knew Him when he saw Him. Approaching the puzzled couple, he took the baby Jesus into his arms (Luke 2:28). Although not understanding the full import of what was happening, something about this old man must have given Mary peace that this stranger was a friend. She did not resist placing Him in Simeon's arms.

Looking down into the face of the Baby, Simeon immediately knew He was the One. Accordingly he blessed God, stating:

> "Now Lord, You are releasing Your bond-servant to depart in peace, according to Your word; for my eyes have seen Your salvation, which You have prepared in the presence of all peoples, a light of revelation to the Gentiles, and the glory of Your people Israel" (Luke 2:29-32).

After Simeon's proclamation concerning Jesus, Luke added in the next verse, "And His father and mother were amazed at the things which were being said about Him" (Luke 2:33). Yet, we generally take this the wrong way. Mary and Joseph were not amazed at what Simeon said—they marveled at how accurate and how similar it was to what the angels long before had informed them. Everything that they heard from Simeon they had heard either from their own encounter with the angels, or from John the Baptist's parents, Elizabeth and Zacharias, especially as Mary had stayed three months with her relative Elizabeth (Luke 1:56). With joyful delight Elizabeth would disclose to Mary the angel's revelation to Zacharias concerning his child that she herself carried—as well as about the One that Mary would bear. Mary's baby had a God-ordained forerunner given Him (Luke 1:17). Mary *knew* her baby was God's Son; she did not fully understand, but she knew it to her core. Gabriel's discourse with her in Luke 1:31-35 disclosed deep wells of theology we still do not grasp in their entirety:

> "And behold, you will conceive in your womb and bear a son, and you shall name Him Jesus. He will be great and will be called the Son of the Most High; and the Lord God will give Him the throne of His father David; and He will reign over the house of Jacob forever, and His kingdom will have no end."
> Mary said to the angel, "How can this be, since I am a virgin?"
> The angel answered and said to her, "The Holy Spirit will come upon you, and the power of the Most High will overshadow you; and for that reason the holy Child shall be called the Son of God."

Joseph, too, had his own divinely-sent messenger who identified the Child who would be born and His saving mission:

> "Joseph, son of David, do not be afraid to take Mary as your wife; for the Child who has been conceived in her is of the Holy Spirit.
> "She will bear a Son; and you shall call His name Jesus, for He will save His people from their sins" (Matt. 1:20-21).

When John (the Baptist) was born, Zacharias, under the power of the Holy Spirit, described a major aspect of the Forerunner's ministry: "To give to His people the knowledge of salvation by the forgiveness of their sins" (Luke 1:77).

So when Simeon declared that he had witnessed God's salvation, "a light of revelation to the Gentiles, and the glory of Your people Israel," this was not new revelation—this was new affirmation. Not that Mary and Joseph needed personal assurance, but it no doubt crossed their minds as to how many others also knew the true identity of their Child.

Their amazement was not about the content of Simeon's statement as much as it was about how this stranger had access to these truths. If Mary and Joseph said anything, it would not have been, "What do you mean?" Instead, it would be more along the lines of, "How do you know this" or "Who told you these things?"

Why, God did, of course.

In the midst of a high priesthood that did not believe in the spiritual world, God sent one as a prophetic witness in the midst of spiritual darkness. It is not a random occurrence that in three successive verses Luke penned a reference to the Holy Spirit of God. Simeon was a man whom "the Holy Spirit was upon Him" (Luke 2:25). "And it had been revealed to him by the Holy Spirit that he would not see death before he had seen the Lord's Christ" (Luke 2:26). For one who walked so closely with God, it should not be surprising that his rendezvous would likewise come from God's leading: "And he came in the Spirit into the Temple" (Luke 2:27). And so Simeon, by the Spirit, identified the same One whom John the Baptist had identified even while in his mother's womb.

What Simeon disclosed was actually more than what the shepherds had understood. They were told about the birth—and went to see—the promised Messiah. Simeon knew that more was needed: God's Salvation; God's Light; God's Savior—God's Glory. Appropriately, though, Simeon identified that the Light and the Glory had returned—briefly—to the Temple of God where God's special presence had not resided for over six hundred years.

However, it would not be the last time. God had much, much more glory to disclose in His own house — and ultimately to the world.

He comes from the Mount of Olives, surrounded by the masses, yet unmistakably alone. He does not enter Jerusalem this time "gentle riding on a foal" (Zech. 9:9). He rides astride a white horse of majesty and grandeur. His conquered domain covers the entire inhabited earth. Worldwide domain, power and authority — divinely granted for His exercise.

How fitting that since the glory of God departed over the Mount of Olives, the advent of the Promised One should be there too. He enters Jerusalem from the East, fulfilling the prophecies that have long been predicting His arrival.

Only once before has the city of Jerusalem partaken in such commotion, and that was what is called the "Triumphal Entry" thousands of years before. Only this time there will be no rejection — only acceptance, reverence and worship.

This time the masses greatly exceed those of the Triumphal Entry. This is not merely a historical event; this is much more. This is fulfilled prophecy coming to life in the presence of humanity; it is an intensely spiritual event. All the attendants sense it. Glory and power pour forth from this Coming One. The worshipers pour out repeated waves of love and devotion on the One they deem so worthy.

He crosses the Brook Kidran amidst the rapturous clamor of the multitude. He enters the Old City amidst the calls of "Hosanna!"

The ancient prophecies foretold a promise:

Thus says the LORD of hosts, "Behold, a man whose name is Branch, for He will branch out from where He is; and He will build the Temple of the LORD. Yes, it is He who will build the Temple of the LORD, and He who will bear the honor and sit and rule on His throne. Thus, He will be a priest on His throne, and the counsel of peace will be between the two offices" (Zech. 6:12-13).

Further, the Holy Word states, "The Lord, whom you seek, will suddenly come to His Temple" (Mal. 3:1). He who has built the Temple comes — and the world knows it. He arrives today to take what is rightfully His with the full intention to see that the prophecies become a reality — and His worshipers have long anticipated His advent.

He, so long ago prophesied, has arrived at last. The Temple — rebuilt after almost two thousand years—functions again as God had designed. The ancient sacrifices and feasts become operative again after so long a stay. A functional priesthood performs the ancient rites down to the smallest detail. Most important is that this Herald of Peace has come to Jerusalem to receive what is rightfully His, and he makes His way to the Temple of God. Once at the Temple, He turns to face the multitude, much as the high priest did on the Day of Atonement. No land area exists within His sight where His worshipers are not tightly congregated to worship the One, as blankets of humanity collectively gape to catch even a small glimpse of their King.

He understands precisely what He is to do. He turns to enter the holy place—and then to go beyond. Pausing, perhaps to savor the import of what He is about to do, He then enters into the very holy of holies of God.

Only there is a significant difference.

He is the Antichrist, the son of perdition, "who opposes and exalts himself above every so-called god or object of worship, so that he takes his seat in the Temple of God, displaying himself as being God" (2 Thess. 2:4; Dan 9:27; Matt. 24:15).

And God—by His holy counsel and eternal and infinite wisdom—grants him the authority to do so (Rev 13:5-8).

He comes astride a white horse, but He does not come alone.

During the temptation, Satan had offered Jesus worldwide dominion, saying, "I will give You all this domain and its glory; for it has been handed over to me, and I give it to whomever I wish" (Luke 4 6). Jesus readily rejected the offer; the Antichrist will by no means reject it. The Apostle John wrote of one to whom Satan will give "his power and his throne and great authority" (Rev. 13:2). The totality of satanic power—power even acknowledged by the angels of God (Jude 9)—will be exercised by one man. Couple with this the fact that God will remove the Restrainer of Second Thessalonians 2:5-7, and the Beast will have a divinely-given window to do anything his evil heart can conceive. The world's collective emperors and dictators in all of human history will not equal the power, dominion, and authority given to this one. The world at large will marvel ("Who is like the beast, and who is able to wage war with him?" Rev. 13:4) and worship ("All who dwell on the earth will worship him" Rev. 13:8).

"Who is like the beast, and who is able to wage war with him?" The earth dwellers are about to encounter Him:

> And I saw heaven opened, and behold, a white horse, and He who sat on it is called Faithful and True, and in righteousness He judges and wages war. His eyes are a flame of fire, and on His head are many diadems; and He has a name written on Him which no one knows except Himself. He is clothed with a robe dipped in blood, and His name is called The Word of God.
> And the armies which are in heaven, clothed in fine linen, white and clean, were following Him on white horses.
> From His mouth comes a sharp sword, so that with it He may strike down the nations, and He will rule them with a rod of iron; and He treads the wine press of the fierce wrath of God, the Almighty.
> And on His robe and on His thigh He has a name written, "KING OF KINGS AND LORD OF LORDS" (Rev. 19:11-16).

The Son will exercise His divine power by devouring the Antichrist and his worshipers (Rev. 19:19-21). But in addition to this conquest, something else must happen. Jesus does not merely exercise God's judgmental capacity—He returns in glory, as the Scriptures repeatedly state. Some samples reveal—and there are many more—that the glory of God returns to earth when Jesus does. For instance, in the verses that precede the Transfiguration, Jesus promised, "For the Son of Man is going to come in the glory of His Father with His angels" (Matt. 16:27). In His teaching about the last time events, Jesus revealed in Matthew 24:29-30:

> But immediately after the tribulation of those days the sun will be darkened, and the moon will not give its light, and the stars will fall from the sky, and the powers of the heavens will be shaken.
> And then the sign of the Son of Man will appear in the sky, and then all the tribes of the earth will mourn, and they will see the Son of Man coming on the clouds of the sky with power and great glory.

In the same Olivet Discourse Jesus explained, "But when the Son of Man comes in His glory, and all the angels with Him, then He will sit on His glorious throne" (Matt. 25:31), literally translated, "throne of His glory." However, the return of Jesus does not end the glory aspect of God; it only begins new and expanding demonstrations of displays and wonders. God has so much more in mind.

In spite of his unequaled power and dominion, the Antichrist's rule will be lacking the glory of God. For blind inhabitants of the earth who will "not receive the love of the truth so as to be saved" (2 Thess. 2:10) and who will "not believe the truth, but took pleasure in wickedness" (2 Thess. 2:12), nothing else dazzles them as much as Satan's power and glory. The Antichrist will have only the glory of the nations (Luke 4:5-6). For people who have no true standard of assessment, the glory of the fallen world often substitutes for the glory of God. Paul revealed in 2 Corinthians 4:3-4, "And even if our gospel is veiled, it is veiled to those who are perishing, in whose case the god of this world has blinded the minds of the unbelieving so that they might not see the light of the gospel of the glory of Christ, who is the image of God." During the Tribulation, this blinding will be on a much more intensive scale.

At the return of Jesus, the world will recognize the difference between the glory of God and anything else; however, for the vast majority, it will be an understanding only as they receive the divine judgment. We should also note another important truth: the Antichrist will be able to seat himself in the rebuilt Temple during the Tribulation, much as the pagans before him entered into the abandoned Holy of Holies. God's glory does not return until Jesus returns (Matt. 16:27); therefore, the Temple of the Tribulation will not have God's glory. Whereas Nebuchadnezzar of Babylon's troops could not enter the holy of holies until God had removed His glory, so the Antichrist will be able to enter only because of the absence of God's glory—and by God's sovereign decree.

But eventually, that will change.

In the last nine chapters of his prophecy, Ezekiel recorded a vision of what will be fulfilled in the end times. So often we are casual readers of Scripture instead of dropping down into the world of the original participants. Put yourself in Ezekiel's position: you are exiled into a pagan Gentile land (Ezek. 1:1); God has allowed you to see a representation of His glory (Ezek. 1:4-28), and sadly, His glory departing (Ezek. 8–11). Six months after the actual event, God's faithful prophet received the report that he knew would eventually come: "Now it came about in the twelfth year of our exile, on the fifth of the tenth month, that the refugees from Jerusalem came to me, saying, '"The city has been taken"'" (Ezek. 33:21). If this is where the story ended, one should expect a regathering to the land as God had repeatedly promised throughout His Word, such as He plainly states in Leviticus 26:40-46:

> "If they confess their iniquity and the iniquity of their forefathers, in their unfaithfulness which they committed against Me, and also in their acting with hostility against Me—I also was acting with hostility against them, to bring them into the land of their enemies—or if their

uncircumcised heart becomes humbled so that they then make amends for their iniquity, then I will remember My covenant with Jacob, and I will remember also My covenant with Isaac, and My covenant with Abraham as well, and I will remember the land.

"For the land shall be abandoned by them, and shall make up for its sabbaths while it is made desolate without them. They, meanwhile, shall be making amends for their iniquity, because they rejected My ordinances and their soul abhorred My statutes.

"Yet in spite of this, when they are in the land of their enemies, I will not reject them, nor will I so abhor them as to destroy them, breaking My covenant with them; for I am the LORD their God.

"But I will remember for them the covenant with their ancestors, whom I brought out of the land of Egypt in the sight of the nations, that I might be their God. I am the LORD."

These are the statutes and ordinances and laws which the LORD established between Himself and the sons of Israel through Moses at Mount Sinai.

So many other verses have already presented the promised regathering, including Deuteronomy 30:1-6. Whether Ezekiel received the wonderful future promises for Israel that God had given through Jeremiah (especially Jeremiah 30–33), we do not know. Nonetheless, the same God who judged the city and His people exactly as He said He would ended this section with a reference to doubters—those present when originally spoken and those present today—of what He would most assuredly accomplish at some undisclosed time in the future:

And the word of the LORD came to Jeremiah, saying, "Have you not observed what this people have spoken, saying, the two families which the LORD chose, He has rejected them? Thus they despise My people, no longer are they as a nation in their sight.

"Thus says the LORD, 'If My covenant for day and night stand not, and the fixed patterns of heaven and earth I have not established, then I would reject the descendants of Jacob and David My servant, not taking from his descendants rulers over the descendants of Abraham, Isaac, and Jacob. But I will restore their fortunes and will have mercy on them' " (Jer. 33:23-26).

If these promises were not sufficient—which they are—God chose to reveal so much more. In a new section of Ezekiel (Ezek. 40–48), he recorded these words that are rarely noted and even less understood:

In the twenty-fifth year of our exile, at the beginning of the year, on the tenth of the month, in the fourteenth year after the city was taken, on that same day the hand of the LORD was upon me and He brought me there. In the visions of God He brought me into the land of Israel, and set me on a very high mountain; and on it to the south there was a structure like a city (Ezek. 40:1-2).

Most modern readers do not get the sense of what Ezekiel would have known immediately: He was not merely Ezekiel the prophet; he was also "Ezekiel the priest" (1:3) who had been meticulously trained in the manner of the priesthood and the Temple services. The prophet received this divine vision in 573 BC (Ezek. 40:1), almost thirteen years after the Temple had been destroyed in 586 BC. No one needed to explain to the prophet-priest that "at the beginning of the year, on the tenth of the month" would have began the annual ten-day preparation for Passover that, sadly, would not be observed in Jerusalem that year — or again for decades — since the Temple was destroyed and the people were exiled. Nonetheless, the ten-day preparation for Passover was and is relevant to God's covenanted people. This was true in history past for the Jews since the Exodus; it was true the week that Messiah was betrayed; it will be true for the future as well.

While many argue about whether this prophecy is even true, whether it already had occurred in history past, or whether it is related to the Church instead of to the nation of Israel, Ezekiel would not have joined in any debate. After all, it is not just the rebuilding of God's Temple that God disclosed, but something immensely beyond the importance of the structure will transpire, as Ezekiel 43:1-2 reveals:

Then he led me to the gate, the gate facing toward the east; and behold, the glory of the God of Israel was coming from the way of the east. And His voice was like the sound of many waters; and the earth shone with His glory.

Although many Bible readers often do not note two massively important revelatory nuggets in these two verses, Ezekiel no doubt immediately did. First, the glory that God had shown him in Ezekiel chapter one and which had evacuated God's Temple in chapter 8–11 would return, returning through the same east gate from which the Glory had departed years earlier in Ezekiel 10:19 and 11:22-23. Same prophet; same gate; same Glory of God, but this time in reverse order.

Second, how appropriate it is that the glory of the Lord has a voice — "His voice," not "Its voice" — "was like the sound of many waters" (Ezek. 43:2). The Apostle John later acknowledged this, "and His voice was like the sound of many waters" (Rev. 1:15). We will get to study this in more detail in future studies, but simply put, Jesus is the radiance of the Glory of God (Heb. 1:3) — always has been in every book of the Bible; always will be throughout eternity. The Glory of God is not a what — the Glory is a Who, as Psalm 24:7-10 and many others make eternal proclamation:

> Lift up your heads, O gates, and be lifted up, O ancient doors, that the King of glory may come in! Who is the King of glory? The LORD strong and mighty, the LORD mighty in battle. Lift up your heads, O gates, and lift them up, O ancient doors, that the King of glory may come in!
> Who is the King of glory? He is the King of glory.

Ezekiel made sure that his readers understand this same eternally important connection:

> And it was like the appearance of the vision which I saw, like the vision which I saw when He came to destroy the city. And the visions were like the vision which I saw by the river Chebar; and I fell on my face.
> And the glory of the LORD came into the house by the way of the gate facing toward the east.
> And the Spirit lifted me up and brought me into the inner court; and behold, the glory of the LORD filled the house.
> Then I heard one speaking to me from the house, while a man was standing beside me. He said to me, "Son of man, this is the place of My throne and the place of the soles of My feet, where I will dwell among the sons of Israel forever" (Ezek. 43:3-7a).

The Glory will return to inhabit not only the future Temple, but also when this occurs "the earth [will shine] with His glory" (Ezek. 43:2).

God filled His tabernacle with His glory (Exod. 40:34).

God filled His Temple built by Solomon with His glory (2 Chron. 5:11-14).

The glory of God eventually departed from His Temple (Ezek. 8–11).

The Word became flesh and dwelt among us, "and we beheld His glory" (John 1:14) — especially at the Transfiguration (Luke 9:32).

Jesus was raised in glory at His ascension (1 Tim. 3:16).

The Antichrist seats himself in the Temple, showing the world that he is God (2 Thess. 2:4) — but with no glory of God present, only that of Satan and himself.

Jesus will return in glory at His second advent to earth (Matt. 25:31).

He will then fill the earth with His glory (Ezek. 43:2).

All the prophecies of the end times ultimately conclude with some aspect of the Glory of God, whether directly stated or collectively grouped. This is only fitting since the culmination of all of God's promises relate directly to His Glory; one cannot exist without the Other. Many displays of God's glory still await their fulfillment. In spite of God's previous displays of His glory throughout the world's history, they all pale when "compared with the glory that is to be revealed to us" (Rom. 8:18).

But all of this is in the future. What about the present? In the meantime, where does God's glory currently reside? Or stated better, where does God choose to place His glory now?

Unless God Himself had revealed the answer in Scripture, we would never believe it. It is far too grand a story for human minds ever to concoct, almost too great a doctrine for mortal minds to comprehend even when disclosed in the Holy Word. You would never believe what the Stone has done—and is doing—for us. Yet, Scripture clearly indicates where God's glory currently dwells.

12

THE GLORY

*M*oses returned from the mountain with a monumental stone testimony given to him by God Almighty: "When He had finished speaking with him upon Mount Sinai, He gave Moses the two tablets of the testimony, tablets of stone, written by the finger of God" (Exod. 31:18). While Moses had communed in the very presence of God, the newly redeemed nation was in the process of quickly abandoning their covenant-making God. Even God's high priest Aaron, who would eventually wear the newly made golden plate inscribed with "Holy to the LORD" attached to his turban (Exod. 28:36), assisted in the rebellion. Yet, Aaron and the short-memory nation were not acting according to God's holy standard:

> Now when the people saw that Moses delayed to come down from the mountain, the people assembled about Aaron and said to him, "Come, make us a god who will go before us; as for this Moses, the man who brought us up from the land of Egypt, we do not know what has become of him."
> Aaron said to them, "Tear off the gold rings which are in the ears of your wives, your sons, and your daughters, and bring them to me." Then all the people tore off the gold rings which were in their ears and brought them to Aaron. He took this from their hand, and fashioned it with a graving tool and made it into a molten calf; and they said, "This is your god, O Israel, who brought you up from the land of Egypt" (Exod. 32:1-4).

God's reaction to this blatant sin was, "I have seen this people, and behold, they are an obstinate people. Now then let Me alone, that My anger may burn against them and that I may destroy them; and I will make of you a great nation" (Exod. 32:9-10). Moses reasoned with God regarding the eternal nature of the Abrahamic Covenant—as God had intended all the time—imploring the LORD that He must "remember Abraham, Isaac, and Israel, Your servants to whom You swore by Yourself, and said to them, 'I will multiply your descendants as the stars of the heavens, and all this land of which I have spoken I will give to your descendants, and they shall inherit it forever'" (Exod. 32:13). Moses pleaded, quite reverently, "You cannot do that God!" Based on the faithfulness to His own Word, God stayed His wrath against the nation (Exod. 32:14).

The account continues, specifying again regarding the stone tablets specifically given by God in Exodus 32:15-16:

> Then Moses turned and went down from the mountain with the two tablets of the testimony in his hand, tablets which were written on both sides; they were written on one side and the other.
> The tablets were God's work, and the writing was God's writing engraved on the tablets.

Although God did not completely destroy the nation, He did inflict punishment that resulted in the deaths of about three thousand Hebrews (Exod. 32:25-28). Feeling compassion for the people, Moses attempted to intercede: "You yourselves have committed a great sin; and now I am going up to the LORD, perhaps I can make atonement for your sin" (Exod. 32:30). The conversation between God and Moses follows in Exodus 32:31-34:

> Then Moses returned to the LORD, and said, "Alas, this people has committed a great sin, and they have made a god of gold for themselves. But now, if You will, forgive their sin—and if not, please blot me out from Your book which You have written!"
> The LORD said to Moses, "Whoever has sinned against Me, I will blot him out of My book. But go now, lead the people where I told you. Behold, My angel shall go before you; nevertheless in the day when I punish, I will punish them for their sin."

An aspect of what God said startled Moses. God said, "Behold, My angel shall go before you." Although this would be comforting in many situations in life, this was not encouraging news for Moses. In essence, God would send someone, but He implied in this that Yahweh Himself would not go before them, which is what the next chapter indicates in detail:

> Then the LORD spoke to Moses, "Depart, go up from here, you and the people whom you have brought up from the land of Egypt, to the

land of which I swore to Abraham, Isaac, and Jacob, saying, 'To your descendants I will give it.'
"I will send an angel before you and I will drive out the Canaanite, the Amorite, the Hittite, the Perizzite, the Hivite and the Jebusite.
"Go up to a land flowing with milk and honey; for I will not go up in your midst, because you are an obstinate people, and I might destroy you on the way" (Exod. 33:1-3).

God, who gave the plans for the Tabernacle so that He might dwell in the very midst of His people (Exod. 25:8), said that He would not go up in their midst. Exodus 33:5 reiterates that this is actually an act of grace on God's part: "Say to the sons of Israel, 'You are an obstinate people; should I go up in your midst for one moment, I would destroy you.'"

Using real life visual aides for this spiritually weak and sinful generation, God removed His presence to a distance outside the camp. The wilderness generation witnessed God's visible presence, but it was away from the midst of the people:

Now Moses used to take the tent and pitch it outside the camp, a good distance from the camp, and he called it the tent of meeting. And everyone who sought the LORD would go out to the tent of meeting which was outside the camp. And it came about, whenever Moses went out to the tent, that all the people would arise and stand, each at the entrance of his tent, and gaze after Moses until he entered the tent.

Whenever Moses entered the tent, the pillar of cloud would descend and stand at the entrance of the tent; and the LORD would speak with Moses. When all the people saw the pillar of cloud standing at the entrance of the tent, all the people would arise and worship, each at the entrance of his tent.

Thus the LORD used to speak to Moses face to face, just as a man speaks to his friend (Exod. 33:7-11).

God removed His visual presence from the people, and yet He would speak to Moses face to face. Fortunately, God allows us a peak at what the two friends spoke. For Moses, there was still that major problem that needed God's immediate attention: "Then Moses said to the LORD, 'See, You say to me, "Bring up this people!" But You Yourself have not let me know whom You will send with me'" (Exod. 32:12). God had promised to send His angel, but not Himself—and this greatly concerned Moses. The following conversation expresses Moses' anguish as a leader as well as his heart's desire as an individual:

And He [God] said, "My presence shall go with you, and I will give you rest."
Then he [Moses] said to Him, "If Your presence does not go with us, do not lead us up from here. For how then can it be known that I have found favor in Your sight, I and Your people? Is it not by Your going with us, so that we, I and Your people, may be distinguished from all the other people who are upon the face of the earth?" (Exod. 33:14-16).

The presence of God dwelling in the very midst of the people was not just some spiritual novelty. As far as Moses was concerned, it was mandatory; essential; life-giving. Moses and the nation were there that day only because of the presence and covenant faithfulness of Yahweh. Although neither the tabernacle nor the Temple had yet been built, if God removed His presence from their midst, they may as well not go any farther—especially since they would soon perish from either the physical elements or from their enemies.

An interesting exchange follows next:

The LORD said to Moses, "I will also do this thing of which you have spoken; for you have found favor in My sight and I have known you by name."
Then Moses said, "I pray You, show me Your glory!" (Exod. 33:17-18).

In addition to the presence of God, Moses desired more. The way that God answered Moses' request to behold His glory must have initially seemed contradictory:

And He said, "I Myself will make all My goodness pass before you, and will proclaim the name of the LORD before you; and I will be gracious to whom I will be gracious, and will show compassion on whom I will show compassion."
But He said, "You cannot see My face, for no man can see Me and live!" (Exod. 33:19-20).

The same One who "used to speak to Moses face to face, just as a man speaks to his friend" (Exod. 33:11), informed Moses, "You cannot see My face, for no man can see Me and live." If Moses had questions—which he must have had—they are not recorded in Scripture.

God continued:

Then the LORD said, "Behold, there is a place by Me, and you shall stand there on the rock; and it will come about, while My glory is passing by, that I will put you in the cleft of the rock and cover you with My hand until I have passed by.

"Then I will take My hand away and you shall see My back, but My face shall not be seen" (Exod. 33:21-23).

Although something marvelously strange took place, it, nevertheless, was not exactly what God had promised. Exodus 34:1-7 explains:

> Now the LORD said to Moses, "Cut out for yourself two stone tablets like the former ones, and I will write on the tablets the words that were on the former tablets which you shattered. So be ready by morning, and come up in the morning to Mount Sinai, and present yourself there to Me on the top of the mountain. No man is to come up with you, nor let any man be seen anywhere on the mountain; even the flocks and the herds may not graze in front of that mountain."
> So he cut out two stone tablets like the former ones, and Moses rose up early in the morning and went up to Mount Sinai, as the LORD had commanded him, and he took two stone tablets in his hand.
> The LORD descended in the cloud and stood there with him as he called upon the name of the LORD.
> Then the LORD passed by in front of him and proclaimed, "The LORD, the LORD God, compassionate and gracious, slow to anger, and abounding in lovingkindness and truth; who keeps lovingkindness for thousands, who forgives iniquity, transgression and sin; yet He will by no means leave the guilty unpunished, visiting the iniquity of fathers on the children and on the grandchildren to the third and fourth generations."

The response by Moses was appropriate for such a divine display: "Moses made haste to bow low toward the earth and worship" (Exod. 34:8).

While God's descent was obviously awe-inspiring to Moses, a close examination of the text reveals something odd: this was not a fulfillment of what had God promised in the previous chapter of Exodus 33. For instance, there is no rock. There is no glory. The LORD passed by, but not His glory (cf. Exod. 33:22). God provided no cleft—and He did not cover Moses with His hand. Something important had taken place, but it was not the fulness of what God had promised. And as majestic as this display was, the core issue of God's presence continually concerned Moses, as Exodus 34:9 indicates: "If now I have found favor in Your sight, O LORD, I pray, let the LORD go along in our midst, even though the people are so obstinate, and pardon our iniquity and our sin, and take us as Your own possession." Moses would find no peace until Yahweh assured him that He Himself would go with them.

One final episode in this section is pertinent to our study. Exodus 34:27-28 presents the timeframe of Moses' stay with God: "Then the

LORD said to Moses, 'Write down these words, for in accordance with these words I have made a covenant with you and with Israel.' So he was there with the LORD forty days and forty nights; he did not eat bread or drink water. And he wrote on the tablets the words of the covenant, the Ten Commandments."

And then—a most unusual sight occurred that never had before:

> It came about when Moses was coming down from Mount Sinai (and the two tablets of the testimony were in Moses' hand as he was coming down from the mountain), that Moses did not know that the skin of his face shone because of his speaking with Him.
> So when Aaron and all the sons of Israel saw Moses, behold, the skin of his face shone, and they were afraid to come near him. Then Moses called to them, and Aaron and all the rulers in the congregation returned to him; and Moses spoke to them. Afterward all the sons of Israel came near, and he commanded them to do everything that the LORD had spoken to him on Mount Sinai.
> When Moses had finished speaking with them, he put a veil over his face. But whenever Moses went in before the LORD to speak with Him, he would take off the veil until he came out; and whenever he came out and spoke to the sons of Israel what he had been commanded, the sons of Israel would see the face of Moses, that the skin of Moses' face shone. So Moses would replace the veil over his face until he went in to speak with Him. (Exod. 34:29-35)

When Moses wrote this section of Exodus, he recorded it as an event that had happened. No following explanatory statement regarding its importance was given—at least not at that point. Nonetheless, the Holy Spirit decided that it was an account that was be recorded forever in God's Holy Word.

Do you know what really is incredible about this Old Testament passage? The Holy Spirit inspired another biblical author to explain its significance. Approximately fifteen hundred years later, Paul used this entire section of Exodus to explain the content of his own ministry—but even more so, to explain the unfathomable vastness of the riches of God's glory for those who abide in Christ Jesus.

Paul, the humble bond-servant apostle, was forced by the carnal minded church at Corinth to defend both himself and his ministry. Having arrived in Corinth, having evangelized the city, having founded the church, then having patiently discipled them for eighteen months,

Paul continued on his missionary journey (Acts 18:1-11).

Paul received disturbing reports from Chole's people about severe problems within the church (1 Cor. 1:11) and also from a letter sent by the Corinthians (7:1). Paul responded by writing the epistle of First Corinthians. It is a strongly corrective book. In the first nine verses Paul attempted to put the focus on whose church it really was, namely Jesus', writing "in Christ" or "in Him" ten times. That is virtually the last good thing he said about the Corinthian assembly until the end of the epistle. Everything they were doing—other than their initial acceptance of Jesus—was wrong. Paul wrote of factions, an incestuous relationship that those in the Corinthian church knew about but did nothing to stop, and lawsuits among the believers. He had to deal with Christian divorce and remarriage. Some hailed their Christian liberty as a cloak for doing whatever they wanted to do. Paul had to correct them, teaching them the repeated biblical principle that great spiritual privilege necessitates great spiritual responsibility. Some of the Corinthian church members even came to the Lord's Table drunk.

Their collective "worship" service was not only a bazaar in its cacophony, it was also demonically influenced. Paul began a three-chapter section on spiritual gifts as instructions to them, "Therefore I make known to you that no one speaking by the Spirit of God says, 'Jesus is accursed'; and no one can say, 'Jesus is LORD,' except by the Holy Spirit" (1 Cor. 12:3). "Jesus is accursed?" —*anathema*—"Jesus is damned by God?"

Again, two problems were present. One, blasphemous "prophecies" were being uttered in the assembly under the supposed influence of the Holy Spirit. Two, nobody had the spiritual insight to recognize that heretical proclamations were being spouted. To top it off, the church of Corinth had some people teaching doctrine similar to that of the Sadducees—namely, that there was no resurrection (1 Cor. 15). Paul reminded them, among other things, "But if there is no resurrection of the dead, not even Christ has been raised; and if Christ has not been raised, then our preaching is vain, your faith also is vain" (1 Cor. 15:13-14). They called themselves Christians; yet, if Christ had not been raised, why call Him Christ? Why assemble as a Christian church at all? Why refrain from any sin if there is no resurrection—and no judgment?

In addition to all these heresies, also scattered throughout the epistle is the fact that the Corinthians had great pride in themselves. It is one thing to be sinful and repentant—it is quite a lower spiritual life form that is both arrogant and ignorant in massive proportions. If people say that their favorite book of the Bible is First Corinthians, they delight either in intense human and demonic conflict, or else they have not read the book very closely. Actually, the previous sentence is an over-statement: First Corinthians is wonderfully rich and useful in that several of the same problems that Paul repeatedly encountered at Corinth still plague many churches today. It is an excellent God-given resource in addressing the same church problems today that Paul repeatedly encountered.

However, Paul's strong approach in First Corinthians did not go over very well with the original readers. They were highly offended — very much like many in today's churches are equally offended by the teachings of this inspired work. We know from various texts that Paul actually made a short trip to Corinth in an attempt to remedy some of the deep problems there (cf. "third trip" in 2 Cor. 12:14). The second trip was a disaster. Paul came back defeated spiritually — not in his own walk, but rather because of the obstinate Corinthians. It was the low point of his ministry. Jesus already knew that it would be, and had already prepared Paul, to a certain extent, for what lay ahead. In Acts 18:9-10 an unusual event took place as Paul began his ministry at Corinth:

> And the Lord said to Paul in the night by a vision, "Do not be afraid any longer, but go on speaking and do not be silent; for I am with you, and no man will attack you in order to harm you, for I have many people in this city."

Jesus appearing in a vision to any of the apostles was rare. This event was even more perplexing because Paul had already been frequently beaten, once stoned, and many times had been run out of towns. He knew from day one of his conversion that he would suffer (Acts 9:16). Furthermore, by the time he wrote Second Corinthians, Paul disclosed that he was taken up to heaven for a preview fourteen years before (2 Cor. 12:1-2). Yet, Jesus said, "Do not be [or literally, "Stop being"] afraid" (Acts. 18:9). When considering everything else that Paul had already endured, what else could Paul possibly fear? Or asked differently, why would Paul be so afraid at Corinth?

When pieced together, it seems that the best reason was that Jesus knew the spiritual hardships that awaited Paul. They would be deeper than even what Paul had experienced before. Also, it is not coincidental that Paul wrote more about Satan and spiritual warfare in Second Corinthians that he did in all of his other works combined. He was in for a very rough time.

What brazenness, then, on the part of the Corinthians that they should request from Paul "letters of commendation to you or from you?" (2 Cor. 3:1). This church was bloated with factions, incest, law-suits, abuse of the Lord's Table, demonic-inspired prophecies in their assembly, misinformed teaching that there is no resurrection—and *they* request letters of commendation *from Paul*? Pure, unadulterated Corinthian gall of the vilest vintage that these carnal-minded, arro-gant, worse-than-babes Christians demanded from Paul credentials so *they* will decide whether to accept *him*. Maybe that is why God did not make me an apostle. I doubt I would have been so gracious. Paul, by God's great grace, loved these Corinthian hard-heads with the love that only God can inspire for those so unlovable.

By God's grand design, Paul wrote his second inspired letter to the Corinthians, which, of course, became part of the Word of God that will not pass away. In effect, Second Corinthians is Paul's most person-al letter. It is a sad epistle, at least until chapter seven, because Paul had to answer charges against his character and his ministry. So Paul wrote very patiently and very openly to the Corinthians about his past con-duct with them (chap. 1–2:13), and then, for our purpose at hand, he wrote about his own ministry (2:14–chapter 7).

It is vital that Paul did not write about his ministry techniques or his activities; he wrote about the content of his message. And of all things, Paul used the account of Moses and the stone tablets and the events that followed (Exod. 32–34) as the basis for his logic. Chapter three of Second Corinthians is loaded with references to the Exodus account:

> Are we beginning to commend ourselves again? Or do we need, as some, letters of commendation to you or from you? You are our letter, written in our hearts, known and read by all men; being manifested that you are a letter of Christ, cared for by us, written not with ink but with the Spirit of the living God, not on tablets of stone but on tablets of human hearts.
> Such confidence we have through Christ toward God. Not that we are adequate in ourselves to consider anything as coming from ourselves, but our adequacy is from God, who also made us adequate as servants of a new covenant, not of the letter but of the Spirit; for the letter kills, but the Spirit gives life.
> But if the ministry of death, in letters engraved on stones, came with glory, so that the sons of Israel could not look intently at the face of Moses because of the glory of his face, fading as it was, how will the ministry of the Spirit fail to be even more with glory? For if the ministry

of condemnation has glory, much more does the ministry of righteousness abound in glory. For indeed what had glory, in this case has no glory because of the glory that surpasses it. For if that which fades away was with glory, much more that which remains is in glory.

Therefore having such a hope, we use great boldness in our speech, and are not like Moses, who used to put a veil over his face so that the sons of Israel would not look intently at the end of what was fading away. But their minds were hardened; for until this very day at the reading of the old covenant the same veil remains unlifted, because it is removed in Christ. But to this day whenever Moses is read, a veil lies over their heart; but whenever a person turns to the Lord, the veil is taken away.

Now the Lord is the Spirit, and where the Spirit of the Lord is, there is liberty. But we all, with unveiled face, beholding as in a mirror the glory of the Lord, are being transformed into the same image from glory to glory, just as from the Lord, the Spirit (3:1-18).

Some points that Paul made are obvious in similarities and in contrasts. The Corinthians were the letter written by God, not on tablets of stone but on the heart. Moses received the Law with glory; the ministry of the New Covenant has more glory — glory to such a degree that it makes the glory of the Exodus account seem almost non-existent by comparison. As Moses was veiled, in a different way a veil lies over someone's heart who is currently an unbeliever. When someone turns to the Lord in faith, the veil is removed. Since the veil is removed when one believes, obviously believers approach God "with unveiled face."

But still — something is not right. It does not seem to fit that in some ways the analogy that Paul — and the Holy Spirit — employed has more contrasts than similarities. We would think there should be more relevance than this. You certainly would not read Exodus 32–34 and conclude that this is obviously true for the Apostle Paul. After all, if I were a Corinthian critic of Paul and if I had received this chapter, I would question him, "If your gospel is so glorious, why do not people stampede to it?" Paul would answer:

> And even if our gospel is veiled, it is veiled to those who are perishing, in whose case the god of this world has blinded the minds of the unbelieving so that they might not see the light of the gospel of the glory of Christ, who is the image of God (2 Cor. 4:3-4).

How appropriate that Satan blinds the minds of unbelievers, specifically so that they might not see the light of the gospel of Christ's glory. Trinkets of materialism, pride, sex, worldly fame — whatever works.

Blind them to the glory of God—keep them in veiled bondage, ignorant of both the glory and the solution. That is all Satan has to do to keep one from a saving relationship with Jesus. Broad, indeed, is the way to destruction (Matt. 7:13).

Still, if I were a critic of Paul, I would have another question. "How can you claim your ministry has much more glory than Moses' ministry had? If your ministry has more glory, why does your face not shine? I've seen you often. Not once did your face shine with God's glory. Why not—if, in fact, the content of your ministry is superior?"

Excellent question.

An even more excellent answer awaits.

Moses implored God in fervent prayer, "I pray You, show me Your glory!" (Exod. 33:18). God would grant the request, but in a most limited fashion. Part of this was due to limitations because Moses inhabited a human body:

> And He [God] said, "I Myself will make all My goodness pass before you, and will proclaim the name of the LORD before you; and I will be gracious to whom I will be gracious, and will show compassion on whom I will show compassion."
> But He said, "You cannot see My face, for no man can see Me and live!" (Exod. 33:19-20).

God permitted an alternative:

> Then the LORD said, "Behold, there is a place by Me, and you shall stand there on the rock; and it will come about, while My glory is passing by, that I will put you in the cleft of the rock and cover you with My hand until I have passed by. Then I will take My hand away and you shall see My back, but My face shall not be seen" (Exod. 33:21-23).

As we saw earlier, aspects of this did come true in Exodus 34:

> The LORD descended in the cloud and stood there with him as he called upon the name of the LORD.
> Then the LORD passed by in front of him and proclaimed, "The LORD, the LORD God, compassionate and gracious, slow to anger, and abounding in lovingkindness and truth; who keeps lovingkindness for thousands, who forgives iniquity, transgression and sin; yet He will by no means leave the guilty unpunished, visiting the iniquity of fathers

on the children and on the grandchildren to the third and fourth generations" (Exod. 34:5-7).

Other elements, however, of what God had promised awaited the fullness of times, when the Word became flesh and tabernacled among His own. This passage is loaded with so many deep spiritual truths that we cannot go into detail now. One such foundational truth that must be marked concerns the rock's identity, as Paul revealed in First Corinthians 10:1-4:

> For I do not want you to be unaware, brethren, that our fathers were all under the cloud and all passed through the sea; and all were baptized into Moses in the cloud and in the sea; and all ate the same spiritual food; and all drank the same spiritual drink, for they were drinking from a spiritual rock which followed them; *and the Rock was Christ.*

Wonderfully deep spiritual truths regarding Jesus lie embedded in these verses, but we must move on.

Centuries after Moses' death, the Word became flesh and dwelt (literally, "tabernacled") among us. Beginning His ministry, Jesus selected twelve disciples to accompany Him. Over a period of time, Jesus the Stone — and Jesus the Rock — repeatedly led His disciples into deeper spiritual truths, especially concerning His identity and His mission. In Matthew 16 two foundational events took place. One, Peter, by means of the revelation of God Himself, declared of Jesus, "You are the Christ, the Son of the living God" (Matt. 16:16). With the Messiah being properly identified, Jesus then presented a new theological truth that would not be readily accepted by His followers. "From that time Jesus began to show His disciples that He must go to Jerusalem, and suffer many things from the elders and chief priests and scribes, and be killed, and be raised up on the third day" (Matt. 16:21). Yet, although the disciples (especially Peter) reacted in terrified dread, events would transpire precisely as Jesus had spoken. These were necessary for the world's salvation; they were also necessary for God to show forth His glory. Jesus' death was necessary for the resurrection to occur. The resurrection was necessary for His ascension to the Father (Ps. 110:1). The ascension was necessary for His return to earth in His glory. In the parallel account in Luke, Jesus noted the glory associated with His second advent, "For whoever is ashamed of Me and My words, the Son of Man will be ashamed of him when He comes in His glory, and the glory of the Father and of the holy angels" (Luke 9:26). He then added, "But I say to you truthfully, there are some of those standing here who will not taste death until they see the kingdom of God" (9:27).

These are the verses that immediately precede the Transfiguration of Jesus. "Some eight days after these sayings, He took along Peter and John and James, and went up on the mountain to pray" (Luke 9:28). The parallel accounts of Matthew and Mark describe the unveiling of Jesus' glory: "And He was transfigured before them; and His face shone like the sun, and His garments became as white as light" (Matt. 17:2; cf. Mark 9:3). Matthew noted a surprising development marked by the word "behold" – "And behold, Moses and Elijah appeared to them, talking with Him" (Matt. 17:3).

We must leave out so many truths here as well as in this monumental occurrence. For the time being, we will limit our study to Moses' previous request of God to "Show me Thy glory!" – and God's ultimate answer.

"Show me Thy glory!"

"I will – on the Mount of Transfiguration." As Luke 9:32 testified, "Now Peter and his companions had been overcome with sleep; but when they were fully awake, they saw His glory and the two men standing with Him."

God had told Moses, "I Myself will make all My goodness pass before you, and will proclaim the name of the LORD before you" (Exod. 33:19) – and He did. Matthew 17:5 records the event, "While he was still speaking, a bright cloud overshadowed them, and behold, a voice out of the cloud said, 'This is My beloved Son, with whom I am well-pleased; listen to Him!' "

Although we have left out more than we have put in about this account, we have set the table for what we need for our present study. We need to make the appropriate connections in Scripture. One item to note is that the word "transfigure" is from the Greek verb from which we get our English word *metamorphosis*. Another very important consideration is that the word "transfigure" – this same word used to describe the Transfiguration of Jesus – occurs in only two other places in Scripture. One is in the famous verses of Romans 12:1-2:

> Therefore I urge you, brethren, by the mercies of God, to present your bodies a living and holy sacrifice, acceptable to God, which is your spiritual service of worship. And do not be conformed to this world, but *be transformed* by the renewing of your mind, so that you may prove what the will of God is, that which is good and acceptable and perfect.

The same type of transforming (or transfigured, the same Greek word for the Gospel accounts) that Jesus had, we are to have in our lives. Notice the usage is passive, "be transformed" — not the active "transform yourselves." We draw near to God. We become spiritual sacrifices. We are not to be conformed to the world's standard and procedures — and then God will do the transforming, as our minds are renewed, especially by feeding on God's Word and by being in communal fellowship with Him.

Paul wrote a command in Romans 12:2 that believers are to be transformed by the renewing of their minds. He also wrote the only other remaining use of this word in the New Testament. But this time he wrote a statement, not an instruction. By this other usage of the word "transform" he uncovered a startling spiritual truth. Other than in the Transfiguration accounts in the Gospel and the one reference in Romans 12:2, the only other time this word for transfigure or transform occurs is back in the section of Second Corinthians where Paul used Moses as a contrasting example for the glory of the New Covenant — and a definitive statement of where God's glory currently dwells.

Because Paul used the account of Moses and the glory on his face as a contrast to the greatness of the New Covenant, perhaps it would be useful to consider again one of the questions that Paul's critics could have asked: "If your ministry has much more glory than that in the old covenant (2 Cor. 3:7-11), why does your face not shine as Moses' face did?"

That is a good place to begin. In fact, it is important to note that Moses' *face* shone with glory. Three times in the Exodus 34, specific references are made to the skin of Moses' face. For instance, Exodus 34:29: "It came about when Moses was coming down from Mount Sinai (and the two tablets of the testimony were in Moses' hand as he was coming down from the mountain), that Moses did not know that the skin of his face shone because of his speaking with Him." Again in Exodus 34:30, "So when Aaron and all the sons of Israel saw Moses, behold, the skin of his face shone, and they were afraid to come near him" (cf. 34:35).

So Paul began a series of comparisons and distinctions between the ministry under the New Covenant versus the Old. Initially, just as Moses had something written by God Himself, so did Paul:

> You are our letter, written in our hearts, known and read by all men; being manifested that you are a letter of Christ, cared for by us, written

not with ink but with the Spirit of the living God, not on tablets of stone but on tablets of human hearts (2 Cor. 3:2-3).

Believers are just as much a work of God as the stone tablets were because we have His writing upon us.

But there is more. While Moses came down the mountain with a reflected glory lingering on his skin, those in Christ have something significantly beyond: "But we all, with unveiled face, beholding as in a mirror the glory of the LORD, *are being transformed* into the same image *from glory to glory*, just as from the LORD, the Spirit" (2 Cor. 3:18).

Those in Christ are presently being transformed—the same Greek root word used for the Transfiguration of Jesus. When used of Jesus in the Gospels, it was a description of an event. When used of believers, it is a present passive statement of continuous, on-going transfiguration from glory into glory—from initial glory at the moment of salvation to an expanded glory throughout eternity.

"Well, I didn't know God's glory was in me."

No matter; Moses did not know his face shone either (Exod. 34:29).

"Well, I cannot presently see God's glory on you or anyone else."

You could not see it on Jesus either until God revealed it at the Transfiguration (Luke 9:32).

"Well, why if it is greater glory, does your face not shine a little, just like Moses?"

It will—one day. But in the meantime God has determined that instead "we have this treasure in earthen vessels, so that the surpassing greatness of the power will be of God and not from ourselves" (2 Cor. 4:7).

An aspect of God's eternal design is for us to accept by faith that God is presently producing glory in the lives of His children. This is hard to do at times, especially when it seems that He is doing the opposite—if He is doing anything at all. Nevertheless, we are to accept His promise by faith:

Therefore we do not lose heart, but though our outer man is decaying, yet our inner man is being renewed day by day. For momentary, light affliction is producing for us an eternal weight of glory far beyond all comparison, while we look not at the things which are seen, but at the things which are not seen; for the things which are seen are temporal, but the things which are not seen are eternal (2 Cor. 4:16-18).

God's own glory within us—yet God's glory that grows and is presently being produced in us.

But there is even more.

By God's own design, He once placed His glory inside a lowly tent in Old Testament times. By God's marvelous grace, He still chooses to place His glory today within other earthly tents, namely, our own physical bodies:

> For we know that if the earthly tent which is our house is torn down, we have a building from God, a house not made with hands, eternal in the heavens.
> For indeed in this house we groan, longing to be clothed with our dwelling from heaven, inasmuch as we, having put it on, will not be found naked. For indeed while we are in this tent, we groan, being burdened, because we do not want to be unclothed but to be clothed, so that what is mortal will be swallowed up by life.
> Now He who prepared us for this very purpose is God, who gave to us the Spirit as a pledge (2 Cor. 5:1-5).

The abiding glory of God — the same transfigurational glory of the Lord Jesus Christ — will one day be revealed in fullness at the Bema Seat Judgment. Second Corinthians 5:10 discloses, "For we must all appear before the judgment seat of Christ, so that each one may be recompensed for his deeds in the body, according to what he has done, whether good or bad." Our present earthly tent — temporary and transitory in nature, just like the original tabernacle — will one day be eternally changed by Christ. As Philippians 3:20-21 promises: "For our citizenship is in heaven, from which also we eagerly wait for a Savior, the Lord Jesus Christ; who will transform the body of our humble state *into conformity with the body of His glory*, by the exertion of the power that He has even to subject all things to Himself."

But the analogy with Moses does not end there. Not only does God's glory currently dwell in our earthly tents, God's glory currently dwells in the current spiritual temple comprised of His church. Paul continued his reasoning in Second Corinthians 6:14-16:

> Do not be bound together with unbelievers; for what partnership have righteousness and lawlessness, or what fellowship has light with darkness? Or what harmony has Christ with Belial, or what has a believer in common with an unbeliever?
> Or what agreement has the temple of God with idols? For we are the temple of the living God; just as God said, "I will dwell in them and walk among them; and I will be their God, and they shall be my people."

How appropriate that Paul quoted from Exodus 29 and Leviticus 26, (and perhaps made an allusion to Exodus 25:8: "Let them construct a sanctuary for Me, that I may dwell among them") in teaching the Corinthians about the wondrous status of the Body of Christ. The context of Exodus 29 fits Paul's reasoning:

"I will meet there with the sons of Israel, and it shall be consecrated by My glory. I will consecrate the tent of meeting and the altar; I will also consecrate Aaron and his sons to minister as priests to Me. I will dwell among the sons of Israel and will be their God" (Exod. 29:43-45).

So also does the context of Leviticus 26 from which Paul selected content:

"Moreover, I will make My dwelling among you, and My soul will not reject you. I will also walk among you and be your God, and you shall be My people" (Lev. 26:11-12).

Taking this into consideration, we can see why Paul used the Exodus account of Moses to explain the unspeakable majesties of the New Covenant. What sublime contrasts exist between the two covenants in Second Corinthians:

Face of Moses (3:7) — face of Christ (4:6).
Limited to Moses (3:7, 13) — includes all the redeemed with unveiled faces (3:18).
Fading glory (3:7, 13) — remaining, abiding, "eternal weight of glory" (4:17)
Temporary change for Moses (3:7) — eternal change for the redeemed (4:18).
Moses: outside effect on his skin — for those in Christ, inside out (4:16-18).
Moses: immediately visible but fading — for us: invisible now, but growing.

Moses observed the refracted glory of Another.

We possess Another's glory.

Thus, the glory presence repeatedly shown before the advent of Messiah becomes a preview of who we are in Christ. God's glory to a tent, the tabernacle; God's glory to the Temple; God's glory in His Son.
God's glory in a tent (5:1-4) — individual, temporary dwelling.
God's glory in His Temple — which we currently are (2 Cor. 3:18) until the King of Glory returns to the Temple (Mal.3:1) that He Himself

will ultimately rebuild (Zech.6:12-13).

The God who chose Moriah still chooses His dwelling place, His abiding residence today, inside the hearts of His children.

The God who filled the Tabernacle with His glory currently does so in our earthly tents.

The God who filled the Temple makes us His Temple and dwells in our very midst.

That which Moses observed, we possess as a grace gift from God.

God's glory in a tent. God's glory in His Temple. God's glory in His Son. And then beyond that—God's glory in His children, historically and throughout all eternity.

Of this church I was made a minister according to the stewardship from God bestowed on me for your benefit, so that I might fully carry out the preaching of the word of God, that is, the mystery which has been hidden from the past ages and generations, but has now been manifested to His saints, to whom God willed to make known what is the riches of the glory of this mystery among the Gentiles,

which is Christ in you,

the hope of glory —

Therefore if you have been raised up with Christ, keep seeking the things above, where Christ is, seated at the right hand of God. Set your mind on the things above, not on the things that are on earth. For you have died and your life is hidden with Christ in God.
When Christ, who is our life, is revealed, then you also will be revealed with Him

in glory

— Colossians 1:25-27; 3:1-4.

So then you are no longer strangers and aliens, but you are fellow citizens with the saints, and are of God's household, having been built on the foundation of the apostles and prophets, Christ Jesus Himself being the Corner Stone, in whom the whole building, being fitted together, is growing into a holy temple in the LORD, in whom you also are being built together into a dwelling of God in the Spirit.

— Ephesians 2:19-22

And coming to Him as to a Living Stone which has been rejected by men, but is choice and precious in the sight of God, you also, as living stones, are being built up as a spiritual house for a holy priesthood, to offer up spiritual sacrifices acceptable to God through Jesus Christ.
For this is contained in Scripture: "Behold, I lay in Zion a Choice Stone, a

precious Corner Stone, and he who believes in Him will not be disappointed."
This precious value, then, is for you who believe; but for those who disbelieve,
"The Stone which the builders rejected, this became the very Corner Stone,"
and, "A Stone of stumbling and a Rock of offense," for they stumble because
they are disobedient to the word, and to this doom they were also appointed.

— 1 Peter 2:4-8

Then I saw a new heaven and a new earth; for the first heaven and the first
earth passed away, and there is no longer any sea. And I saw the holy city,
new Jerusalem, coming down out of heaven from God, made ready as a bride
adorned for her husband.
And I heard a loud voice from the throne, saying, "Behold, the tabernacle of
God is among men, and He will dwell among them, and they shall be His
people, and God Himself will be among them."

— Revelation 21:1-3

And he carried me away in the Spirit to a great and high mountain, and
showed me the holy city, Jerusalem, coming down out of heaven from God,

having the glory of God.

Her brilliance was like a very costly Stone, as a Stone of crystal-clear jasper.
I saw no Temple in it, for the LORD God the Almighty and the Lamb are its
Temple.
And the city has no need of the sun or of the moon to shine on it, for the glory
of God has illumined it, and its lamp is the Lamb.

— Revelation 21:10-11, 22-23